ECONOMICS OF AGING
The Future of Retirement

About the Editor

Malcolm H. Morrison, Ph.D. is Director of
major national studies being conducted to
examine the consequences for employers and
employees of new retirement age policies.
He currently serves as Chief of the Research
Support Staff of the Employment Standards
Administration, U.S. Department of Labor
and is the Department's representative for
the 1981 White House Conference on Aging
and the 1982 United Nations World Assem-
bly on Aging. He is also on the faculties of
Johns Hopkins University and George Washington University. Internationally known as
an expert on employment and retirement
problems of middle-aged and older workers,
Dr. Morrison has lectured and written extensively on trends and developments in employment and retirement.

ECONOMICS OF AGING
The Future of Retirement

Edited by

Malcolm H. Morrison, Ph. D.

 VAN NOSTRAND REINHOLD COMPANY
NEW YORK   CINCINNATI   TORONTO   LONDON   MELBOURNE

"The opinions expressed in this book do not necessarily represent the official opinion or policy of the U.S. Department of Labor. The editor and authors are solely responsible for the contents of this book."

Van Nostrand Reinhold Company Regional Offices:
New York   Cincinnati

Van Nostrand Reinhold Company International Offices:
London   Toronto   Melbourne

Copyright © 1982 by Van Nostrand Reinhold Company

Library of Congress Catalog Card Number: 81-207
ISBN: 0-442-25553-5

Manufactured in the United States of America

Published by Van Nostrand Reinhold Company
135 West 50th Street, New York, N.Y. 10020

Published simultaneously in Canada by Van Nostrand Reinhold Ltd.

15 14 13 12 11 10 9 8 7 6 5 4 3 2 1

Library of Congress Cataloging in Publication Data

Main entry under title:

Economics of aging.

    Includes index.
    1. Retirement—Economic aspects—United States
—Addresses, essays, lectures.   I. Morrison,
Malcolm H.
HQ1062.E36   305.2'6   81-207
ISBN 0-442-25553-5   AACR2

CONTRIBUTORS

Dorothy C. Bauer

Dorothy Bauer is Senior Program Associate at the National Council on the Aging, Inc. (NCOA) Washington, D.C. Mrs. Bauer is an expert on national employment programs for older workers and has served as Director of the NCOA Senior Community Service Employment Program. She has been directly involved in providing technical assistance to national and state employment services in designing more effective programs for older workers. Most recently she designed, developed and administered for the U.S. Department of Commerce a project on Economic Development of the Older Worker, and is presently involved in instituting seminars on age discrimination and age related personnel practices in industry.

Ruth C. Blank

Ruth Blank, a national expert in retirement planning programs, presently serves as an Assistant Editor of the journal *Aging and Work* published by the National Council on the Aging, Inc. (NCOA). Mrs. Blank is also involved in preparing a series of Task Force Reports for the 1981 White House Conference on Aging. Previously, she served as Assistant Program Associate for the NCOA Industry Consortium Retirement Planning Program.

Charles S. Harris, Ph. D.

Dr. Charles Harris is the former Director, Department of Research and Evaluation at the National Council on the Aging, Inc. (NCOA). He is presently on the staff at the Bureau for Social Science Research, Inc., Washington, D.C. Dr. Harris has been responsible for numerous national studies of the problems of older persons including "Employment Opportunities for Older Workers" for the National Committee on Careers for Older Americans and "Development of Models for Evaluating Three Older Americans Volunteer Programs" for the ACTION Agency. Dr. Harris is the editor of the nationally recognized publication *Fact Book on Aging: A Profile of America's Older Population* (1978).

Gary Hendricks

Gary Hendricks was a Senior Research Associate at The Urban Institute in Washington, D.C. where he was responsible for research studies in the Income Security and Pension Policy Program. Mr. Hendricks is presently conducting research at the U.S. Department of Labor. Since 1973, Mr. Hendricks has been conducting a series of socioeconomic studies on the retirement income problems of older workers and public and private pension policies. Mr. Hendricks is a national expert in simulation models of the retirement system in the United States and his work has been incorporated in numerous reports prepared by the Urban Institute for the U.S. Congress, the U.S. Department of Health and Human Services and the U.S. Department of Labor.

Edward F. Howard, J.D.

Edward Howard is the General Counsel for the National Council on the Aging, Inc. (NCOA), Washington, D.C. He advises the Council on legal matters and is responsible for public interest litigation in the field of aging. He also supervises the Council's public policy activities related to legislation. Previously, Mr. Howard served as General Counsel for the Select Committee on Aging, U.S. House of Representatives where he was responsible for much of the Committee's work on the Age Discrimination in Employment Act and the Older American's Act.

Eric R. Kingson, Ph. D.

Dr. Eric Kingson is presently a member of the faculty at the University of Maryland School of Social Work where he is responsible for courses in social welfare policy, income maintenance and social policies for the aging. Dr. Kingson is presently preparing a Task Force paper on employment for the 1981 White House Conference on Aging. He is a recent graduate of the Florence Heller Graduate School for Advanced Studies in Social Welfare of Brandeis University where his major area of study was the retirement patterns of older workers.

Nancy M. Peavy

Nancy Peavy is the Editor of the journal *Aging and Work* (formerly Industrial Gerontology) a quarterly journal published by the National Council on the Aging, Inc. (NCOA). In addition, Ms. Peavy writes a regular column reporting on recent decisions, settlements and pending cases under the Age Discrimination in Employment Act. Ms. Peavy is actively involved in preparing Congressional testimony, coordinating seminars and conferences and reviewing original research projects on employment and retirement problems of middle aged and older workers.

Elizabeth L. Meier

Elizabeth Meier is a Senior Economist on the Staff of the President's Commission on Pension Policy. In this capacity she has been directly responsible for analysis and preparation of papers on issues related to retirement trends, income adequacy and employment of older workers. Previously, Ms. Meier was a Research Associate and faculty member at the Institute on Aging, Portland State University where she was co-principal investigator on an early national study measuring the impact on industry of the Age Discrimination in Employment Act. Ms. Meier has also been on the staff of the U.S. Senate Special Committee on Aging and is the author of numerous articles and monographs on retirement income and employment of older workers.

Malcolm H. Morrison, Ph. D.

Dr. Malcolm Morrison, currently serves as Chief, Research Support Staff, Employment Standards Administration, U.S. Department of Labor, and is the Director of major national studies being conducted to examine the consequences on employees and employers of involuntary retirement and the effects of raising the mandatory retirement age limit in the 1978 amendments to the Age Discrimination in Employment Act. These studies will be utilized by Dr. Morrison in preparing reports to the President and Congress in 1981 and 1982 on the consequences of the Age Discrimination in Employment Act. Dr. Morrison, who also serves on the faculty of the Johns Hopkins University and George Washington University, is a recognized national and international expert on employment and retirement problems of middle-aged and older workers and has lectured and written extensively on trends and developments in employment and retirement. His current interests involve the establishment and implementation of protective international labor standards for older workers, establishment of flexible retirement policies and research on future labor force participation by older workers.

Lauren Selden

Lauren Selden was most recently the Coordinator of the Age Discrimination Project of the National Retired Teachers Association—American Association of Retired Persons. He is the author of numerous articles on discrimination, retirement, employment training and employee benefits, and has testified before Congressional and State legislative committees on the constitutional and administrative implications of discriminatory age practices. Mr. Selden was previously on the staff of the American Civil Liberties Union serving as Director of the Virginia and Washington State Offices.

Harold L. Sheppard, Ph. D.

Dr. Harold Sheppard now Associate Director, National Council on the Aging, Inc. (NCOA), was Counselor on Aging to the President of the United States, and is recognized throughout the world as America's foremost expert on the problems of older workers. Dr. Sheppard has had a long and distinguished career as a researcher, policymaker, and advocate in the field of aging and has had more influence than any other individual on policies and programs for older workers in the United States. He has been directly involved for over 25 years with research and policy studies concerning middle aged and older workers and has served on numerous national and international advisory groups and committees. He is the author of numerous articles and monographs and of several books the most recent being—*The Graying of Working America: The Coming Crisis of Retirement Age Policy* (1977). Previously, Dr. Sheppard served as staff director and research director of the U.S. Senate Special Committee on Aging and was Senior Research Fellow and Director of the Center on Work and Aging, American Institutes for Research, Washington, D.C.

James R. Storey

James Storey is Director of the Income Security and Pension Policy Program at The Urban Institute, Washington, D.C. Mr. Storey is responsible for numerous research projects on mandatory retirement policy, state, and local pensions, financial incentives for retirement and public welfare programs. He has written numerous papers and monographs for committees of Congress regarding retirement, income maintenance, and public and private pension programs. Mr. Storey's most recent publications include "Emerging Options for Work and Retirement Policy" for the U.S. Senate Special Committee on Aging, "Disincentives for Continued Work by Older Americans" (with Gary Hendricks), and "Policies Affecting the Income and Employment of Older

Americans: A Review of Options for Change." Previously, Mr. Storey conducted studies of welfare and retirement programs for the Office of Management and Budget, Executive Office of the President, the Department of Health, Education and Welfare, the Joint Economic Committee, U.S. Congress, and the U.S. Senate Budget Committee where he was Director of the Human Resources Staff.

Barbara B. Torrey

Barbara Torrey now at the Office of Management and Budget, Executive Office of the President, was Deputy Assistant Secretary for Income Security Policy, U.S. Department of Health and Human Services, where she was responsible for developing national policy regarding retirement income programs. Mrs. Torrey is currently involved in developing a long-term research program on retirement income problems designed to resolve numerous complex issues and provide guidance to Congress in developing new national retirement policies. Mrs. Torrey recently served as Deputy Director of the President's Commission on Pension Policy where she had overall responsibility for management of the Commission's activities. Previously, Mrs. Torrey was a Fiscal Economist, Office of Management and Budget, Executive Office of the President.

FOREWORD

Harold L. Sheppard

Social historians and gerontologists have, in the past two decades, written about retirement as a new phenomenon as far as the history of humankind is concerned. The growing numbers, the rising proportions, but especially the extension of years in retirement, certainly warrant that proposition. The increase in the percentages of older age groups no longer in the labor force has been dramatic over the past twenty years.

Now there seems to be an emerging paradox: the concern that the trend has perhaps gone too far. Malcolm Morrison's discussion in the Introduction to this volume elaborates on that theme. In this country, along with other industrialized societies at roughly the same state of development (especially in a period of slow-down in economic growth), the currents and counter-currents in policy discussions, reflect the need to strike a balance between the needs of the working population and the needs of the retired population, partly because of the rising retirement rate, coupled with an increase in longevity.

The new phenomenon of retirement is partly the result of the increase in "incentives" to leave the labor force, i.e., the level of retirement income benefits in the form of governmental old age pensions and private ones. But we cannot ignore the power of the assumption that job-creation for young, new entrants into the labor force requires the exit of large numbers of older workers. But again, that raises the issue, what is the point beyond which early retirement in the name of job-creation for younger persons becomes an added, net increase in the burden on the working population required to support the growing retired population? The "maturation" of retirement income systems everywhere evokes this and other questions.

The chapters in this book are directly and indirectly related to this issue, among others. The economics of aging is in part a product of the paradox described earlier.

The foci of the contributors here range from demography; past and projected retirement trends; unemployment; age discrimination; new patterns of work-time; and pension programs.

As the United States moves into the last fifth of the 20th Century, its society and economy are marked by other factors and forces that may make our future somewhat different from the post-World War II era, as far as those foci are concerned. In my opinion, one of these is the undeniable, however gradual, process of redefining, in socio-cultural terms, "when is old." Economists as well as other social scientists, and decisionmakers, should be sensitized to the fact that a society's perceptions as to what age should be the typical one for retirement are influenced by its members' images as to when—in the chronological life cycle—men and women generally begin to show outward signs of physical and mental decrements in functions deemed relevant for adequate work performance. These perceptions are no less influential as factors in retirement age policy than so-called economic "realities."

Age discrimination in employment is partly due to such perceptions on the part of the "gatekeepers" in the world of work.

While its authors may provide many other explanations, the 1978 amendment to the Age Discrimination in Employment Act (ADEA)—raising the permissible compulsory retirement age from 65 to 70—is a formalistic milestone in the socio-cultural redefinition process we are undergoing. Regardless of the many motives for passage of that amendment, we cannot deny that at the very least, it signifies that such a redefinition has been formalized. Historical and anthropological gerontologists recognize that in earlier epochs, and in other societies, 40, and then 50 or so, marked the onset of "old age." Until recently, 65 was the typical age. It should not surprise us to see that calendar age passed over.

In saying this, I am by no means rejecting the scientifically valid argument that chronological age *per se* should be irrelevant in setting retirement policy. This is the ideal policy position, reflected partly in the new policy in Federal employment (also emanating from the 1978 amendments to the ADEA) which eliminated any age for compulsory retirement. Nor am I in any way overlooking the role of pension levels, health status, job satisfaction, and discouraging unemployment experiences, as critical conditions for retirement decisions by *individuals*.

But research on these variables does not directly confront the issue of retirement age *policy*. We tend to focus on them because they are measurable and somewhat quantifiable.

This redefinition process may take some time for substantial effects on retirement age trends to show themselves. The mere passage of the legislation does not, overnight, produce such effects. But it will tend to set a tone, and imperceptibly change expectations and norms, regarding actual decisions as to when to retire. In addition, because of the probability that inflation will—by conventional standards—remain high, the 1978 amendments to ADEA will make it possible for workers in their early 60's to think beyond 65 as a retirement age, and actually retire later than otherwise, in order to minimize the retirement income penalties associated with a long retirement life. At the very least, we should expect an increase in the average age of "early" retirement.

These points all have a bearing on the growing disciplines of the economics of aging, and the chapters brought together here by Malcolm Morrison constitute significant contributions to that discipline.

INTRODUCTION

Over the short span of forty years, *retirement* has become an important concern for the American people. Almost every day, articles and commentaries appear in publications throughout the country on the economic, social, and psychological consequences of retirement. Such headlines as "Social Security Costs To Rise," "Age for Mandatory Retirement Increases," and "The Aging of America," are now commonplace.

It is clear that interest in retirement and its consequences has been heightened primarily because of rising costs of public and private retirement benefits, and serious concern as to whether these costs can be afforded in the future. Underlying these significant cost increases for retirement income programs are a series of demographic and economic changes occuring in our society. The results of these changes are just beginning to affect our society, their future consequences will pose serious economic and social challenges in the years ahead.

This book examines the future of retirement by reviewing current economic and social trends in retirement behavior, retirement income, and worklife patterns and discusses their probable consequences in the future. A variety of policy issues are examined concerning the financing of future retirement benefits, changes in future worklife patterns, and alternative policy choices in resolving future financial and social problems connected with retirement.

Almost every industrialized country in the world continues to experience an overall aging of the population and a continuing decline in labor force participation by older workers as a direct result of earlier retirement. With declining birth and death rates, and improved health at older ages, it is clear that most countries will face a significant challenge in supporting increased older populations of the future.

In the United States, due to steadily declining birth and death rates, the population is aging rapidly. Whereas persons age 65 and older were only 4 percent of the population in 1900, by 1975 this percentage had increased to 10 percent and projections indicate that by the year 2000 they will comprise 12 percent of our population. (By the year 2020 this proportion will jump to 15.5 percent, and reach almost 18 percent by 2040.)

The growth of the older population has been accompanied by the development of retirement as a social institution and accompanying retirement benefit programs. Whereas in 1940 less than 100,000 persons received retirement benefits under the Social Security system, and private pensions were virtually unknown, today more than 21 million persons receive Social Security retirement benefits and about 7 million private pension payments. Due to a combination of more liberal retirement benefits, early retirement options, and social attitudes, ever increasing numbers of workers aged 50 and over are retiring. As this trend continues, fewer and fewer active workers must support an increasing number of retirees. The implications of these trends for funding of retirement benefits and for meeting individual economic and social needs are a matter of increasing concern in our society.

As demographic and labor force trends continue to accelerate, more and more questions arise about the future of retirement in this country. These relate both to the development of appropriate public policy on retirement benefit programs and to individual concerns about worklife flexibility, preparation for retirement, and economic security in retirement. The major questions examined in this book can be outlined as follows:

- Population Trends: What are the characteristics of the present and future aged population? In what way is the population distribution changing? What are the future support implications for the retired?
- Changing Worklife and Retirement Patterns: How did retirement become a part of the worklife pattern in the United States? What are the major retirement policy issues? What factors influence the decision to retire? How effective are retirement preparation programs? What are the essential components of retirement income? What factors influence adjustment in retirement? Are there practical alternatives to retirement now utilized by older workers? Is it likely that the retirement age will increase?
- Retirement Trends: What factors influence the labor force participation of older workers? What are current retirement trends and future projections? What leads to early retirement? How prevalent is employment and retirement planning? How will workers support the increasing retired population?
- Age Discrimination and Mandatory Retirement: What are the effects of age discrimination in employment? How prevalent is mandatory retirement? What are employer and employee attitudes about retirement and its consequences? What will be the effects of the new legislation raising the age for mandatory retirement?
- Employment Programs for the Retired: What are the various government programs for employing older persons, how are they utilized

and is their expansion likely? What is the extent of employment assistance for retirees? How extensive are job retraining programs for older workers? What are future employment prospects in the regular labor market?

- Economics of Retirement: What is the economic position of current and future retirees? What are the most important economic problems for retirees? What will be the effects of recent developments in Social Security policy? What are the new proposals under consideration for Social Security? What will be the future role of private pensions? What are some of the significant policy choices for the future of Social Security and private pensions? What will be the individual's response to changing public and private pension policies?
- Retirement Flexibility: What are the new conceptualizations of the worklife? How prevalent are such options as phased retirement, job-sharing, job shifting, part-time employment, job retraining, new careers, etc.? What are the current applications of retirement flexibility in the U.S. and other countries? What adjustments in personnel policies are likely in the future? Will retirement preparation programs be modified in the future toward career life planning programs?
- Future of Retirement: What will be the future patterns of retirement in the United States? How will economic security be provided? How will persons participate in the new patterns of work, leisure, and education? What are the major retirement policy choices?

It is clear that there are multiple and complex interactions between demographic, labor market, economic, and social factors which shape retirement trends. A comprehensive examination of issues and problems associated with the future of retirement in terms of economic and social consequences is necessary for informed policy formulation and subsequent program development.

In the past ten years numerous policy and program developments have occurred which directly impinge on the retirement process. New legislation has been enacted in the areas of Social Security, private pension regulation and age discrimination protection. Many new programs for retirees have been implemented. Much more attention has been devoted to retirement planning approaches and new conceptions of the worklife. Many if not most of these developments have not been examined in terms of future implications for our society. This book fills an important gap in providing a comprehensive review and analysis of current retirement trends and potential future developments. It will be useful to all who have an interest in the future of retirement in American society.

CONTENTS

ECONOMICS OF AGING
The Future of Retirement

1

A CHANGING WORKLIFE AND RETIREMENT PATTERN: AN HISTORICAL PERSPECTIVE

Ruth Crary Blank

"Longer life, freedom from infirmity and illness, a higher level of living, and more free time from the tasks of making a living have been principal objectives of man in every society" (U.S. HEW, CRS, November 1974, p. 1). After many years of socioeconomic change, these objectives have been realized for an increasing number of individuals in the United States. Technological advance has been the fundamental factor leading to life extension and to work free time, and a subsequent changing worklife and retirement pattern. Increased productivity has limited the need for man-hours of labor affecting both arbitrary and mandatory retirement practices. Concurrently, improved health services have contributed to both a relative and a proportionate increase of older people in the population (U.S. HEW, CRS, November 1974).

As Sheppard (1976) relates, there is a larger aging population with a decline in the income earning work-force, but a lengthening in possible individual average work-force participation years. Individuals living longer account for the increase in possible average work-force participation years; however, increased productivity eventuates in a high percentage of people being released from goods and service production (Sheppard, 1976). Consequently, machine culture has afforded a great change in the worklife pattern of modern adults by adding another dimension to the life-cycle: Retirement (U.S. HEW, CRS, November 1974).

THE PREINDUSTRIALIZED WORKLIFE PATTERN

Prior to the 20th century, due to social, philosophical, economic, and demographic patterns in the United States, retirement was not a social institution.

A Social Philosophical Concern

In preindustrialized society, the Puritan heritage gave religious overtones to the virtues of hard work which assigned a positive value to work involvement and commitment. For a "man" to be respected in society, it was necessary for him to hold a steady job. The first full-time job acquisition became a rite of passage that constituted induction into the adult community (Loether, 1975). Agricultural and early industrialized worklife demanded " . . . lifelong sunup to sundown routine . . ." (Hendricks and Hendricks, 1977, p. 67*).

A social doctrine of work was adopted through the Puritan tenet "gospel of work." Idleness was a sin in Puritan thought, and education was used as a device to breed piety that, in turn, strengthened industrious behavior (Loether, 1975). The Protestant work ethic, while a product of many protestant religious sects, was primarily based on Puritan philosophy. Stressing duty and work obligation, the work ethic created guilt feelings in those not maintaining occupational activity (Sheppard, 1970). In addition, traditions of individualism and laissez faire enhanced the value placed on both work and achievement in the young American society (Garraty, 1971). Retirement, partial or complete, was not a part of the social order, and when occurring was not sanctioned by society. Only severe ill health or advanced age, forcing discontinuance of work, provided social acceptance of retirement (Hendricks and Hendricks, 1977).

An Economic Barrier

Sociophilosophical barriers to retirement were accompanied by economic barriers that forced workers to continue working for survival. Farmers and factory workers did not accumulate "nest eggs";

*From *Aging in Mass Society: Myths and Realities* by Hendricks and Hendricks. Copyright © 1977. Reprinted by permission of Winthrop Publishers, Inc., Cambridge, Massachusetts.

and, there was no Social Security to provide a steady retirement income (Hendricks and Hendricks, 1977).

> In the past, when most men were farmers, a man did not suddenly part from activity to inactivity: he worked as long as he could, and neither he nor his society nor government paid much attention to his age . . . (Puner, 1974, p. 178*)

This implies that retirement was not a consideration of the time. In addition, low wages, lack of education, unskilled labor, and farm labor did not encourage work-force mobility. Work transition was slow; and generally, son followed father into the work ranks. Although there were craft unions, the majority of workers were not unionized (Garraty, 1971).

In the late 19th century, initial industrial expansion stimulated immigration, and millions of foreign-born workers entered the United States from Eastern and Southern Europe. Concurrently, an increasing number of black workers migrated from South to North seeking employment. Although some immigrants worked the farmlands, most workers were absorbed into the fledgling industries. Many of the "new" immigrants were penniless, unskilled, uneducated, clannish, and committed to lifelong work for survival. These new immigrants were desperately poor and without any resource other than their ability to work (Garraty, 1971).

Discrimination against both the European and black immigrant constituted another factor that limited work opportunities and/or job advancement. In many instances, individuals with special skills and education were forced, for reasons of economic survival, to seek employment below their ability.

According to Atchley (1976), it was generally individuals in the higher economic status who lived to an advanced age; consequently, the early American leisure class was designated by social class. Workers in the lower socioeconomic strata either continued to work or turned to the family for economic assistance. This resulted in support of older people being a form of conspicuous consumption (Atchley, 1976). In preindustrialized society, it was almost impossible to ". . . earn the right to an income without a job or owning enough property to provide it" (Atchley, 1976, p. 10).

---

*From *To the Good Long Life: What We Know About Growing Old* by Morton Puner. Universe Books, New York, 1974.

**Table 1-1. Absolute Increase and Percent of Older People
in Total Population.
(United States)**

Year	Absolute Number 65 + in Society	Increase	Percent of Total Pop.
1800s (late)	2.0 million		3.5
		1 million	
1900	3.0 million		4.1
		6 million	
1940	9.0 million		6.8
		11.2 million	
1970	20.2 million		9.8
		10.4 million	
2000 (proj)	30.6 million		9.7 (appx.)

Sources: A composite of figures from Kimmel, 1974; Loether, 1975; Woodruff and Birren, 1975; National Council on the Aging, 1978 (see references).

A Demographic Pattern

It was not until the late 1800s that persons aged 65 and over totaled more than 3.0 percent (Table 1-1) of the United States population. This small percentage of older adults numbered less than 2 million, before the 1800s (Loether, 1975), due to an average life expectancy of less than 50 years (Woodruff and Birren, 1975). In the subsistence economy of this period, the population distribution of older people was the outcome of natural conditions where both birth and death rates were high (Ford, 1970). This situation precluded either high relative or proportionate increases in the numbers of older adults in the society until the early 1900s. (Table 1-1) The interrelation of factors underlying a demographic shift and industrialized worklife sponsored a new worklife and retirement pattern.

A DEMOGRAPHIC SHIFT

The demographic transitional theory ". . . relates the type of population growth to the level of technological development of a society," (Cowgill, 1963, p. 270-274) and the following principles are significant in worklife patterns. (1) "A population which is experiencing secular declines in both birth and death rates will also manifest a marked aging trend"; and, (2) "An aging population tends to be predominantly female." (Cowgill, 1963, p. 270–274*)

A Marked Aging Trend

The proportion of older people in a society is a result of fertility and mortality rates as well as of the immigration profile. The fertility rate establishes the absolute size of a cohort, and sets its relative size as to other population age-groups. On the other hand, the mortality rate controls life expectancy with infant mortality decrease most significant in reducing the general death rate (Woodruff and Birren, 1975). While Woodruff and Birren (1975) do not view immigration as an important factor for projection into the 21st century, immigration is important when examining the past demographic shift of an increasing older population with decreasing work-force participation by adults 65 and over (Rhine, 1978).

Life expectancy (Table 1–2) and the proportion of older people in the population (Table 1–3) began to rise in the early 20th century. The rate of increase, along with the absolute increase, expanded the older American population (National Council on the Aging, 1978).

Although there has been some increase in life expectancy at age 65 (see Table 1–2), the major increase in life expectancy arises from changes in life expectations at birth. In 1900, only 4 percent (Table 1–3) of the total population could be designated as older; while in 1975, the 10 percent mark was being passed with a projection of 16.1 percent for 2050.

Table 1-2. Average Life Expectancy at Birth and at Age 65 in the United States.

	1900	1939	1949	1955	1959	1970	1977
At Birth	47.3	63.7	68.0	69.6	69.9	70.9	73.2
At Age 65	11.9	12.8	12.8	14.2	14.4	15.2	18.0 (Appx.)

Sources: Composite of figures from: (1) *Aging: Scientific Perspectives and Social Issues* by Diana Woodruff and James E. Birren. New York: D. Van Nostrand, p. 32, 1975; and (2) U.S. Department of Commerce, Bureau of the Census, *Monthly Vital Statistics Report,* Table 3, Abridged Life Tables by Color and Sex: United States, p. 17, 1977.

*From "Transitional Theory as General Population Theory," *Social Forces,* 41, March 1963.

Table 1-3. Percent of the Total Population 65 and Over:
1900-2050

Year (July 1)	Percent	Year (July 1)	Percent
1900	4.1	1980	11.0
1910	4.3	1990	11.7
1920	4.6	2000	11.7
1930	5.4	2010	11.9
1940	6.8	2020	14.6
1950	8.1	2030	17.0
1960	9.2	2040	16.1
1970	9.8	2050	16.1
1975	10.5		

Source: U.S. Bureau of the Census, *Current Population Reports, Special Studies,* Series P.-23, No. 59, p. 9, May 1976.

Historically, a demographic shift contributed to a changing worklife pattern when there was:

1. A high birth rate in the late 19th, early 20th centuries.
2. A high "new" immigrant rate in the early 20th century.
3. An increase in life expectancy.
4. A proportionate increase in the older population due to a declining birth rate in mid-20th century (National Council on the Aging, 1978).

The preceding relates to a marked aging population trend which brought deep-seated changes in social, political, and economic systems in the United States (U.S. House of Representatives, Select Committee on Aging, *News,* September 27, 1977).

A Predominantly Older Female Population

The increase in an older population resulted in a decreasing ratio of males to females, and was ". . . attributable to the differing trends in mortality rates for males and females" (National Council on the Aging, 1978, p. 14). In 1900, the approximate ratio of males to females was 102/100; by 1960, the ratio was 83/100; and in 1975, there was a ratio of 69/100 in the 65 and older cohort (National Council on the Aging, 1978). U.S. Representative Mario Biaggi

(D–N.Y.) declared that "(B)y the year 2000, there will be 150 elderly women to every 100 elderly men" (U.S. House of Representatives, Select Committee on Aging, *News,* 1977, p. 1).

Social philosophical, economic and demographic factors in American preindustrialized society resulted in a lack of retirement pattern; and until ". . . seventy years ago, over 60 percent of all American men continued working past age 65" (Hendricks and Hendricks, 1977, p. 67*). Traditionally, if work was curtailed, it was a gradual cessation from the work-force (Blau, 1973) due to declining health or complete removal through death.

In the early 20th century, a new worklife and retirement pattern began emerging. The difference arose from a demographic shift (Tables 1–2 and 1–3), and from industrialization which encouraged socioeconomic changes in both the private and public sectors of society.

INDUSTRIALIZATION AND WORKLIFE CHANGES

As industrialization increased productivity, fewer workers were needed in production of output (Atchley, 1977). The increase in machine energy gradually diminished the need for the existing large adult labor force when an economic surplus materialized (Atchley, 1976). A decline in infant mortality when the fertility rate was down (Atchley, 1976), along with a complicated set of technological, cultural and scientific changes (Streib and Schneider, 1971), caused an aging of the United States population (see Tables 1–2 and 1–3).

At a time, when the numbers of older people increased and when their worklife shifted, there was a decline in the honorific position previously assigned to those reaching old age. As management was separated from ownership and as the premium given experience declined, there was a social and economic status reduction for older adults. A new social order with a sharp division in labor, increased corporate bureaucracy and a rising powerful, private sector emerged. Socioeconomic changes of the early 20th century drew response from both the federal government and union interests. Industrialization altered the worklife concept as the need for crafts-

*From *Aging in Mass Society: Myths and Realities* by Hendricks and Hendricks. Copyright © 1977. Reprinted by permission of Winthrop Publishers, Inc., Cambridge, Massachusetts.

manship decreased and jobs became fragmented. There was an increase in secularism which resulted in new views about the Protestant work ethic; and the relationship between sinfulness and the lack of a work role was questioned (Atchley, 1976).

In the Spring of 1928, the Great Depression descended upon the United States. It was not the collapse of the stock market that brought economic disaster, but

> . . . the industrialization and urbanization of the United States in the course of a century; too much of the wealth of the nation had fallen in too few hands with the result that consumers were unable to buy all the goods produced (Garraty, 1971, p. 333).*

The financial system fell under the strain of plant close-downs, laid-off workers, and closing banks. The industrial depression soon spilled into agriculture; and, all economic indicators reflected the collapse by 1930. In some areas of the country, one-third of the state population was on relief; and both private and state agencies were fundless due to the vast number of workers seeking financial aid (Garraty, 1971).

Without a doubt, the older worker was heavily burdened during this period. In fact, Kreps has observed that in any pressured economic system ". . . older workers are among the last hired and the first fired to accommodate these economic fluctuations" (Kasschau, 1976, p. 13).

In 1935, two events occurred, in response to the Depression, that would affect future worklife and retirement patterns. The Committee for Industrial Organization (CIO) was organized; and the Social Security Act (SSA) was designed. The CIO brought workers into one union regardless of craft lines, increasing union power and strength. The Social Security Act set up a national system of old-age insurance, recognizing work/retirement problems of older workers (Garraty, 1971) from an economic standpoint.

Consequently, the Great Depression of 1929, and the plight of the elderly worker, led to Federal intervention through introduction of retirement, Social Security laws and a public pension system (Blau,

*From *The American Nation: A History of the United States* by J. A. Garraty. Reprinted by permission of Harper & Row, Publishers, Inc., New York.

1973). In addition, union extension over the rank-and-file led to establishment of a private pension system for specific workers.

Public Pension Plan Initiation

The Social Security Act of 1935 ". . . set up a national system of old-age insurance, financed partly by a tax on wages, partly by tax on payroll"* (Garraty, 1971, p. 348), and legitimized retirement at age 65 (Hendricks and Hendricks, 1977). The development of a national government with a growing bureaucracy responded to older worker need through pooling of resources that allowed a segment of the population to be supported after leaving the work force (Atchley, 1977). However, Social Security benefits were never intended to be the only source of support for retired older workers (Hendricks and Hendricks, 1977), who in 1930 had comprised only 5.4 percent of the population (see Table 1-3).

Massive Federal intervention, as an aid to older workers/retirees, was necessary to alleviate worklife and retirement problems encountered in the Great Depression of 1929; but, the intended effect of the Social Security Act changed over time.

Social Security Program Effect

Americans had labored under the belief that saving for old age was an individual problem but the Great Depression dispelled confidence in the assumption. Life savings had been swept away; and the Townsend Old Age Revolving Pension Plan, promising to provide $200 per month for every individual over 60-years-old, encouraged some type of government intervention. While there were employer misgivings about the one percent to be paid on employee salaries, by each employer and employee, popular demand was for liberalization of the Social Security Act (Barch and Blake, 1965). By January 1, 1937, workers were making compulsory contributions to a personal retirement fund. Arguments abounded as to the feasibility of a contributory tax ever being returned to individuals after retiring (Schlesinger, 1960).

Social Security Act Amendments of 1939 favored social adequacy

*From *The American Nation: A History of the United States* by J. A. Garraty. Reprinted by permission of Harper & Row, Publishers, Inc., New York.

and dependents' benefits. Consequently, individual equity or receipt of pensions as contributed was weakened; and universal, compulsory protection became the goal under the social insurance plan. A welfare criterion, measuring benefits against the standard of living rather than lifetime contribution, was instituted (Munnell, 1977).

Over the years, Social Security has affected retirement in three ways:

1. . . . retirement benefits moderate the reduction in income that workers must face when they retire. Consequently, there is a pure income effect that encourages older workers to choose leisure instead of work.
2. . . . the earnings test makes it impossible for most workers to receive benefits without cutting back on work effort.
3. . . . social security may condition both employers and employees to the idea that sixty-five is the "normal" retirement age (Munnell, 1977, p. 63*).

Munnell (1977) observes that compulsory retirement, set by private industry, may be a result of Social Security system expansion. Union contracts and industry practices increased compulsory retirement provisions after World War II, as trade unions enlarged the private pension system.

The Private Pension Plan Movement

According to Clague et al. (1971), the private pension plan movement, covering industrial workers, began in the early 20th century as a consequence of the increasing older population. Originally, individual firms formed pension plans to bind employees more securely to the work place. But, concurrently, employees were guaranteed an income upon retirement (Clague et al., 1971).

Brooks (1964) cited union strikes and conflict as being the impetus toward new "corporate welfarism" with profit sharing, social insurance, and pensions being the ". . . cement of the new order" (Brooks, 1964, p. 126*). In the early years, the majority of private

* Alicia H. Munnell, *The Future of Social Security*, Washington, D.C.: Brookings Institution, 1977. Copyright © 1977 by the Brookings Institution.
* Excerpted from the book *Toil and Trouble* by Thomas R. Brooks. Copyright © 1964, 1971 by Thomas R. Brooks. Reprinted by permission of DELACORTE PRESS.

pension plans were for executive, administrative and white-collar, clerical workers, with blue-collar workers being included sometimes. Larger firms, such as public utilities, were usually the ones involved in pension plan formation. While some unions, in the early 20th century, had pension plans, only a small percentage of American industrial workers had coverage. Private pension plans suffered badly in the Depression of 1929 with railroad-industry pensions being saved by the Railroad Retirement Act of 1935. There were few payments made to workers laid off during this period. This was one of the factors contributing to the initiation of the Social Security system (Clague et al., 1971).

After World War II, union interest expanded private pension plans in industry. The National Labor Relations Board and Supreme Court rulings of 1949 permitted concentration on fringe benefits as a part of collective bargaining. This promoted union freedom in establishing retirement policy for private industrial pension plans. Although collective bargaining was directed toward extending the work-years in the early 1950s, business recession and increased unemployment rates of the late 50s and early 60s caused a change in the outlook for older worker employment (Clague et al., 1971). Consequently, prior to 1949, ". . . pension plans were usually voluntary undertakings by companies, and management had a relatively free hand in their design" (Clague et al., 1971, p. 136*).

Work Force Participation Change

Time spent in the work force by an individual worker has decreased proportionately but not absolutely with the growth of industrialization (Atchley, 1976). The increase in life expectancy has been of significance in providing more time available for work. As an example, there has been an increase in average life expectancy (Table 1–2) from 47.3 years in 1900 to 73.2 years in 1977.

However, according to Levitan and Belous (1977), as the years available for work force participation increased, there was a reduction in weekly and annual hours spent in the work force. While vacation and holiday increases supported decreased working hours, a worklife shift was more significant. Late entrance into the work

*From *The Aging Worker and the Union* by Ewan Clague, Balraj Palli and Leo Kramer. New York: Praeger Publishers, 1971.

force (longer periods of education and training), and earlier retirement reduced what had been a long-term rise toward longer workforce involvement.

Clark and Spengler (1978) state that "labor force participation of older cohorts is expected to decline during the next 30 years" (pp. 10/11). Labor force participation rates, actual and projected, reveal changes for both males and females (Table 1-4). While there is a steady decline shown, actual and projected, in Table 1-4, figures from 1948 (Clark and Spengler, 1978) reveal a constant decline over a 27 year period.

In 1948, there were 46.8 percent of males 65 and over in the work force while in 1975, 21.7 percent were active workers (Table 1-4). In the 55-64 male cohort, 89.5 percent were work-force participators in 1948; by 1975, this group had dropped to 75.7 percent active members in the work force (Table 1-4).

Although in 1948 only 24.3 percent of women aged 55-64 were in the labor market (Clark and Spengler, 1978), by 1975, 41.0 percent of this group were work-force participants. Although work-force participation for females 65 and over is not dramatic (Table 1-4), if coupled with the demographic fact that the older population is predominantly female, then the figures are more significant as the worklife pattern changes.

Sex ratio change, the numbers of females in relation to numbers of males, is important in work-force participation changes. According to the National Council on the Aging (1978), the expanding female population produces an increased married, female work force. In addition, there is a relatively high rate of widowed,

Table 1-4. Labor Force Participation Rate.

	Actual				Projected		
	1970	1975	1980	1985	1990	2000	2010
Males							
55-64	81.8	75.7	74.3	71.6	69.9	66.6	63.2
65 and over	26.9	21.7	19.9	18.0	16.8	13.8	10.8
Females							
55-64	42.5	41.0	41.9	42.2	42.3	43.3	43.9
65 and over	9.6	8.2	8.1	7.8	7.6	7.1	6.6

Source: U.S. HEW, *Aging*, "Population in the Twenty-First Century," by Robert Clark and Joseph Spengler, No. 279-28, January/February, 1978.

separated and divorced women entering the work force. Many of these women could be considered "displaced homemakers": a displaced homemaker being an individual who has lost family income and position due to death, divorce or illness of a spouse.

The birth cohort effect may also impact upon work force participation changes. According to Maddox and Wiley (1976), the ". . . position in the stream of historical environments, indexed by date of birth, differentiates one cohort from another with respect to broad classes of behavior" (p. 19). Consequently, the birth cohort, by influencing behavior, may account for worker expectation of a worklife and retirement pattern, and impact upon employer and government actions regarding these issues. In addition, changing social values, beliefs and norms, impinging upon worklife and retirement, may arise due to the birth cohort effect.

Commentary

It is evident that a changing worklife and retirement pattern is grounded in the historical background of the United States as socioeconomic evolvement from preindustrialized to industrialized society materialized. Certainly, both public (Social Security Act) and private (union/industry) pension plan development occurred as a consequence of worklife problems in a growing socioeconomic system.

Organized labor made an important contribution to the older worker/retiree status when encouraging new private pension plans and augmenting existing plans. Because unions found it possible to gain pension plan supplements rather than wage increases, it can be assumed that financial protection for retirees has been an important element in bargaining agreements. However, the counteractive element of mandatory retirement must not be overlooked where union rules and regulations may not at all times be at the preference of nor in the best interest of the older worker. In some cases, there are indications that age discrimination in employment may be encouraged by those same rules that provide retirement benefits.

The Social Security Act is of major importance to all older workers/retirees. However, complete reliance on Social Security as retirement income is not possible in a time of fluctuating economy. Although Social Security benefits are tied to a cost-of-living increase, inflation decreases the retiree's purchasing power immediately. The effect of inflation may perpetuate additional changes in worklife and retirement patterns as return to employment becomes an economic necessity for some retirees.

Worklife and retirement changes, when viewed as a group or collective action, occurred in a sociohistorical time-frame as a birth cohort effect. Industrialization, with a steadily increasing older population that declined in work-force participation, led to the contemporary worklife and retirement pattern in the United States. This pattern engendered a new social institution to accommodate many older workers entering a "workless" life. In analyzing the institutionalization of retirement, a social change was seen as materializing to alter past worklife horizons by including the dimensions of retirement.

RETIREMENT: A SOCIAL INSTITUTION

Berger and Berger (1972) describe the process of institutionalization through the basic characteristics of: (1) Externality; (2) objectivity; (3) coerciveness; (4) moral authority; and (5) historicity. The changing worklife pattern, over the past 75 years, has followed this process; and, retirement has been institutionalized as a new socially expected life phase.

Retirement has arisen outside of the individual worker through industrialization and a changing demographic profile (externality). Social, philosophical, political, and economic input into the retirement trend has established a realness to retirement's existence (objectivity). Increasing numbers of retirees have persuaded the society of a "retirement status" and a "retiree role" (coerciveness). Federal sanction of retirement through the Social Security Act, as well as union/industry sanction through private pension plan development, have established rules and regulations for pension receipt (moral authority). Economic, political, and sociohistorical change, from the early 1900s, has authenticated the historicity of retirement. These distinguishing markers, as outlined by Berger and Berger (1972) and used in describing retirement as an institution, are supported by the following statements:

Retirement is a generalized social pattern, institutionally sanctioned in practically all industrialized countries (Monk, 1972, p. 63).

With amazing speed over a 25-year-period, occupational retirement has become institutionalized in America (Blau, 1973, p. 12*).

. . . Social Security was established, and with its introduction the institution of retirement came of age in the United States (Atchley, 1977, p. 142).

Atchley (1977) observes that ". . . the average job holder has come to accept the idea that people can legitimately live in dignity as adults without holding jobs. . . " (p. 142), that is, if the right has been earned. Atchley (1976) outlines the criteria for dignified retirement as follows:

1. People were living long enough.
2. The economy could support nonworking adults.
3. The work force was restricted.
4. There was an increase in both the national state and unionism, and a possibility of diverting economic surplus for retiree support through pension funds.
5. Workers could accept retirement without negative feelings after Federal and union sanction.

However, Sheppard (1976) notes that it would have been possible to decrease the numbers of workers, due to changes in technology, without an aging population. From 1890 to 1970, Atchley (1976) finds retirement closely paralleling: (1) An increased gross national product; (2) population increase in urban areas; and (3) machine energy in production.

As is evident, social, philosophical, economic, and political factors had an effect on the institutionalization of retirement. In addition, retirement is still a new and somewhat difficult life phase in American society, which has only recently been subject to definitive examination (Atchley, 1976; Praigg, 1977).

THE DIMENSIONS OF RETIREMENT

The dimensions of retirement include an earned right as well as a shift in both the amount and the source of income. Although work never ceases entirely, retirement does refer specifically to work cessation, and the stoppage of a role for which payment is received (Atchley, 1977).

The full dimension of retirement can best be explored through a sociopsychological perspective and through factors that affect retirement qualification and the retirement decision. As a major milestone marking the move from middle-age to old-age, retirement is a transition point designating the end of worklife and the beginning of a "leisure" life. Retirement includes the elements of an event, a status, a role, a process, and a social pattern.

Retirement From a Sociopsychological Perspective

Usually, the retirement event takes place at the age of 65 primarily due to Social Security legislation of 1935. However, socioeconomic factors vary, and may affect the timing of this event by either increasing or decreasing retirement age. As illustrations:

1. Increased productivity may reduce the retirement age when declining labor force need results in older workers leaving the job market at earlier ages.
2. Lack of a mandatory retirement age may increase the retirement age when older workers, who are functionally capable and personally motivated, remain on the job past the customary retirement age of 65.

The retirement event concentrates on work cessation, emphasizing past achievement and *not* future opportunities and responsibilities. However, ". . . retirement offers by definition an income free from job responsibilities. . . " (Atchley, 1976, p. 54) with an opportunity for individualism and autonomy. Ceremony is seldom a part of this event although retirement may be considered a rite of passage (Kimmel, 1974; Atchley, 1976; Atchley, 1977).

The status of retirement brings a new social position with different roles, expectations, and responsibilities. Most often, there is a narrowing of roles and responsibilities with a lowering of living standard that may not be in line with preretirement worker expectation. While this may be judged a negative change, an increase in leisure time may be considered a positive aspect of retirement (Kimmel, 1974).

According to general theory, there are at least three concepts that may be employed when considering retirement as a role:

1. Activity Theory—the job role will be replaced with another major activity at about the same energy level, and constitute an active retirement role.
2. Continuity Theory—the concentrated activity toward work will decrease; and energy will be redistributed among other roles (husband, stamp collector, etc.) without a new major role emerging.
3. Disengagement Theory—the job role will be dropped without change in other role activities or in adding new activities, consequently, diminishing roles in retirement (Atchley, 1976).

The retirement role may be seen as vague and individualistic; but there are certain behaviors typically performed by retirees that conform to society's view of a retirement role. The role "retired person" assumes rights of economic support and time from the work force without social stigma, and with receipt of particular social privileges; all to be carried forth while living within a reduced income (Atchley, 1977).

Anticipatory status and both conscious and unconscious adaptation and preparation for a new role are the first steps in the retirement process (Monk, 1972; Kimmel, 1974). However, there is generally little anticipatory socialization for retirement; and entrance into a retirement planning program could signify the beginning of the retirement process (Atchley, 1976). A retirement planning program thus becomes the symbol of a life transition stage. Kimmel (1974) stresses the biological, socio-cultural and psychological elements as important in the retirement process.

Retirement, a unique and modern phenomena, is a social pattern in Western industrialized nations (Streib and Schneider, 1971), and a

"social artifact" according to Jaffee (1972). The social pattern occurs when: (1) people live long enough; (2) the economy can tolerate
worker transfer to nonworker status; and (3) social insurance of
some form is available (Streib and Schneider, 1971; Atchley, 1976;
Sheppard, 1976).

Retirement Qualifications

The U.S. Census cites working previously, not searching for a job,
and not working presently as denoting retirement status. Private
pension systems specify various conditions, such as, minimum age
and length of employment service, to qualify for retirement (Blank,
1979). Hendricks and Hendricks (1977) view retirement as a matter
of degree when work/nonwork specifications are not the important
criteria; but receipt of retirement benefits defines the retirement
position.

An important qualification, in the United States, occurs as a result
of the Social Security Act. In this case, retirement status rests
on a monetary component when a "retirement test" becomes a
criterion. A worker/retiree must pass this means test, not earning
more than a specified sum, when receiving Social Security income
(Sheppard, 1976).

The position of Hendricks and Hendricks (1977) defines retirees as
those who receive pensions but continue to work for supplemental
income or in a voluntary capacity. However, the U.S. Census
Bureau definition follows closely the retirement test qualifications
under the Social Security Act.

Retirement Decision Factors

An inexhaustible number of factors influence the retirement decision: financial adequacy, health status, mandatory and flexible
retirement regulations, self-employment, availability of jobs as well
as the prevailing social attitude (Hendricks and Hendricks, 1977).
Atchley (1976) agrees with the factors cited by Hendricks and Hendricks, and adds the following: (1) Discrimination policies against
older workers; (2) individual preference for leisure time; (3) individual ability/inability to accept the retirement concept; and (4)

a worker's positive or negative personal view of his/her current job. Another important decision element is involved when social acceptance increases–then retirement becomes more individually appealing. In this circumstance, a commitment change away from a "world of work" philosophy impacts on personal resistance to retirement (Atchley, 1976).

Sheppard (1976) mentions the importance of job strain, worker autonomy, worker evaluation of task attributes, and mechanized versus nonmechanized types of work in relation to worklife and retirement decisions. The type of occupation, the features of explicit job tasks, as well as job skill level, are relevant in the retirement decision among both blue- and white-collar workers. Age, social class, occupation, family context, climate preference, and education are among other variables mentioned by Sheppard (1976), as having a definite connection with individual worklife and retirement judgments.

According to Munnell (1977), recent Social Security Administration findings specify health and Social Security availability as significant in worklife/retirement influences.

While these many factors on which the retirement decision depends may be anticipated, exploited, or guarded against, they are not too often controllable due to heredity, education, ambition, motivation, social orientation, sex, race, health, etc. In addition, the three stages of retirement, active, sedentary and terminal, are subsidiary components to be considered as more people live through a longer life experience due to increased longevity (Cooley, 1972), and reach the confining period of extreme old age.

Retirement, as an event, a status, a role, a process, and a social pattern, is a recent phenomenon in the United States with retirement qualifications and decision-making factors being current areas of study. However, contemporary retirement issues are of significance in the present changing worklife and retirement pattern.

CONTEMPORARY RETIREMENT ISSUES

Contemporary issues in retirement addressed by past-Secretary Joseph A. Califano, Department of Health, Education and Welfare (July 17, 1978) were:

1. The increase in life expectancy of almost ten years since 1940.
2. The coming appearance of the "senior boom" due to the World War II "baby boom."
3. The increase in earlier retirement even though individuals are living longer.
4. The changing ratio of active workers to retired or dependent ex-workers.

The increase in life expectancy (Table 1-2) and the senior boom (Table 1-3) are demographic facts. However, there are social, economic, political, and psychological circumstances that may be analyzed for possible social policy intervention when examining: (1) the early retirement trend; (2) federal action impacting on worklife and retirement factors; (3) escalating retirement problems; and (4) future needs of older workers/retirees. Each of these points is a significant contemporary retirement issue.

Early Retirement: A Consequence of Interacting Factors

Using the age of 65 as the traditional age of retirement, early retirement is defined as retirement before the age of 65. Mandatory retirement is retirement due to work rules that demand exit from the work force at a prescribed age. Many factors operate together in reinforcing and supporting the early retirement trend: Union and industry policies, private pension plans, a public pension plan and other federal legislation, worker expectation and lack of other options. Regardless of the elements affecting early retirement, it is the interaction between the factors that has sustained the early retirement movement.

Union/Industry Promotes Early Retirement. Faltermayer (1965) believes that unions were responsible for the drift toward early retirement through establishment of private pension plans with options for early retirement. The early retirement effect counteracts the effects of a functioning seniority system wherein older worker priorities reign in such areas as preferential work shifts and general working conditions. The union retirement system operates ". . . as a check and balance to the seniority system so that older union members are transferred into retirement and the young trade unionists are offered more opportunity" (Streib and Schneider, 1971, p. 176).

Innovations in private retirement and health plans as well as a surge in union activity made it increasingly possible to retire earlier than age 65. As examples: The United Auto Workers increased benefits for early retirees; and pension plan change led to workers selecting earlier retirement (Streib and Schneider, 1971). Since 1963, Teamster Union members have been allowed to retire at age 57 in some parts of the United States. In 1964, the United Auto Workers won a supplementary payment that gave early retirees a larger pension than previously retired 65-year-olds (Faltermayer, 1965). The United Mine Workers lowered the age of pension eligibility from 60 to 55 in 1965. At the same time, United Rubber Workers reduced the mandatory retirement age to 62 making pension rights possible at an earlier age without actuarial deductions. Chemical and Atomic Workers negotiated similar retirement agreements inviting earlier retirement (Faltermayer, 1965).

Atchley (1976) found that employers and unions generally subsidized the worker until eligibility for Social Security benefits was reached. In a study conducted by Banker's Trust Company of New York City, 84 percent of collective bargaining plans permitted early retirement with some type of pension benefit (Faltermayer, 1965). Rhine (1978) observed that added retirement benefits generally included some form of built-in mandatory retirement age requirements.

Mandatory retirement rules have been a powerful instrument in supporting the early retirement trend. The significance of employer mandatory retirement regulations can be recognized from a study conducted by Louis Harris and Associates (NCOA, 1978). Thirty-six (36) percent of all working people polled revealed that their companies, with pension and/or other employee benefits, carried a fixed mandatory retirement age (National Council on the Aging, 1978).

Private pension plans and mandatory retirement ages are generally linked; and with a swing toward age reduction requirements for benefit receipt, these plans are strongly influential in the early retirement trend.

Private pensions make retirement more attractive (U.S. HEW,

1976); and unions generally provide this service (Clague et al., 1971; Mercer Corporation, 1978). Companies providing bonus subsidy, payments until Social Security income is available, and redesigned pension funds (Davidson, 1969) are elements that reinforce union activity in promoting earlier retirement.

Federal Legislation Encourages Early Retirement. In 1961, economic pressure from business and union lobbying resulted in reduction of the possible pensionable age to 62, with accompanying actuarial deduction, under the Social Security Act. Though this was an economic measure responding to a recessionary period (Hendricks and Hendricks, 1977; Jaffe, 1972) the outcome led to earlier retirement. According to Mercer Corporation (1978), "(M)ore than 80% of Social Security retirement benefits (excluding those for disability) are now made to persons under 65 as compared to 12 percent twenty years ago" (p. 6).

The Social Security Act, as amended in 1974, provides a cost-of-living increase that is an added support to earlier retirement. However, it must be recognized that each new piece of legislation, encouraging older worker retirement, has been a result of economic, social and/or political pressure arising from changes in the worklife pattern of industrialized society.

Worker Expectation and Preference Supports Early Retirement. Worker expectation and/or preference for leisure time is an additional endorsement of early retirement. Preference for leisure is accentuated for those with good health and adequate income among white-collar workers (Green et al., 1969; Loether, 1975; Hendricks and Hendricks, 1977) as well as for blue-collar workers in dissatisfying, tiring, unpleasant and boring positions (Puner, 1974; Loether, 1975). Or, as Atchley (1976) notes, the worker's interpretation of the job has an impact upon his/her worklife and retirement impression.

Clark Tibbitts (Faltermayer, 1965) predicted that providing retirement income and "cultural outlets" would eventually encourage retirement before the age of 60. Atchley (1977) found that adult expectation of retirement was generally correlated with income (high income-early retirement), but believed that retirement income expectations were unrealistic for many workers.

Lack of Other Options Forces Early Retirement. Technological advance, with machine productivity, resulted in an increasing number of older workers with obsolete skills, lack of education and contemporary training, being driven from the job market. In addition, social philosophy, economic, political, and psychological maintenance were not, and are not, available for older workers desiring worklife and retirement flexibility. According to experts, job retraining, education, job relocation, trial retirement, job redesign or restructuring, second careers, job sharing and/or career and life counseling could introduce worklife and retirement flexibility into interested older worker's lives. A deficiency of these features offering worklife and retirement flexibility encourages early retirement.

When older workers leave the work force, in addition to a lack of worklife and retirement flexibility, they experience difficulty in obtaining new employment (Church, 1978). When work-force re-entry is abandoned, this is not an arbitrary or voluntary retirement, but rather a "discouraged worker syndrome" (Rhine, 1978). A major finding by the U.S. Department of Health, Education and Welfare (1976) reveals that workers claim entitlement to retirement benefits under conditions ranging from extreme hardship to comfortable positions. This follows the line of thought that lack of options supports early retirement, and that workers retiring in poor economic circumstances may be a result of worklife and retirement inflexibility where choices are slim.

Factors Interact to Reinforce Early Retirement. The interrelation of factors contributing to the early retirement trend is complex, and each factor impacts upon the other. Union and industry policies, private pension funds, federal legislation and worker expectation and preference as well as the lack of options, contribute to the current early retirement trend. In addition, early retirement may originate from mandatory factors of injury, occupational disease, and/or declining health.

The current worklife and retirement pattern in the United States is a result of a demographic shift, sociohistorical movement toward industrialization, the institutionalization of retirement, and the early retirement trend. Two other contemporary issues that are instrumental in defining the present situation are: (1) Federal intervention measures; and (2) escalating social and individual worklife/retirement problems.

FEDERAL INTERVENTION AND THE WORKLIFE AND RETIREMENT PATTERN

Recently, there has been federal action, in response to the changing worklife and retirement pattern, that encourages retirement on the one hand, and advocates flexibility of retirement options on the other hand.

Social Security Act as Amended in 1974

The economic position of the retiree is elevated, somewhat, by changes in the Social Security Act in 1974. The developments are: (1) the raising of Social Security benefits across the beneficiary group; (2) automatic adjustment of benefits for all recipients to keep within the cost of living; (3) SSI income guarantee for the elderly, blind, and disabled without adequate financial assets; and (4) a special Social Security benefit minimum based on length of covered employment (U.S. HEW, 1976).

Because these measures do benefit the retiree, they can be assumed to support retirement.

Employee Retirement Income Security Act (ERISA)

ERISA, enacted on September 2, 1974, has been ". . . hailed as major reform legislation which would insure the pension rights for workers covered by private plans" (Meier and Bremberg, 1977, p. 6). Workers covered by private pension plans increased from 450,000 workers in 1960 to 6.4 million in 1974 (Meier, 1977) revealing the scope of older worker/retiree pension programs covered by this piece of legislation.

Employee protection from pension loss through ". . . company or pension plan bankruptcy, merger or mismanagement" (Quirk, 1974, p. 62) was the main objective of ERISA legislation. Federal regulations were to be followed by all companies and unions both under existing plans and when establishing new plans. The major provisions were:

1. Eligibility—all employees reaching the age of 25 or having one year of service may join a plan.
2. Vesting—nonforfeitable right to a retirement pension benefit must be selected from one of three plans. These plans, I, II and III, spell out vesting alternatives.
3. Pension Insurance—a Pension Benefit Guarantee Corporation (PBGC) was set up within the Department of Labor to protect benefits in terminated plans.
4. Survivor Benefits—at least half of the benefit due the pension plan participant must be paid to a survivor (Quirk, 1974).

While Individual Retirement Account (IRA) and Keogh plans are not of great consequence to workers covered by private pension plans, they are a part of ERISA, and they are important in establishing worklife and retirement flexibility for those workers, *approximately 50 percent of the work force,* who do *not* have a private pension program.

The Individual Retirement Account (IRA) is a mechanism to provide pension coverage for those workers without a private pension plan. IRA allows individuals to establish a plan with a tax free deduction from the salary. The maximum deduction is $1500 or 15 percent of the worker's wages per year. The pension fund may be withdrawn as early as 59½ years of age, but no later than 70 years of age. Taxes are paid when the pension is withdrawn (Meier, 1977; Hendricks and Hendricks, 1977; Hutchison, 1978), which would generally be at a time of decreased income, creating a tax advantage.

Keogh plans were liberalized through ERISA; and the self-employed, without other plans, are allowed retirement savings at 10 percent of yearly income or $2500 annually. The first $750 earned may be used to establish a plan regardless of yearly income. The maximum allowed for tax exemption was $7500. Employees must be included in the employer's plan (Meier, 1977, Kovach, 1978).

Though less than one-half of the working population is covered through private pension plans, federal activity is significant, through ERISA, in attempting to assist workers without a work-related pension plan. Together, Social Security, SSI, and ERISA, appear to encourage the current worklife and retirement pattern, and possibly the early retirement trend, by protecting the older worker/retiree under both public and private pension plans. While this pension protection system is necessary, other federal legislation and activity indicate interest in a more flexible worklife and retirement system.

Age Discrimination in Employment Act (ADEA)

The Age Discrimination in Employment Act of 1967 covers workers aged 40 to 69, and prohibits discriminatory practice in employment because of age in hiring, job retention, compensation, firing and/or promotions. The older worker is to be evaluated on functional ability and *not* on chronological age. The law is enforced through the Equal Employment Opportunity Commission. The ADEA Amendments of 1978 raise the upper age limit of mandatory retirement to age 70. Mandatory retirement is eliminated for Federal Civil Service employees, age 40 and above (Grunewald, 1972; Rhine, 1978; House, 1978).

Comprehensive Employment and Training Act of 1973 (CETA)

CETA ". . . consolidated a variety of traditional categorical manpower development and training programs" (Flahive, 1975, p. 110). Clients must be poor, unemployed, or under-employed and jobs targeted for youth, American Indians and older workers. CETA stresses the establishment of a flexible and decentralized system to provide job training and employment opportunities in federal, state and local systems. Flahive (1975) continues that those serving the older worker must be ready to ". . . make sacrifices in order to institutionalize older worker service by integrating the entire manpower system" (p. 116). An example of CETA functioning for older workers is a pilot program, "New Ways to Work," which provides job-sharing opportunities (U.S. DOL, May 1978).

However, there are questions on the effectiveness of CETA for older workers. Schran and Osten (1978), in an analysis of CETA data, found relatively few older people being served by the program, with job concentration assistance being given to youthful workers.

Capitol Hill Examines Worklife/Retirement Flexibility

Through May, June and July of 1977, Hearings were held before the Subcommittee on Retirement Income and Employment of the Select Committee on Aging, House of Representatives, seeking testimony from expert witnesses regarding alternatives of retirement. Chairman Fred B. Rooney stressed the need of flexible hours, job-sharing and part-time work to alleviate the future economic impact of the changing worklife and retirement pattern. Flexible retirement was deemed necessary to offer options to workers across the life span (U.S. House of Representatives, Select Committee on Aging, 1977). Rooney (1978) observed that both those alternatives to retirement that presently exist and those under development in the public and private sectors should be examined.

On May 18, 1978, Representative Claude Pepper introduced a package of Bills into the House of Representatives that would function to terminate age discrimination in the United States (U.S. House of Representatives, May 18, 1978), and pave the way for decreasing the numbers of older workers *forced* into retirement.

In July of 1978, a U.S. Senate Special Committee on Aging, chaired by Senator Frank Church, conducted a Hearing on "Retirement, Work and Lifelong Learning." The demographic shift to an older population, slower economic growth, inflation, early retirement, demands for medical care, a shortage of younger workers, the dependency ratio, the coming "senior boom" and market demand shifts, were some of the factors viewed as having an impact on the contemporary and the future worklife and retirement pattern (U.S. Senate Special Committee on Aging, 1978).

Nearly all of the witnesses said that ways should be found to delay retirement and extend working life as a means of easing the strain on the Social Security, pension and welfare systems as well as on the labor market (Shabecoff, July 30, 1978, p. 16*).

Commentary

Federal activity, affecting the contemporary worklife and retirement pattern, could be considered ambiguous; but this is due to federal

*Copyright © 1978 by the New York Times Company. Reprinted by permission.

response to socioeconomic pressure in a historical context. The Social Security Act, as amended, adjusts to public need as inflation creates inroads into the economic security of retirees; and ERISA responds to the benefit problems within the private pension field. Although these pieces of legislation may be viewed as encouragement toward retirement, they are necessary measures to protect the ever increasing retired population.

On the other hand, the Age Discrimination in Employment Act, the Comprehensive Employment and Training Act of 1973, and action before the U.S. House of Representatives and the U.S. Senate, indicate interest in more flexible worklife and retirement possibilities for older workers/retirees. While these examples are not indicative of an across-the-board mandate for worklife and retirement alternatives, they do address a changing attitude among many specialists in the fields of aging, work, and retirement. However, many workers neither adequately understand the ramifications, nor even know of the existence of : (1) ERISA; (2) ADEA; (3) CETA; and (4) Capitol Hill activity. These could be among areas of study under the lifelong learning process recommended by the 1978 U.S. Senate Special Committee on Aging. The lifelong learning concept is also advised by the Office of Education, Department of Health, Education and Welfare through a ". . . comprehensive Joint Working Agreement between the Office of Education and the Administration on Aging" . . .for ". . . working on implementation plans and activities" (Chandler, May 2, 1978). Another element that could assist with worklife and retirement education is examination of the American Association of Community and Junior College (1978) project of careers for older adults. In addition, the majority of large universities, across the country, are in the process of designing classes for older adults.

The early retirement trend and federal activity in work, retirement, adult education, and flexibility for these life phases are not the only issues affecting the contemporary worklife and retirement pattern. There are escalating problems of both an individual and a social nature that contribute to the existing situation. In addition, questions concerning the future needs of older workers must be answered if worklife and retirement flexibility is to be realized.

WORKLIFE/RETIREMENT PROBLEMS IMPACT ON SOCIETY AND THE INDIVIDUAL

Both widowhood and retirement, traumatic experiences, happen abruptly; and social practices that ease these role changes are Social Security benefits, private pension funds, profit-share receipt, annuities and life insurance (Blau, 1973; Puner, 1974). All of these are economic interventions.

Because occupation is used as a measure of class position, social stratification occurs along occupational lines. Without a job role, there is a decrease in social status, and a lowering in social rank for most retirees. Professionals may keep titles associated with a position, and hold on to prestige; but this is not true for most workers/retirees (Puner, 1974; Streib, 1976).

Lack of a Retirement Role or a National Retirement Policy

There is neither a clear rite of passage nor social gain, role continuity, or social expectation (Blau, 1973) that affords a positive social role transition into retirement. Lack of preparation, inexperience, and/or no form of anticipatory socialization regarding retirement may bring discontinuity into old age. In other words, without concentrated work activity and/or without retirement education or worklife/retirement options, energy is not redirected among other roles. There is neither a continuation of activity level nor a new role emergence in senior life for many adults. It is this situation that isolates many older adults when they disengage from the work force.

Streib and Schneider (1971) stress "role set" as being role continuity through redistribution of work energy to spouse, children, neighbors, etc., when the worker is no longer active with employer and fellow workers. Roles in senior life should involve anticipatory socialization; and without the making of specific plans, ambiguity will enter late adulthood. If informal and formal retirement planning programs do develop, then a point of anticipatory socialization could be available for establishing a retirement role (Streib and Schneider, 1971).

If retirement becomes a recognized social role, then problems of

role discontinuity may well rest on social decisions that would expand worklife and retirement education. However, Blau (1973)
credits retirement as presently resting ". . . ultimately on a social
judgement that the interests of the society are better served by excluding older people from work" (p. 32). This does not appear to
project a positive future for either flexibility in worklife/retirement
options or a shining social role for retirees. A current study
(Research and Forecasts, Inc., 1979) recognizes the impact that an
increasing older population could have in the social sphere, and the
demands this group could make, possibly altering the future worklife
and retirement pattern.

The individual problem, lack of a social role, is compounded by a
social problem of great magnitude. As expressed by Senator Frank
Church, "The United States has no retirement policy" (Shabecoff,
July 30, 1978, p. 16). This fact may well be the central issue that
limits both the general opportunity for education and flexibility
of older workers'/retirees' options in worklife/retirement decisions.
The lack of a national social policy on retirement contributes
to negative forces affecting the older worker/retiree, but most
especially to the approximately 50 percent of workers without a
private pension plan. Workers/retirees without a private pension
plan do not have access to retirement education which is usually
undertaken by unions and large industry (Blank, 1979). While a
decline in role or role obligations through retirement may open new
role opportunities, presently there is neither an institutionalized
form of anticipatory socialization nor a national retirement policy
to delineate worklife and retirement possibilities in senior life.

Failing Health, Being Female and Limited Job Opportunities

The majority of men retire involuntarily below the age of 65 because
of ill health, and above the age of 65 due to the restrictions of old
age. According to Monk (1972), this is indicated through educated
older workers and workers in demand remaining in the work force
past age 65. The 1969 Retirement History Study by the Social Security Administration (Sheppard, 1976) places health as the most common reason given for early retirement. In a study conducted for the

National Council on the Aging, *The Myth and Reality of Aging in America,* poor health is cited as the major reason for not working by those 65 and over though other reasons were also given (NCOA, 1977). However, older citizens are becoming progressively more active, healthy, and youthful due to health and nutrition innovations (Califano, 1978), which could reverse the trend of retirement because of failing health.

Although early retirement may be predicated upon individual health problems, Dr. Julius B. Richmond, former Surgeon General of the United States, cautions that sudden changes in living style ". . . can create the severe emotional stress which has been associated with serious physical illness or even premature death" (Rosenberg, October 14, 1979, p. 8). Puner (1974) pinpoints the highest mortality rate for retired workers as being in the first year *after* retirement. Brickfield (1978) views mandatory retirement as detrimental to health, and sees extension of the worklife as possibly prolonging the lives of some workers who retire at 70 rather than 65.

With one exception, studies on retirement ". . . have been marked by total exclusion of females . . . " (Jaslow, 1976, p. 212*). Moser (1974) observes that the discouraged worker syndrome is a problem for females who become victims of limited job opportunities when attempting to re-enter the job market. When first entering the workforce close to retirement age, older females, displaced homemakers, and widows encounter social, economic, and psychological problems with career and employment direction unavailable (Foss, 1978). However, the highest workforce participation rates for females, increasing 40 percent from 1947 to 1973, is among nonmarried females: older single, widowed, divorced, and separated women who are centralized in low status, service positions (Sheppard, 1976). Consequently, those socioeconomic variables affecting the older male worker/retiree, in the contemporary worklife and retirement pattern, are exacerbated for the older female worker/retiree.

Limited job opportunities for older workers, who have left a job either arbitrarily or on-demand, are common. In many instances, the work force is abandoned when the prospect of obtaining a new posi-

* With the permission of the *J. of Gerontology,* 1976.

tion becomes disheartening. There are a multiplicity of reasons that obscure the job scope of older workers, such as (1) lack of educational background; (2) obsolete skills; (3) employment in declining industries; (4) increasing health problems; and (5) decreased mobility with an inability to follow a new job market (Rhine, 1978). In addition, even when well qualified, an older worker may be passed over for a youthful worker (Rhine, 1978). Sheppard (1976) presents plant shut-downs, mass layoffs, regional economic growth rates, national economic profile, education, physical capability, and prior experience as underlying the unemployment problems of older workers. Sheppard (1976) adds that a "culture of age-ism" places emphasis on chronological age as the criterion for working capacity which results in a reduction of job availability. Once the older worker leaves the work force, increased health problems and fruitless job-seeking encourage retirement (Sheppard, 1976).

According to Fisher (1978), unemployment problems of older workers were compounded by an overexpansion in the 1960s. Furthermore, recession periods are extremely difficult on older workers who are pressed into retirement when other financial and career alternatives do not exist. Fisher (1978) points out that encouragement toward early retirement does not address the possibility of locating future jobs.

The lack of a retirement role and a national retirement policy along with individual problems of declining health, being female, and limited job opportunities point directly to the most explicit change when older workers confront retirement—a decrease in income.

Economic Problems Compounded by Spiraling Inflation

Economic problems are two-fold within the contemporary worklife and retirement pattern. There is an economic impact on both the older worker/retiree and on the society upholding the public pension system. Inflation aggravates the situation at all times; but when double-digit inflation occurs, the economic problems become very difficult for most workers and retirees.

The early retirement profile reveals workers who have led less successful work lives, accrued lower Social Security benefits, and need old age assistance (U.S. HEW, 1976). Kreps (1978) states that the sharp drop in retirement income makes it difficult for retiree adjustment, and that living expenses, while declining, do not decline as much as retirement income. In examining the Department of Labor's three Retired Couple's Budgets, Robert N. Butler (1975), Director of the National Institute of Aging, finds that the budgets are founded on the assumption that older couples have ". . . accumulated much of what they will need for the rest of their lives" (p. 28).* Butler questions this premise especially when considering the future retiree: healthier, more active, more highly educated and with more years to live. The utility of free time is directly related to income level (Kreps, 1976); and while there have been economic gains, money is needed the most by older people (Comfort, 1976).

Economic pressure is obviously great on older workers/retirees; and as the ratio of retired workers to nonretired workers (the dependency ratio) increases, an added burden is placed on the entire economic system (Cowan, 1978). Ray Marshall (1978), Secretary of Labor, demonstrates a demographic change significant to the dependency ratio over time. Presently, there are 25 million people who are 65 and over in the United States or approximately 11 percent of the population. The projected figures for the year 2050 are 38 million, or 19 percent of the total population. Marshall (1978) believes this will result in a hardship for the working force and for the Social Security system. Therefore, employment options to insure older worker/retiree flexibility should be approached as "(I)t will be increasingly difficult for all older Americans to experience a comfortable retirement if we depend primarily on 'transfer' systems supported by smaller cohorts of younger workers" (Marshall, 1978, p. 9).

When examining the actuality of these "transfer" payments, current employee/employer contributions sent to the Social Security Administration are not placed in an account for the particular contributor, but rather, are used for some past retiree who may or may not have contributed to the system or who contributed at a lower

*From *Why Survive? Being Old in America* by Robert N. Butler. Reprinted with permission of Harper & Row, Publishers, Inc.

rate. If the aging of the population (Table 1-1) continues, with a decreasing birth rate, then the dependency ratio could become unfeasible. The economic impact on both the individual and society, under the present worklife and retirement pattern, is further complicated by inflation and its effect.

Rising inflation (in excess of 7 percent per year) has created a loss of purchasing power detrimental to those on a fixed income, such as, monies received from a private pension plan. Social Security, while carrying a cost-of-living increase clause, has become the mainstay of retiree support, which it was not intended to be.

Government figures revealed an increase of 8.2 percent in a retired couple's cost of living for fall of 1978. Within the same time frame, Social Security income increased by 6.5 percent; and as stated previously, in many cases, Social Security formed the basis of retirement income. Retirees, using investment as supplementary income, found that inflation reduced their fixed assets by 8.2 percent. Consequently, it was necessary to increase the retirement "nest egg" to stay up with the inroads of inflation (Armstrong, October, 14, 1979, p. 3).

The 1979 Study of American Attitudes Toward Pensions and Retirement (Harris, Louis and Associates, Inc., 1979) uncovered inflation and the quality of retired life as the prime concerns of employees, retirees, and business leaders. Retirees not receiving private pension funds, were affected most seriously by inflation with an actual reduction in the standard of living. Business leaders found inflation to be a disadvantage in company pension plans. Both retirement income needs and expectations were found to be increasing among employees/retirees. A cost-of-living component in private pension plans was deemed important (Harris, Louis and Associates, Inc., 1979).

The Research and Forecast, Inc. (1979) study found the positive view toward retirement diminished by continuing inflation, and questions on retirement postponement arising for those aware of the effect on retirement income. Inflation and its impact on fixed or partially fixed income brought a decrease in early retirement according to 88 percent of personnel directors surveyed (Research and Forecast, Inc., 1979).

These studies support the finding of the National Council on the

Aging (1978) that inflation destroys the security of old age when a fixed income is paramount.

Social, individual, and economic problems result, in many instances, in psychological problems for the older worker/retiree trapped in a changing work and retirement standard.

Psychological Problems Attend Retirement Adjustment

Erik Fromm observes that there is a difference between "freedom from" and "freedom for what" (Blau, 1973). Loss of a work role does not establish what work-free time is for. Streib and Schneider (1971) view "loss of automatic, job-defined roles" as possibly retirement's greatest problem. Rolelessness can lead to an increasingly poor self-image, and produce feelings of uselessness, isolation, loneliness, demoralization and aimlessness (Monk, 1970; Blau, 1973; Freese, 1977). Female dislocation is equally devastating, particularly if accompanied by divorce, widowhood, and/or child rearing role loss (Rosow, 1974). Rosow (1974) continues that there is little done to define or to prepare a "distinctive role" in retirement—or to help in finding meaningful substitutes for work. There is no training for the majority of people entering the retirement phase of life, except in,

> . . . the genuflection of preretirement counseling programs . . . These programs are not widespread and tend toward superficiality with limited content. There is possibly . . . an hour or so between one and five times before retirement, usually in the last five months (Rosow, 1974, p. 26*).

There are a complex set of variables that determine retirement adjustment with the very definition of adjustment being of importance. Voluntary/involuntary retirement, retirement income, personal happiness, nature and degree of individual activity, preretirement adjustment and attitude, physical and mental health, preretirement occupation, education, physical capacity, and mobility are among factors examined by Sheppard (1976) as having influence on retire-

* Copyright 1974 by the Regents of the University of California. University of California Press, Berkeley, California.

ment adjustment. Sheppard (1976) advises that differences in study results may be attributable to definitions of all terms, the sample, time frames, etc.

Commentary

The worklife and retirement problems that impact on the individual and society can only be solved when they are systematically addressed. At this time, the lack of a national retirement policy prohibits the orderly formulation of plans and procedures that could reduce current and future worklife and retirement uncertainties. These major issues should be open to general scrutiny because of their profound effect on older worker/retiree practical concerns such as: financial planning, health, housing, leisure opportunities, employment, training and education, interpersonal relationships, etc. These items are among the realities that each older worker/retiree must account for when establishing personal needs, resources, priorities, expectations, and actions within an ever-changing worklife and retirement scene.

Fluctuating socioeconomic and political circumstances increase the necessity for worker/retiree understanding of issues that directly and indirectly effect the worklife and retirement pattern. There are indications that future older workers/retirees may face more significant problems if the demographic shift continues and if inflation is not controlled. Education appears to be the solution, and could be the basis of a National Policy on Work, Retirement and Lifelong Learning. Retirement education is hardly a new idea; but a generally accessible method that would motivate and involve all workers/retirees in worklife and retirement examination has not been attempted. Retirement education has traditionally been carried forth in retirement planning programs within unions and large industry which automatically excludes a large portion of the work force (Blank, 1979).

In addition, questions surrounding the significance, necessity, and the application of retirement planning programs are some of the areas that have undergone extended review since initial program development.

RETIREMENT EDUCATION DEVELOPMENT

Studies on retirement education began shortly after development of group discussion programs at the University of Michigan and the University of Chicago. Hunter (1968), in examining studies undertaken from 1950 to 1963, came to certain conclusions:

- Industrial preretirement planning programs paralleled private pension plan growth.
- Large industrial organizations were more likely to initiate programs than were small employers.
- Method of delivery was primarily on an individual interview basis—perhaps only a single interview.
- Beginning in the 1950s, program content expanded into such areas as health, leisure time, family life, housing.
- Group discussion type programs showed some growth in large companies.
- Programs were not viewed as a major company element, and were not participant or employer evaluated.
- Community involvement was limited, with inhouse personnel conducting the programs.
- Financial aspects of retirement were the priority feature.

Hunter (1968) concluded that a review of retirement planning programs, sponsored by union and industry, failed ". . . to reflect the growth of programs which were being sponsored by universities and colleges, public schools, libraries, the various branches of military service, governmental agencies at both the federal and state levels, YM—YWCA's and church organizations" (p. 17).

In 1974, Kasschau questioned the many authors who had ". . . hailed the increasing trend among employers to provide preretirement counseling. . ." (p. 42) when evidence suggested little change in retirement planning programs over the past decade. According to Kasschau (1974), programs generally offered only pension benefits information and were impossible to evaluate until ". . . systematically conceived, designed and implemented . . ." (p. 42) with rigorous research. Manion (1974) found preretirement education carried out primarily by progressive employers, employee interest groups, and nonprofit organizations. The patterns of change, recognized by Manion, were: (1) Employee awareness of need; (2) employer awareness of responsibility; and (3) university involvement which provided new insight for program content and delivery method.

Maddison (1974) discovered that advanced retirement education programs were to be found in the areas of origin: the University of Michigan and the University of Chicago. In these locations, programs had evolved into weekly group discussion sessions, usually seven in number, with an expanding range of topics including finances, health, leisure, housing, employment, etc. Community activity, as well as community programs, were viewed as an important element of retirement planning. New activity in community colleges (California and New York), and increased university (Utah, Southern California) involvement revealed a growth in program development according to Maddison (1974). Professional developers, such as Action for Independent Maturity (AIM), were recognized as important developers of programs (Maddison, 1974).

In a study conducted by Reich (1977), the majority of retirement planning programs were found to be based on an individual approach, but with a growing interest in the group approach. Most programs did not include participants below the age of 60, even though professionals were advising earlier ages for participation. While programs varied in length, companies and universities generally offered weekly sessions of seven to nine meetings—each two hours in length. Worker and spouse were encouraged to participate together, voluntarily, on a variety of issues—finances, housing, health, etc. Finances and health were of major concern in short-term programs with added topics in programs of greater length. Reich (1977) saw a need for inclusion of "more feelings in group programs" to bring a valuable experience to the middle-aged person.

O'Meara (1977) observed that "(R)elatively few employers are providing either pre- or post-retirement assistance for their employees" (p. 1). In this study of 800 companies, the economic, social, and psychological problems encountered by retirees were addressed as well as the little being done by employers to alleviate the situation. Guidelines were provided for those companies that were either revising programs or instituting new programs.

Mulanaphy (1978), surveying higher education retirement preparation programs, found that only 4 percent, or 96 of 2,210 institutions, presented a formalized retirement planning program. Participation was voluntary; and spouses were invited to combined one-to-one and group session presentations. Although program content varied, retirement benefits and financial concerns were always favored. Housing and leisure time were included in more than one-half of the programs; health and legal affairs were covered in 68 of the 96 programs. Program evaluation was undertaken in less than one-half of the programs, and follow-up procedures in less than one-fourth (Mulanaphy, 1978).

Siegel and Rives (1978), in a study of existing and planned programs, concluded that programs were generally designed by company personnel, and held during business hours with financial planning the main area of interest. Although the research analysis was based on a 34 percent response rate, the researchers felt the programs under examination were too narrow in scope.

RETIREMENT EDUCATION STUDY RESULTS VARY

These study results, covering from 1950 (Hunter, 1968) to 1978 (Mulanaphy; Siegel and Rives, 1978), differ in conclusions as they examine various dimensions of retirement planning programs. Hunter's (1968) study and Maddison's (1974) review provide a state-of-the-art approach. The six intervening years allow for some alterations in program content and delivery method. Each of the studies reveals the strong influence of the University of Michigan and the University of Chicago as retirement planning program developers.

While the studies uncover a montage of problems and changes, as viewed by the individual researchers, there is no indication that program proliferation, if in fact true, contributes to general program accessibility. In addition, retirement planning program application results leave some unanswered questions when approaching the feasibility of a national policy on retirement that would include education opportunities. In other words, is general retirement planning program accessibility possible, and if so, does program material exist that would offer a comprehensive and comprehensible vehicle with maximum flexibility in senior life?

CURRENT RETIREMENT PLANNING PROGRAM AVAILABILITY STATUS REPORT

In a recent study (Blank, 1979), the factors examined in following the proliferation of retirement planning programs were: (1) Federal activity; (2) university research and development; and (3) free enterprise response of universities and private nonprofit-making organizations in producing packages for sale. Each of these areas were expected to be instrumental in either inhibiting or expanding retirement planning program availability and growth; and if expanding growth, then the expectation was that program content and delivery method would improve. Concurrently, if expansion was revealed, then the assumption could be made that proliferation was a response to the factors responsible for the current worklife and retirement pattern: longer life expectancy; increased older population; industrial productivity; liberalized earlier retirement; mandatory retirement; private and public pension plan growth and job scarcity. Each of these socioeconomic changes impacted upon the worker and society, and contributed to worklife and retirement changes which may now demand general education for alleviating future problems.

Federal Activity Aids Program Proliferation

The Administration on Aging, established by the Older Americans Act of 1965, is of interest to this status report, in that it legitimized assistance to older people, and made grant funds available for research and demonstration projects on aging. Activity in the aging field showed a growth surge because of federal legislation affecting the Administration on Aging, and because of related federal legislation creating and enlarging other governmental agencies serving the aging population (Department of Education, Department of Labor, Department of Commerce, etc.). *

* Note: For additional information, see Legislation in the 93rd Congress Relating to the Elderly, Enacted and Introduced (CRS, Library of Congress, HD—7106 A, 1975).

As examples: The Older Americans Act, under Title IV—Training and Research, authorizes grants for research and demonstration in the field of aging (U.S. House of Representatives, August 1976). There is a Comprehensive Joint Working Agreement between the Office of Education and the Administration on Aging that promotes interagency activity for older people. The fiscal 1978 Labor—HEW Appropriation Act (H. R. 7555) earmarks over $800 million for older Americans' programs (U.S. HEW, *Aging,* November/ December, 1977).

In addition to these examples of federal activity that provided legitimization and grant funds for retirement planning research and development, the 1971 White House Conference on Aging sanctioned the need for program proliferation:

Preretirement education and counselling should be provided throughout the nation by trained instructors, starting at least five years before normal retirement age. Government at all levels, employers, unions, and educational institutions (especially through adult education agencies and the use of television) should encourage and promote preretirement counselling by trained instructors. Special courses for those nearing retirement are urgently needed (White House Conference on Aging, 1973).

The White House Conference on Aging of 1971 was focused toward establishing a national policy on aging from which can be inferred that a National Policy on Retirement was also a target. Interest at the federal governmental level, and available funds, provided the impetus for increased university research and development and a free enterprise response.

University Research and Development Increases

With funds available through research and development grants, university activity in retirement planning programs increased.

Drake University set up a three-year demonstration project under a joint grant from the Administration on Aging and the Manpower Administration, Department of Labor. The program was to test the feasibility of improving meaningful retirement activity through education and to train representatives in methods of organizing and delivering programs. In the process of the research, a retirement planning program was designed, guide books prepared and two-day training sessions started (United States Department of Health, Education and Welfare, "How Retirement Planning Works," 1970).

The University of Massachusetts conducted a two-year demonstration program with three small union groups. The investigation was partially supported by the Administration on Aging, and revealed that successful retirement programs must include a systematic training component for recruiters, a knowledge of worker-participant background and of retirees' attitudes on retirement (O'Rourke, 1972).

The Manpower Administration, U.S. Department of Labor, sponsored a ten-year study by a Ohio State University research team investigating the work lives of middle-aged men. While not a retirement planning research project, the report showed that economic changes affected early/late retirement, that age, earnings, and productivity were linked; and that health problems reached a minority of the preretired group (Perlman, 1975); all of which are significant to retirement program planning.

The Rocky Mountain Center of Gerontology, University of Utah, representing a consortium of universities (Brigham Young University, Southern Utah State, Weber State, Utah State and the University of Utah), conducted research on social, biomedical, psychological, legal, and environmental aspects of retirement. Short-term training for professors and summer workshops were offered by this program, financed by the Administration on Aging (Maddison, 1974).

A comprehensive retirement planning program was developed at Duke University through an experimental match-control design. The project, partially funded by AOA, used Duke employees to demonstrate multimedia, lecture, group discussion, exercises, and worker notebook components (Duke University, 1977).

These examples of university action in retirement planning program research and development were an invaluable aid to program proliferation as well as to the extension of content material and program presentation modes. While the free enterprise response was partially located within universities that were activists in retirement planning program development, private nonprofit organizations, using grant funds, produced services and materials that further expanded program possibilities.

Free Enterprise Response Assists Program Application Possibilities

A free enterprise response is evident through the proliferation of salable retirement planning programs, services and materials being offered to industry, unions, and others.

University Producers. The University of Georgia offers "New Wrinkles on Retirement," a series of eight half-hour color TV programs and U-matic cassettes among its retirement plan components on a rental or purchase basis. The University of Michigan-Wayne State presents "Preretirement Education Programs and Services" that includes consultant services, pilot programs, leadership training, leader's manuals, reading materials, seven 16 mm sound-track films, and program evaluation services. Pace University, New York City, in its Active Retirement Center, offers courses for personnel staff, retired human service workers, and individuals wishing to plan a personal retirement. "Planning and the Third Age" is the title of the University of Nebraska's retirement planning program which is an ultrasophisticated package. In addition, the University of Southern California, Duke University, and the University of Chicago are among other universities producing retirement planning services and/or materials (Blank, 1979).

Private Producers. *Action for Independent Maturity (AIM)* may be the largest of the retirement planning package distributors. AIM's services include both preretired and retired memberships and employer package arrangements. Employee membership services cover areas from reduced pharmaceutical rates to insurance and travel services. Employers may purchase training programs and sophisticated multimedia materials. The *American Consultant Team* offers to customize a program, "One Third of Your Life," narrated by Dave Garroway. ACT produces program service along with elegant multimedia materials. The program is designed for use by a trained discussion leader and for ease in localizing and updating material. The series includes an eight-session slide-tape discussion covering a range of retirement considerations, as well as workbooks, discussion guides, etc. The *Manpower Education Institute* promotes a package, "Ready or Not," with continuing updated material, carried on both video cassette and 16 mm film. Material may be rented or purchased, and covers areas of basic needs, priorities, and alternatives for retiree examination. The materials are recommended for company, educational and other organizational group use, and have been used on public television. Personal assessment manuals, leader's guides and monthly news letters are a part of the package. *Retirement Advisors, Incorporated (RAI)* stresses individualization of program material for large or small manufacturers, financial and professional organizations, governmental agencies, etc. The program offers a variety of services, the price of which is established through tailoring to employer/employee need. *Retirement Program Services* advertises tailored programs for an organization's individual needs. *Retirement Services, Incorporated* in "Plan Now for Your Retirement, Free to Do, Free to Be," offers a series of ten articles on various aspects of retirement, and provides services for retirement preparation. The *Pre-Retirement Planning Institute* invites organizations to Pre-Retirement Counselor Training Workshops; makes available leadership training, group skills, facilitating techniques, personal retirement concern examination; suggests promotion tools and recruitment methods; and offers films, materials, charts, questionnaires, budgets, evaluations, projection aids, etc. *Retirement Living Magazine* produces a set of retirement booklets for use by organizations. The pamphlets cover a variety of subjects with a personal information and records inventory of monthly budget assessment. *The National Council on the Aging* has developed a new retirement planning program package. The input of thirteen major industrial and union groups has led to a comprehensive and comprehensible program. Audio visual materials, special background materials, participant workbooks and leaders' training sessions are available. The program puts major emphasis on setting goals and objectives and on assessing individual needs, priorities, expectations, and resources (Blank, 1979).

Federal activity and the availability of grant funds have encouraged proliferation of retirement planning programs, with universities and private nonprofit organizations responding through increased research and development. The professionalism arising in the retirement planning field can be recognized through the establishment, in 1975, of a Society for Preretirement Program Planners. The Society functions as a clearinghouse for information, organizes conferences and training programs (Blank, 1979).

These available retirement planning programs offer a variety of services and materials which, generally, can be purchased either packaged or piecemeal. If for no other reason than competition, professionalism of program development has augmented both program content and presentation methods.

Program Growth Broadens Application Possibilities

Because of professional application, retirement planning program possibilities are enhanced. Although selection for simplistic to complex program design may be made by consumers, generally, a packaged program is available that may be tailored to fit the most sophisticated need. With earlier program participation (National Council on the Aging suggests age 40, The Manpower Education Institute cites age 50) being recommended, the majority of professional producers include employment, second careers, and/or factors necessary for career changes in mid- to late life. Participant workbook type materials are available, and are devoted to increasing the planning skills and to introducing new planning skills to participants (Blank, 1979).

Monthly news services may be purchased, and cover a multiplicity of worklife/retirement related subjects: Educational opportunities, trust funds, federal legislation changes, etc. Programs that include participant planning through goals and objectives is another approach available to consumers. Professional program developers, both universities and private organizations, usually offer a consultant service to interested employers or other perspective customers. Special training programs for program leaders and an impressive range of multimedia material, in many instances based on sophisticated educational and/or behavioral techniques, are purchasable (Blank, 1979).

An interesting development, which further expands application possibilities of some programs, is an emphasis on participant needs assessment of worklife and retirement resources, expectations, priorities and establishment of a specific individual action worklife/retirement plan. Evaluative methods are available, and measure participant behavior change pre- and postprogram contact. Special interest areas, such as women and their future, finances and health, personal safety features for the older retiree, financial planning and inflation, may be added to the standard program fare when using specific developers offering these features (Blank, 1979).

It appears that professional program developers have broadened application possibilities which react to current concerns of flexibility in worklife, retirement and education options for older workers/retirees. A flexible planning aspect seems to place emphasis on an individual's past life planning ability which, with a little assistance, could be enhanced in later life. As the inclusion of employment and second career modules become program components, a life-planning possibility enters the changing worklife and retirement situation rather than the current quick transition from work to retirement.

There has been retirement planning program proliferation that was encouraged by federal activity providing legitimization for older worker/retiree assistance and grant funds. Both sanction of worker/retiree aid and available monies resulted in an increase in university research and development of retirement education. Concurrently, a free enterprise response, by universities and private, nonprofit organizations, assisted expansion in the retirement planning field, and broadened application possibilities for consumers. However, although program growth and extension of flexibility are evident, retirement planning program accessibility for general worker/retiree participation has not become a trend (Blank, 1979).

Retirement Planning Program Accessibility
Rests on Specific Criteria

A retirement planning program is usually accessible to those people who:

1. have a private pension plan
2. belong to a union

3. are employees of a large industry
4. live near a retirement planning program presentation unit
5. are church affiliated
6. are 55+
7. are married
8. are the "volunteer" type
9. have *free* nonworking hours, and
10. are *employed* (Blank, 1979)

These explicit factors may be joined by implicit factors of:

11. being a blue-collar/white-collar worker
12. being male

These criteria must be present in some form, of either one or more, for an individual worker/retiree to have easy access to worklife and retirement education. In addition, these criteria become necessary to promote worker expectation and motivation in seeking a means to examine worklife and retirement processes.

"Accessibility Criteria" Inhibit
General Worklife and Retirement Education

When inhibiting criteria of any sort exist, accessibility is curtailed for entering a group regardless of individual need, resources, expectations or priorities. In this case, the criteria are elements that limit or retard "general" worker/retiree entrance into worklife and retirement education.

As an example, the following statement demonstrates that "have a pension plan" criterion automatically eliminates 53 percent of current workers from programs in the private sector:

An estimated 47 percent of wage and salary workers in the private sector are currently participating in retirement plans. . . . In 1977, 30 percent of married couples and 15 percent of nonmarried persons receiving Social Security retirement benefits also received other pension income. This includes government employees and railroad retirement programs as well as private pensions. . . .The most recent data available indicate that over 40 percent of married couples, and over a quarter of nonmarried persons, who are beginning to collect Social Security benefits also receive another pension (Marshall, July 18, 1978, p. 3).

Consequently, 60 percent of married couples and 75 percent of nonmarried persons, recently retired, are without second pension plans. This infers that worklife and retirement education accessibility has been an improbability for these individuals.

As an added insight on accessibility, when related to a second pension fund, ". . . such pension plan coverage generally is concentrated on those persons with higher than average wages during their lives" (Marshall, July 18, 1978, p. 5). This injects a socioeconomic factor into work and retirement education accessibility.

The total civilian labor force, male and female, as of December 26, 1978, was 94.373 million (U.S. Department of Labor, CPS Base Table, 1978). The total union Employee Association membership was 22.506 million (Becker, Department of Labor Statistics—1976 Data Base, 1978). Using "belong to a union" as a retirement planning program accessibility criterion, there are approximately 72 million workers who do *not* belong to a union; and therefore, retirement planning program accessibility is unlikely.

As another example, using the average entrance age to programs as a median of 55 + (Blank, 1979), there are approximately 14 million workers in this age category, and about 34 million workers in the 35 to 55 age range (U.S Department of Labor, CPS Base Table, 1978). When speaking of early worklife and retirement planning, the age "accessibility criterion" excludes over one-half of those being encouraged to plan early.

These examples of accessibility criteria reveal the possible exclusion of 53 percent of all workers/retirees (private pension plan criterion), or of 72 million workers (union membership criterion), and/or 34 million workers (age 55 + criterion, excluding ages 35–55). Admittedly, there is overlap in these categories; however, the data is used to demonstrate the numbers of workers/retirees who may find worklife and retirement education programs inaccessible.

While the balance of "accessibility criteria" will not be related to demographic data, many workers: (1) Are not employed by large industry; (2) do not live near a program presentation unit; (3) are not affiliated with a church group; (4) are single, divorced or widowed and not a spouse; (5) are not a volunteer type; and (6) do not have time free from work. Probably, the most limiting factor is to be unemployed, underemployed or have a sporadic employment history; all of which negate the opportunity for worklife and retirement education. It could be inferred that the older population most in need of planning is the least likely to be afforded participation (Blank, 1979).

O'Meara (1977) and Mulanaphy (1978) address the "lack of formal programs" among employers. According to the Blank (1979) study, some of the same accessibility criteria may be reversed to read: small business, nonunion enterprises, rural location, female work force, lack of private pension plan, and reflect the reason for lack of programs among employers. The premise, when using "accessibility criteria" is that the lack of worklife/retirement education depends upon the worker/retiree position in the work force as well as upon employer status in the business sector.

Program Inaccessibility is a Form of Cultural Lag

Current retirement planning program inaccessibility for all workers/retirees, in relation to program proliferation and application possibilities, is viewed as an area of "cultural lag" wherein national social policy intervention measures are necessary.

William Ogburn (Berger and Berger, 1972) designates cultural lag as ". . . a discrepancy between different processes of change" (1972, p. 313*). Generally, this concept is used to describe ". . . drastic transformation of the economy and technology of a society while its family institution or its moral values still retain their traditional forms"* (1972, p. 313). however, in this case, cultural lag is used to draw attention to the discrepancy between the majority of older workers/retirees without worklife and retirement education accessibility, and the fact that these individuals are participating in a changing worklife and retirement pattern where planning is necessary to offer flexibility in senior life. The cultural lag is a product of the industrialization of worklife, and is a product of the changing worklife and retirement pattern.

According to Toffler (1970), technology feeds on itself with three

*From *Sociology: A Biographical Approach* by Peter L. Berger and Brigitte Berger. p. 313. Copyright © 1972 by Peter and Brigitte Berger. Published by Basic Books, Inc., New York.

stages of innovation: (1) A creative, feasible idea; (2) a practical application of the idea; and (3) diffusion of the idea through society. The process is complete, and the loop closes when diffusion helps to generate new ideas (Toffler, 1970).

Retirement was a new process accompanying industrialization as a creative and feasible idea to alleviate a social problem of too many workers for too few jobs. However, the practical application of the process revealed that a possible transition period was necessary for successful transfer from work to retirement. As the idea of retirement spread through society, problems arose that generated a new idea that would provide a transition stage between work and retirement. Consequently, retirement planning program development began, but these programs have not become accessible to all older workers/retirees.

This appears to be the area of cultural lag, wherein social emphasis is placed on retirement without a concurrent emphasis on worklife and retirement education that is generally accessible. In addition, easy-access worklife and retirement planning programs should provide study opportunities for keeping abreast with constantly changing factors in the society, and offer a wide range of worklife/retirement options for flexibility in senior life.

Experts Continue to Recommend Retirement Education and Flexibility

Monk (1970) recommended visibility and diffusion of retirement plans, lowering of the attending age, and retirement planning programs to be delivered in three stages. Delivery was to be between the ages of 50–64, and include special manpower resources. Two years later, Monk (1972) stated:

> Preparation for retirement should become a generalized social concern. Free information and referral services must become functional attributes of our present-day society available to all and not based on economic need (Monk, 1972, p. 63).

Sheppard (1970) believed that work behavior as well as future retirement behavior was influenced by the topic of retirement and retirement preparation. This could denote a positive behavioral change because retirees with precounseling were found by Greene et al. (1970) to be better adjusted with a great difference between those counseled and those not counseled. According to Greene et al. (1970), retirement counseling reduced resistance to retirement which, along with increased morale and work performance, was beneficial to both employee and employer.

Counseling helped employees to develop positive attitudes toward retirement and to adjust to socioeconomic aspects of retirement (Conklin, 1973). Kasschau (1974) stated that there was need for retirement planning programs to be studied through research methods, and for incorporation of specific goals within retirement planning programs. Puner (1974) found ". . . critical need for all those burgeoning pre- and post-retirement planning programs, those and many more in the future that can penetrate into the main stream of life" (p. 170*).

Puner's statement reflects a future oriented and general program accessibility need in worklife and retirement planning education, as do the following ideas: (1) There should be a national strategy to elevate the position of older workers, over 40, through second careers (Batten and Kestenbaum, 1976); and (2) retirement planning program and retirement employment needs could be met in community colleges through education and retraining of older workers (Galvin et al., 1975).

These recommendations and viewpoints give added credence to the conclusion that all older workers/retirees should have an available easy-access worklife and retirement model that affords alternative life choices in the ever-evolving worklife and retirement pattern.

CONCLUSION AND RECOMMENDATIONS

Primary issues addressed in this chapter related to a changing worklife and retirement pattern viewed from an historical perspective. A subtle time and industrial connected aging problem was revealed through a demographic shift and other socioeconomic and political changes that contributed to an emerging retirement phenomena, and subsequent inflexible worklife and retirement options. Contemporary retirement issues of early retirement, federal

*From *To the Good Long Life: What We Know About Growing Old* by Morton Puner. Universe Books, New York, 1974.

legislation impacting on worklife and retirement, and escalating individual and social problems were reviewed, and justified the need for an expansion of worklife and retirement education through easy-access worklife/retirement planning programs, offering flexibility in senior life.

In addressing general retirement planning program accessibility, it was found that there had been: (1) Retirement planning program proliferation; and (2) broadened program application possibilities along with the increase in professional developers. However, general program accessibility for all older workers/retirees was not a consequence of content and delivery technique expansion. Specific "accessibility criteria" were found to exist that described the population who would "most likely" have worklife and retirement education.

Program inaccessibility, viewed as a form of cultural lag, automatically rejects a certain portion of the older worker/retiree population from examining the intricacies of worklife and retirement, and consequently, from obtaining flexibility in senior life. As the worklife and retirement pattern must continue to fluctuate, due to the changing socioeconomic scene, the necessity for an easy-access worklife and retirement planning program with a wide range of options increases. In addition, educational programs of this type are recommended by experts in the fields of gerontology, economics, psychology, sociology, and others, and have been cited as important for worklife/retirement transition since the 1950s.

Federal sanction, through legitimization of aging programs and available grant funds, has provided the possibility for program proliferation, and concurrent content and delivery method expansion. This is another reason, if not the most important, that worklife/retirement education should be accessible in some form to *all* older workers/retirees who assisted in the financing of these undertakings through personal taxation.

RECOMMENDATIONS

There are certain elements available in the social system that could provide the necessary ingredients for a national social policy intervention measure that would facilitate generally accessible worklife and retirement education.

A Need for Social Policy Intervention

Although the value of existing, functioning retirement planning programs is not discounted, current worklife/retirement issues reveal problems that should be recognized and possibly reduced through a national social policy with an emphasis on lifelong learning for older workers and retirees. Worklife and retirement examination, to be effective, must be generally accessible, and must prove flexibility by responding to individual needs, resources, and priorities as well as to socioeconomic change.

Demographic shifts, an earlier retirement trend and ramifications, along with changing federal legislation (ERISA, CETA, ADEA, SSA, etc) and possible social and individual problems are elements that should be open to inspection and review by older workers/retirees. In addition, individual survival concerns–financial planning, legal arrangements, housing, health, community resources, education and employment opportunities, leisure possibilities, life and interpersonal relation assessment as well as restricted life inevitabilities should be reviewed when involved in worklife/retirement decisions. The ideal point for examination of both social and individual changes and for new skill development is within an easy-access worklife and retirement planning program.

The Elements to Construct an Easy-Access Worklife/Retirement Program

The U.S. Department of Health, Education and Welfare (1977) has a guide for organizing a retirement planning program, *Planning and Conducting Pre-retirement Seminars,* which could serve in establishing basic action steps. The Blank (1979) study reveals the existence of ample retirement planning program materials, with sophisticated educational and behavioral presentation techniques, for application possibilities. The multiplicity of programs, and the availability of comprehensive and comprehensible "packages" should permit the establishment of programs with options for flexible worklife and retirement choices. Activity plans, drawn from this source, could provide a basis for competitive bidding among professional groups with available retirement plans.

There is a Joint Working Agreement between the Office of Education and the Administration on Aging for interagency activity that could enhance a lifelong learning focus into a worklife and retirement social policy. These two agencies could provide additional input to augment the current U.S. HEW retirement planning program guidelines.

The American Association of Community and Junior Colleges (AACJC) has an Older Americans Program for response to the needs of older adults. The AACJC, if motivated toward worklife and retirement planning education interest, could promote an "entrypoint" for older worker/retiree "easy-access" programs at a community level, within community and junior colleges.

Employer interest should be actively solicited as the point where worker expectation and motivation could be increased.

These initial elements in forging an easy-access worklife and retirement program should bring together federal, community, employer and employee input in developing a national social policy for worklife and retirement. However, it is felt that the Social Security Administration, which holds pertinent retiree/worker data, must be the initial developing point in establishing a national social policy.

Initiation and Invitation Point of Easy-Access Work/Retirement Planning Programs

The Social Security Administration, with its extensive data bank, could automatically issue projected public pension statements to workers reaching the 35th birthday. Along with projected income statements, invitations to public "easy-access" worklife retirement planning programs should be included. In addition, programs could be advertised by all government agencies involved in worklife/retirement/education issues. Invitations and announcements would follow at specified intervals.

Initial invitation by the Social Security Administration would be a prime motivator in encouraging workers/retirees to examine an easy-access program. In addition, federal recognition of worklife and retirement as a key social issue would legitimize the need for the worker/retiree seeking flexibility in senior life. An automated system of providing projected pension plan benefits, within a period where options are possible, would be an added motivation to examining career changes, extended education, job retraining and other worklife/retirement possibilities.

Social Policy Intervention Necessary

It is recognized that the suggestions given to initiate such a broad social movement for older workers/retirees are a simplistic design in relation to the needs for development of a worklife and retirement education system with easy access. In addition, there are economic, social, and individual barriers to be considered that will further complicate design, development, and implementation of such a program. In order to conduct a social action of this type, national social policy intervention is necessary. The magnitude of an undertaking of this type demands federal government legitimization and sponsorship as well as community, employer and worker/retiree interest, cooperation and shared responsibility. A systems approach to an easy-access worklife/retirement planning program, that underscores the human worth of older workers/retirees, offering flexibility in senior life should be a social policy goal. The ingredients are attainable; it is social policy intervention that is necessary.

REFERENCES

American Association of Community and Junior Colleges. Utilizing older Americans through community colleges. *Newsletter,* Washington, D.C.: American Association of Community and Junior Colleges, 1978.

Armstrong, Douglas D. You can learn to cope with squeeze of inflation. *The Milwaukee Journal,* Sunday, October 14, 1979, 3.

Atchley, Robert C. *The Sociology of Retirement,* New York: Schenkman Publishing Company, Inc., 1976.

—————. *The Social Forces in Later Life,* California: Wadsworth Publishing Company, Inc., 1977.

Barck, Oscar T., Jr. and Blake, Nelson M. *Since 1900—A History of the United States In Our Time,* New York: The Macmillan Company, 1965.

Batten, M. and Kestenbaum, S. Older people, work and full time employment. *Social Policy,* November 1976, 30–33.

Becker, Eugene. Department of Labor Statistics Bureau. *Telephone interview,* Washington, D. C.: Department of Labor, 1979.

Berger, P. and Berger, B. *Sociology: A Biographical Approach,* New York: Basic Books, Inc., 1972.

Blau, Z. S. *Old Age in a Changing Society,* New York: New Viewpoints, 1973.

Blank, Ruth Crary. *Current retirement planning program proliferation, application and accessibility: A state-of-the-art paper,* unpublished, Baltimore, Maryland: Antioch University; Washington, D.C.: Library of Congress, Copyright number 14588, June 21, 1979.

Brickfield, Cyril. Mandatory retirement can be hazardous to your health. *Dynamic Years,* January/February, 1978.

Brooks, Thomas R. *Toil and Trouble,* New York: A Delacorte Press Book, 1964.

Butler, Robert N. *Why Survive? Being Old in America,* New York: Harper & Row, Inc., 1975.

Califano Jr, Joseph A. Testimony before U.S Senate Special Committee on Aging. *Hearing on Retirement, Work and Lifelong Learning,* Washington, D.C.: U.S. Senate, July 17, 1978.

Chandler, Barbara A. Education Program Specialist, U.S. Department of Health, Education and Welfare, Division of Adult Education. *Correspondence,* May 2, 1978, Washington, D.C.: U.S. Department of HEW, 1978.

Church, Senator Frank. Opening statement before U.S. Senate Special Committee on Aging. *Hearing on Retirement, Work and Lifelong Learning,* Washington, D.C.: U.S. Senate, July 17, 1978.

Clague, E. et al. *The Aging Worker and the Union Employment and Retirement of Middle-Aged and Older Workers,* New York: Praeger Publishers, 1971.

Clark, Robert and Spengler, Joseph. Population aging in the twenty-first century. *Aging,* Nos. 279-280. Washington, D.C.: U.S. Department of HEW, January/February, 1978.

Cooley, L. F. and Cooley, L. M. *How to Avoid the Retirement Trap,* Los Angeles, California: Nah-Publishing Company, 1972.

Comfort, Alex. *A Good Age,* New York: Simon & Schuster, 1976.

Conklin, W. E., Jr. Preretirement counseling. *Hospitals,* November 16, 1973, **47** (22), 86-88.

Cowan, E. A pension aide says people should work long beyond age 65. *The New York Times,* May 2, 1978.

Cowgill, Donald. Transitional Theory as General Population Theory, *Social Forces,* March 1963, 41, 270-274.

Davidson, W. Some observations about early retirement in industry. *Industrial Gerontology,* February 2, 1969, **1**:26-30.

Duke University. *Advances in Research,* **1**(3), Durham, North Carolina: Duke University, Fall, 1977.

Faltermayer, E. K. The drift to early retirement. *Fortune,* May 1965.

Fisher, P. The social security crisis: An international dilemma. *Aging and Work,* **1**(1), Winter 1978, 1-14.

Flahive, M. CETA and the older worker: A planning strategy for local communities. *Industrial Gerontology,* Spring 1975, **2**(2), 110-121.

Foss, H. M. Displaced homemakers/widowed services, *Information Sheet,* University of Oregon, 1978.

Freese, A. S. Adjustments in later life. *Dynamic Years,* November/December, 1977, 37–39.

Galvin, K. et al. Educational and retraining needs of older adults. *Final Project Report,* California: Southern California Community College Institutional Research Association, 1975.

Garraty, J. A. *The American Nation: A History of the United States.* New York: Harper & Row, 1971.

Greene, M. R., et al. Preretirement counseling, retirement adjustment and the older employee. *Industrial Gerontology,* **6,** Summer 1970, 37–38.

—————. *Preretirement Counseling, Retirement Adjustment and the Older Employee.* Eugene, Oregon: University of Oregon Press, October, 1969.

Grunewald, R. J. The age discrimination in employment act of 1967, *Industrial Gerontology,* Fall, 1972, 1–11.

Harris, Louis and Associates: *1979 Study of American Attitudes Toward Pensions and Retirement,* New York: Johnson and Higgins, 1979.

Hendricks and Hendricks, C. D. *Aging in Mass Society Myths and Realities,* Cambridge, Mass.: Winthrop Publishers, Inc., 1977.

House, Sharon L. *Mandatory Retirement,* Issue Brief No LB 77087, Washington, D.C. U.S. Library of Congress, CRS, April 10, 1978.

Hunter, W. *Preretirement education for hourly workers,* Project No. 1422, Contract No. OE-2-10-047, U.S. HEW, Michigan: University of Michigan, October, 1968.

Hutchison, J. D. The compleat fiduciary. *Pension World,* **14**(4), April 1978, 44d.

Jaffe, A. J. The retirement dilemma. *Industrial Gerontology,* Summer 1972, 1–88.

Jaslow, P. Employment, retirement and morale among older women. *Journal of Gerontology,* **31**(2) March 1976, 212.

Kasschau, P. Reevaluating the need for retirement preparation programs. *Industrial Gerontology,* **1**(1), Winter 1974, 42–59.

—————. Retirement and the social system. *Industrial Gerontology,* **3**(1), Winter 1976, 11–24.

Kimmel, D. C. *Adulthood and Aging,* New York: John Wiley and Sons, Inc., 1974.

Kovach, D. Program Associate, Retirement Planning Program. *Interview,* Washington, D.C.: National Council on the Aging, 1978.

Kreps, Juanita M. The economy and the aged, in *Handbook of Aging and the Social Sciences,* (R. H. Binstock and E. Shanas, Eds.), New York: Van Nostrand Reinhold Company, 1976.

—————. The economics of aging, in *The New Old: Struggling for Decent Aging,* (Gross, R. Gross, B. and Seidman, S., Eds.) New York: Anchor Books, 1978.

Levitan, Sar A. and Belous, Richard S. *Shorter Hours, Shorter Weeks: Spreading the Work to Reduce Unemployment,* Baltimore, MD: The John Hopkins University Press, 1977.

Loether, H. D. *Problems of Aging,* California: Dickenson Publishing Company, 1975.

Maddison, A. *Pre-retirement Education in North America,* Plymouth, England: 1974.

Maddox, George L. and Wiley, James. Scope, concepts and methods in the study of aging, in *Handbook of Aging and the Social Sciences* (R. H. Binstock and E. Shanas, Eds.), New York: Van Nostrand Reinhold Company, 1976, 3–34.

Manion, U. V. Issues and trends to preretirement education. *Industrial Gerontology,* 1(4), Fall 1974, 28–36.

Marshall, Ray, Secretary of Labor. Testimony before U.S. Senate Special Committee on Aging. *Hearing on Work, Retirement and Lifelong Learning,* Washington, D.C.: U.S. Senate, July 18, 1978.

Meier, E. ERISA and the growth of private pension income. *Industrial Gerontology,* 4(3) Summer 1977, 147–157.

————— and Bremberg, H. *ERISA: Progress and Problems,* Washington, D.C: National Council on the Aging, 1977.

Mercer, W. M. Incorporated. *The Impact of Mandatory Retirement Legislation on Employee Benefit Plans,* New York: W. M. Mercer, 1978.

Monk, A. Attitudes and preparation for retirement among middle-aged executives and professional men. *Industrial Gerontology,* 5, Spring 1970, 45–46.

—————. A social policy framework for pre-retirement planning. *Industrial Gerontology,* Fall 1972, 63–70.

Moser, C. Mature women—the new labor force. *Industrial Gerontology,* 1(2), Spring 1974, 14–25.

Mulanaphy, James M. *Retirement Preparation in Higher Education,* New York: TIAA, 1978.

Munnell, Alicia. *The Future of Social Security,* Washington, D.C.: The Brookings Institute, 1977.

National Council on the Aging, *Fact Book on Aging: A Profile on America's Older Population,* Washington, D.C.: National Council on the Aging, February, 1978.

—————. The Myth and Reality of Aging in America, Washington, D.C.: National Council on Aging, June, 1977.

O'Meara, J. R. *Retirement: Reward or Rejection,* New York: The Conference Board, 1977.

O'Rourke, J. F. and Friedman, H. L. An inter-union preretirement training program: Results and commentary. *Industrial Gerontology,* 13, Spring 1972, 49–64.

Perlman, L. Probing the preretirement years. *Manpower,* Washington, D.C.: U.S. Department of Labor 7(6), June 1975, 11–15.

Praigg, N. S. Cashing in on experience. *Industrial Gerontology,* 4(3), Summer 1977, 183–189.

Puner, Morton. *To the Good Long Life: What We Know About Growing Old,* New York: Universe Books, 1974.

Quirk, Daniel A. Public policy notes. *Industrial Gerontology,* 1(4), Fall 1974, 62–64.

Reich, M. Group preretirement education programs: Whither the proliferation? *Industrial Gerontology,* **4**(1), Winter 1977, 29–41.

Research and Forecasts, Inc. *Retirement Preparation: Growing Corporate Involvement,* New York: Corporate Committee for Retirement Planning, 1979.

Rhine, S. *Older Workers and Retirement,* New York: The Conference Board, Inc., 1978.

Rooney, Fred B. U.S. House of Representatives. *Correspondence,* Washington, D.C.: U.S. House of Representatives, May 2, 1978.

Rosow, I. *Socialization to Old Age,* Berkeley: University of California Press, 1974.

Rosenberg, Neil D. Emotion affects retiree's health. *The Milwaukee Journal,* Sunday, October 14, 1979, 8.

Schlesinger, Arthur M. Jr. *The Politics of Upheaval,* Boston: Houghton Mifflin Company, 1960.

Schran, Sanford F. and Osten, David F. CETA and the aging. *Aging and Work,* **1**(3), Summer 1978, 163–173.

Shabecoff, Philip. A fast-aging population. *The New York Times,* Sunday, July 30, 1978, 16.

Sheppard, H. L. (Ed.). *Towards an Industrial Gerontology, An Introduction to a New Field of Applied Research and Study,* Cambridge, Massachusetts: Schenkman Publishing, 1970.

—————. Work and retirement. *Handbook of Aging and the Social Sciences,* (R. H. Binstock and E. Shanas, Eds.), New York: Van Nostrand and Reinhold, 1976.

Siegel, Sidney and Rives, Janet. Characteristics of existing and planned preretirement planning programs. *Aging and Work,* **1**(2), Spring 1978, 93–100.

Streib, G. B. Social stratification and aging. *Handbook of Aging and the Social Sciences* (R. H. Binstock and E. Shanas, Eds.), New York: Van Nostrand and Reinhold, 1976, 160–181.

————— and C. J. Schneider. *Retirement in American Society,* New York: Cornell University Press, 1971.

Toffler, A. *Future Shock,* New York: Bantam Books, 1970.

U.S. Department of Commerce. *Current population reports, special studies,* Series P-23, No. 59, Washington, D.C: U.S. Bureau of the Census, May 1976.

—————. *Monthly vital statistics report, table 3, abridged life tables by color and sex: United States,* Washington, D.C.: U.S Bureau of the Census, 1977.

United States Department of Health, Education and Welfare. *How retirement planning works,* combination of AOA and DOL manpower grant research, Des Moines, Iowa: Drake University, 1970.

—————. *Planning for later years,* Washington, D.C.: Reproduced by the Library of Congress, CRS, November, 1974.

—————. *Reaching retirement age,* (Publication No. 017-070-0028701), Washington, D.C.: U.S. Government Printing Office, 1976.

—————. Labor—HEW bill includes $800 million for aging programs. *Aging,* November/December 1977, 277–278.

United States Department of Labor. Job sharing—another way to work. *Worklife,* 3(5), May 1978.

—————. CPS Base Table. *Employment status of the civilian noninstitutional population by age and sex,* Washington, D.C.: U.S Government Printing Office, December 26, 1978.

United States House of Representatives. Select committee on aging, *NEWS,* Washington, D.C.: U.S House of Representatives, September 27, 1977.

—————. Select committee on aging. *NEWS,* Washington, D.C.: U.S. House of Representatives, May 18, 1978.

—————. *Older Americans Act: A Summary,* Washington, D.C.: U.S. Government Printing Office, August 1976.

United States Senate Special Committee on Aging. *Hearing on Retirement, Work and Lifelong Learning,* Statement of Ray Marshall, Secretary of Labor, July 18, 1978.

University of Oregon. *Center for Displaced Homemakers/Widowed Services, Fact Sheet,* Eugene, Oregon: University of Oregon, ND.

White House Conference on Aging. *Toward a national policy on aging,* Vol. II, Washington, D.C.: U.S. Government Printing Office, 1973.

Woodruff, D. and Birren, J. E. *Aging Scientific Perspectives and Social Issues,* New York: Van Nostrand Company, 1975.

2
DEMOGRAPHIC CHANGE AND RETIREMENT AGE POLICY

Elizabeth L. Meier and Barbara Boyle Torrey*

Age distribution of the population is basic to an understanding of the development of our retirement income programs. For pay-as-you-go systems such as Social Security, the aged are the beneficiaries of the pensions and the working age population the contributors. Thus relative proportions of the two groups are important in the economics of these programs. Also important are the definitions of retirement ages in retirement programs since this determines at what ages pension benefits can be paid. These retirement age policies of pension programs interact with demographic factors in determining the size and composition of the retired population and the demand for retirement income.

POPULATION TRENDS

During the last century, the U.S. had high birth rates, high mortality rates, and high immigration. These factors produced a population mix which had a large number of young people and a relatively small proportion of elderly people. But since 1880, birth rates, mortality, and immigration rates have all decreased significantly. By the early 1930s, the birth rate had dropped to the population replacement

*This chapter is based on two working papers prepared for the President's Commission on Pension Policy: *Demographic Shifts and Projections; the Implications for Pension Systems* by Barbara Boyle Torrey and *Varieties of Retirement Ages* by Elizabeth L. Meier and Cynthia C. Dittmar.

61

rate, which is approximately 2.1 children per woman. Immediately after World War II, however, the birth rate rose rapidly to a peak in the late 1950s that was 60% higher than the Depression years "baby bust" trough although still lower than in the last century. Since the late 1950s, the fertility rate has dropped back again, creating another trough on the other side of the baby boom.

The post World War II baby boom produced a demographic tidal wave which has had an enormous impact on society. When this cohort entered elementary schools, it produced overcrowded conditions until new facilities could be built. When it passed out of the schools there was a surfeit of teachers and a surplus of rooms. It had the same effect on college enrollments. Labor markets and housing markets have also felt the large demands made by the baby boom generation. Retirement programs will be the last major social institution to feel the full effects of this unique generation when the first of the cohort becomes 62 in 2009.

The people 65 and over will increase relatively slowly both in absolute numbers and as a percent of the total population between now and the turn of the century. However between 2000 and 2030, the increase will be more rapid as the baby boom retires. Only after 2030 when the baby boom dies may the people over 65 become a decreasing part of the population. The changing and projected proportions of the aged are shown in Figure 2-1.

Projections of the actual number of aged have a degree of certainty about them that many demographic projections do not. All of the people who are being estimated in the 65 and over categories out to 2040 are already alive, the only uncertainty in the projection of their numbers is in their life expectancy. The projections of the proportion of the aged in the society are, however, more speculative because those projections are dependent on assumptions about the size of the total population. That in turn is based on the estimated fertility rate, which will be the single strongest factor in determining the size of the population under 65.

In this chapter population projections are generally based on the Census Series III projections of 1.7 child fertility rate because:

● Series III is the closest series to the present-day fertility rate of 1.8 children per woman;

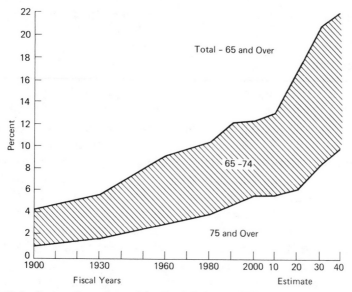

Figure 2-1. Proportion of aged in the total population.

Source: U.S. Bureau of the Census. *Current Population Reports.* Series P-23, No. 59 and Series P-25, No. 704. (Series III)

● The fertility rate since 1974 has been close to Series III;
● Series I and Series II assume that the fertility rate will increase in the future, an assumption that cannot be supported on the basis of present information;
● There is no significant difference in the estimated number of people 65 and over among Series I, II, and III until the year 2042;
● Series III is the most conservative series in estimating the number of future workers who will be available to support the retired population in the baby boom retirement crisis period.

Today the baby boom generation is part of the labor force which contributes to resources for the 11% of our population 65 and over, particularly through their taxes for Social Security. But the generations behind are much smaller. Therefore, when the baby boom retires, the ratio of the number of retired to the number in the labor force could double if population trends continue. This would produce a heavy burden for the future labor force and pension systems to support.

Immigration

In addition to an increase in births the population can also be expanded by an increase in immigration. But today legal immigration does not make the contribution to our population growth that it did in the 19th and early 20th century when it accounted for over 60% of the population growth in some decades. For 1977 immigration was responsible for approximately 20% of the increase in population.

The importance of illegal immigration is unclear. There are large flows, both in and out, across the southern border. Whether the net annual increase in undocumented aliens is substantial is open to question. The Bureau of the Census assumes in their long-term projections that there is a constant 400,000 increase in net immigration for each year. Legal immigration in recent years has been somewhat less than this, but without reliable information on illegal immigration there is no basis on which to modify their long-term estimate.

Life Expectancy

Mortality rates dropped sharply in the U.S. during the first half of the 20th century. Average life expectancy rose from about 47 years in 1900 to almost 60 years in 1930—due largely to improved public health measures such as improved sanitation. By 1950, life expectancy was 68 years. However, the rate of improvement fell off from 1950 to 1970; in fact, during the two decades there was only a 2.7 year gain. But mortality rates have been declining fairly sharply once again during the 1970s, and further significant increases in longevity are again a possibility.

Recent increases in life expectancy have not been evenly distributed among the various age groups. Until World War II, increases were primarily for the young and middle-aged. People were more likely than before to survive childbirth, infancy, and childhood diseases. However, once they reached old age they did not live much longer than elderly people had lived in previous generations. Recently this has changed, as can be seen in Table 2–1.

Increases in life expectancy for people 75 and over since 1965 have come at a time that the gains in life expectancy for the rest of the

Table 2-1. Life Expectancy by Age Group.

	Birth	65 Years	75 Years
1900–02	49.2	11.9	7.1
1939–41	63.6	12.8	7.6
1965	69.5	14.2	8.7
1976	72.8	16.0	10.1

Source: Life Table published by the National Center for Health Statistics, U.S. Public Health Service, and the U.S. Bureau of Census. Reprinted in *Current Population Reports* Special Studies Series P-23, No. 59, May 1976.

population were slowing. This trend, of course, increases the number of elderly in our society and makes it difficult for demographers and pension planners to accurately predict their numbers. Today people are on the average living almost 3 years longer after 65 than they did when the Social Security program began. Since World War II, the life expectancy of the aged has grown at a faster rate than life expectancy at birth, and the older the age the faster the rate of increase has been.

Historically, life expectancies have been consistently under-estimated because past experience gives no hint of future medical breakthroughs. Several illustrations suggest that estimates of the population 65 and over by the year 2000 may be conservative. Comparison of mortality rates with other industrialized countries shows that the five leading causes of death in the U.S might be able to be reduced by 37%. This would increase longevity considerably from 5% at birth to 12% at age 80. Actual population increases that would result from reducing preventable deaths are significant. There would be close to 8 million more people in the U.S. by the year 2000 if the U.S. could reasonably reduce its preventable deaths. Approximately 5 million people would be 65 years old and over, which would be an increase of 15% over present estimates. (Gori and Richter, 1978, Table 4*)

The population 65 and over would also be significantly increased if the adult life expectancy of men and women became equal, a 20% increase by the year 2000. Although both sexes are living longer, there are significant differences in life expectancy between the sexes and races. The difference in male and female life expectancies has

*Copyright © 1978 by the American Association for the Advancement of Science.

implications for both the retirement systems and the way of life of the elderly.

Black males have the lowest life expectancy in our society; white males have the second lowest. These life expectancies implicitly determine some of the general characteristics of the beneficiaries of retirement programs. In 1900 there were as many males as females who were 65 and over. This is in part because of the large immigration of males in the 19th century and the high mortality of women in the childbearing years. But during the 1930s the ratio began to shift until today there are only 69 males for every 100 females 65 and over. Within the older age group, the disparity increases with increasing age and the Bureau of the Census is projecting that this deterioration of the sex ratio will continue out past the turn of the century as is shown in Table 2-2. Thus, the problems of the very old are increasingly the problems of women, and retirement programs are the major sources of support for these women.

Demographic factors alone, however, are not the sole determinants of the beneficiary population of retirement programs. The age of retirement interacts with the demographic trends to define who the beneficiaries will be.

Table 2-2. Sex Ratios. (Males per 100 Females)

	All Ages	65 and Over	75 and Over	85 and Over
1900	104.4	102.0	96.3	NA
1930	102.5	100.4	91.8	NA
1960	97.8	82.6	75.0	63.8
1970	95.8	72.0	63.6	53.2
1980	95.0	67.9	56.0	44.1
1990	94.2	66.1	53.7	39.9
2000	93.8	64.9	52.5	38.5
2010	93.3	65.5	51.8	37.8

Source: U.S. Bureau of the Census, *Current Population Reports,* Special Studies Series P-23, No. 59, May 1976, p. 13.

THE INSTITUTIONALIZATION OF RETIREMENT

At the beginning of this century, only 4% of the U.S. population—about 3 million persons—were 65 and over. More than two-thirds of the men were working. There was very little retirement on a pension income because there was no Social Security and very few private and public pensions. Many persons were still employed on family farms and in small business enterprises which enabled them to remain working as long as possible. As industrialization proceeded, however, older men had more difficulty keeping and obtaining jobs.

In 1935, at the hearing which preceded the enactment of the Social Security Act, William Green, President of The American Federation of Labor (AFL), testified about these trends as follows:

> The mass system of industrial production has still further contributed to old-age insecurity. Under the mass process of production there came into existence new requirements for minimum intensity and speed of effort. There has also appeared a tendency to make this energetic requirement uniform for the entire plant. In the presence of heavy unemployment, each job has been placed in a highly competitive position. The older worker has been placed at a heavy disadvantage. There has appeared a tendency to displace him long before his productive capacity has disappeared or even before it has been appreciably impaired. (U.S. Congress, Senate Committee on Finance, 1935, p. 176, 177)

The Great Depression, of course, greatly worsened this situation as unemployment reached 31%. Many middle-aged and older persons were forced to turn to relief programs, and if they lost their jobs they had little hope of regaining them. The fact that many older persons were thus forcibly retired and in want gave impetus to the enactment of the Social Security retirement programs of national old age insurance and federal-state old age assistance.

SOCIAL SECURITY RETIREMENT AGES

Because the retirement ages provided by the Social Security Act and subsequent amendments have greatly influenced past and current retirement ages, it is worthwhile to examine the choice of 65 in 1935 for benefit eligibility and 62 for early retirement benefits several decades later.

Prior to the passage of the Social Security legislation, President Roosevelt appointed a Committee on Economic Security to study the problems relating to the economic depression and to make legislative recommendations. The Committee consisted of the Secretary of Labor as Chairman, the Secretary of the Treasury, the Attorney General, the Secretary of Agriculture and the Federal Emergency Relief Administrator. Old age security was only a part of the wide-ranging problems that the committee studied, which included unemployment compensation, security for children, and public health.

Staff studies considered the increase of aged persons in the United States, employment difficulties of the older worker, the extent of old age dependency, provisions for the aged in the United States and old age security abroad. Germany's system was examined closely as a staff report relates:

> Since the United States is taking its first steps toward a nation-wide system of old-age benefits and since forecasts are made, actuarial and otherwise as to what will happen to such a system within the next half century, it appears of value to investigate the experience of a country which has had the system in operation for the past 44 years. Germany adopted contributory invalidity and old-age insurance covering its entire working population in 1891 and has retained this system up to the present time. (President's Committee on Economic Security, 1937, p. 469)

Chancellor Bismarck initiated the system, apparently as a political move to appease the German working population after having suppressed the labor movement. Despite the fact that Bismarck is usually given credit for initiating age 65 retirement, the staff study found that the original law provided that pensions be paid from age 70 on. It was not lowered to 65 until 1916. (President's Committee on Economic Security, 1937, p. 487) When the age was lowered, the numbers of persons receiving pensions jumped considerably.

Another system which was studied extensively was that of Great Britain. Its noncontributory pension acts provided for an old age pension at age 70. However, when contributory pensions were enacted the age was lowered to 65.

The agitation to lower the pensionable age to 65 and to provide a universal pension had its fruition in the old-age pension granted to those between 65 to 70 years of age under the provisions of the Widows', Orphans', and Old-Age Contributory Pensions Act of 1925 . . . (President's Committee on Economic Security, 1937, p. 450)

In the United States, a number of states had started their own old age pension systems beginning with Montana in 1923. By 1935, there were 28 states and Alaska and Hawaii which had pension laws. Edwin E. Witte, Executive Director of the Committee on Economic Security, summarized the age requirements as follows, ". . . 14 states have a 70-year age limit, 1 state has an age limit of 68 and the balance 65. So, you have just about half of the group at 70 and half of the group at 65." (U.S. Congress, Senate Committee on Finance, 1935, p. 62).

The choice of age 65 eligibility for both the social insurance program for the future aged and the federal-state system of old age assistance for those already aged and in need is not discussed in any detail in the legislative history. But the experience of foreign countries and the states as well as the unemployment experience of older workers undoubtedly influenced the Committee. Secretary of Labor Francis Perkins (Chairman of the Committee) stated:

Many of the states have the provision that applies at 70 years of age, but the committee recommended 65 rather than 70, because we have come to a realization out of our studies that industrial practices and habits of this country have come to the point where it is very difficult for a man 65 years old to get a job, even though he is physically well and physically able to perform the job. (U.S. Congress, House Committee on Ways and Means, 1935, p. 176).

The president of the American Federation of Labor proposed that the age of eligibility be set at 60. This was also the age proposed by supporters of the Townsend plan named after its originator Dr. Francis E. Townsend. The latter politically popular plan called for a monthly pension of $200 for all those age 60 or over on the condition that they be retired and spend the entire amount the month it was received in order to stimulate the economy.

Ages below 65 were apparently rejected because of cost considerations. (The Townsend plan was certainly rejected for cost considerations.) Secretary Perkins suggested that other programs such as unemployment compensation should take care of older worker problems below the age of 65 as follows:

> All of us are concerned with the fact, for instance, that old age in many instances today begins at 50, if the man who is laid off for some reason or other during the depression finds he cannot get back to work on the theory that he is too old. We could gradually be asked to extend our old-age coverage to cover a man of that age, but no industrial systems which any of us sets up today could possibly afford to maintain all the people over 50 years of age who happened to be without work. But if we think of it as a problem of unemployment, if we think of the man of 50 as being a part of the unemployment problem and realize that the cost of his maintenance should be properly assessible against the unemployment fund, then we begin to treat his problem in a different way. (U.S. Congress, Senate Committee on Finance, 1935, p. 103).

After the Social Security Act was enacted and 65 institutionalized as the "normal" retirement age, withdrawal from the labor force became both more feasible and more obligatory as employers followed the lead of Social Security and made it the normal pensionable age and even the compulsory age of retirement. This did not happen at once, for no Social Security benefits were paid until 1940 and World War II kept many older persons in the labor force. But by 1950 the proportion of men 65 and over who were still working had shrunk to 40 percent as can be seen in Table 2-3.

In the 1950s, coverage of Social Security programs was greatly expanded from the industrial work force originally covered (about 50% of the total work force) until about 9 out of 10 workers were covered. This, together with increases in Social Security benefits, as well as increases in the availability of private pension benefits, influenced the declines in labor force participation. By 1978, only 20% of men over 65 were still in the labor force.

For women, the very small proportion over 65 who are working has remained relatively stable over the years and is currently 8 per-

Table 2-3. Older Worker Labor Force Participation Rates by Sex 1950, 1960, 1970, 1978.

	Male			
	1950	1960	1970	1978
Total				
55–64	83.0	82.6	83.0	73.5
55–59	86.7	87.7	89.5	82.9
60–64	79.4	77.8	75.0	62.0
65 +	39.0	29.4	26.8	20.5
	Female			
	1950	1960	1970	1978
Total				
55–64	23.2	34.6	43.0	41.4
55–59	25.9	39.7	49.0	48.6
60–64	20.5	29.5	36.1	33.1
65 +	7.3	10.0	9.1	8.4

Sources: U.S. Bureau of the Census. *Census of Population 1960; Detailed Characteristics.* U.S. Department of Labor, *Employment and Earnings,* January, 1971, January 1979.

cent. Thus, 92% of the women and 80% of the men 65 and over are retired and out of the labor force.

EARLY RETIREMENT LEGISLATION

Even though unemployment insurance was enacted and became a major federal-state program, unemployment problems of older workers were cited as the main reason for the 1961 provision of early retirement Social Security benefits for men at age 62. Such an actuarially reduced benefit had been provided for women in 1956 with the rationale that women were usually younger than their husbands and they also leave the labor market at younger ages. President John F. Kennedy had advocated the 1961 early retirement measure as part of legislation to promote economic recovery and area redevelopment in a time of economic recession.

Proponents of the legislation did not believe that the reduced benefits would be an inducement for the employed men to retire but would aid the unemployed who have difficulty in finding a job as they near 65. Administration officals gave the following rationale:

> Though there is general agreement that this change does not represent the only or the best solution to the economic problems of older unemployed workers, it does give them some protection. The fact is that the problem of the older worker who cannot get a job continues to exist, in good times as well as bad, and the social security program should be flexible enough to take account of this problem. Men and women make social security contributions over the years in the expectation of receiving insurance benefits when they are too old to work. They should have a degree of protection if they find themselves unable to get work because of conditions beyond their control when they are nearing retirement age, even though they have not reached 65. (Cohen and Mitchell, 1961)

Thus the institutionalization of early retirement with reduced benefits under the Social Security insurance program was based upon the rationale of assisting older persons who may lose their jobs in their sixties and have great difficulty becoming re-employed. The wisdom of using a retirement program to alleviate an unemployment problem has since been questioned. As a Brookings Institution study stated, "The point that requires widespread public understanding is that the retirement program is the incorrect remedy for the problem at hand. The problem, for which public policy seeks an answer, is the *unemployability,* for one of many reasons, of aging workers." (Pechman, Aaron, Taussig, 1968, p. 140*).

EARLY RETIREMENT TRENDS

Whatever the state of the economy, since the institution of early retirement for both men and women the numbers of both sexes retiring early has continued to increase. This is shown in Figure 2-2. Now 54% of all male Social Security beneficiaries and 68% of all women worker beneficiaries have retired with reduced benefits before age 65.

---

*From *Social Security: Perspectives for Reform* by J. Pechmann, H. Aaron and M. Taussig. Copyright © 1968 by the Brookings Institution. Published by the Brookings Institution.

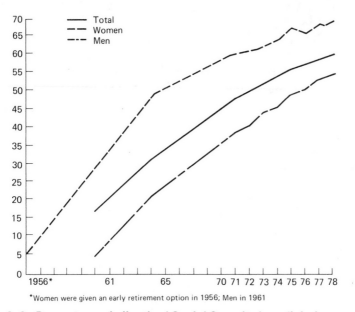

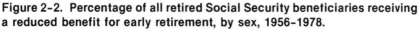

*Women were given an early retirement option in 1956; Men in 1961

Figure 2-2. Percentage of all retired Social Security beneficiaries receiving a reduced benefit for early retirement, by sex, 1956-1978.

Source: Social Security Administration. *Social Security Bulletin.* March 1979, Table Q-4.

Not all persons retire early for reasons of unemployment, however. The Social Security Administration (SSA) has included reasons for early retirement in a number of its studies. In a survey of newly entitled worker beneficiaries in 1968-70, SSA found that only 13% of the men taking reduced benefits said that they had lost their jobs while more than half felt that health was the most important reason for leaving their last job. (Reno, 1976, Chapter 4) Those who stipulated health reasons, however, could have had other reasons for leaving a job including eligibility for a pension or Social Security or job-related reasons. Nearly half of those opting for early retirement (62-64) had second pensions.

The report also found that there were some of the most advantaged and most disadvantaged in the group of men who filed for benefits at the earliest age of 62. About a quarter retired willingly with second pensions while 45% had no pension and did not want to retire when they had to leave their jobs.

Married women workers were the most likely to take reduced early retirement benefits; 85% did so compared to 53% of the nonmarried women (Reno, Chapter 7, 1976, p. 77) Of the women who had been out of the labor force for some time before taking early retirement, 16% of the married and nonmarried alike said that they had lost their jobs. Following the same pattern as men, more of the retirees taking early retirement cited health reasons as the reason for retiring than those retiring at age 65.

Private Pensions

While only a minority of retirees receive private pensions, the relative growth of pension plan coverage and the popularity of early eligibility ages for pension benefits have been important factors in influencing ages of retirement, particularly in some industries. A Conference Board survey report states, "The dramatic retirement fact of the 1970's has been the trend of early retirement. . . The trend has been so strong in some companies as to stretch the concept of a standard retirement age of 65 virtually out of shape. Average actual retirement in some of the companies represented by these executives is reportedly well below 60; and 62 is often the normal retirement age in practice, if not in a formal sense." (Meyer, 1978)

"Normal" retirement age is usually defined as the age when the employee may retire and receive a full benefit. As a Banker's Trust study points out, however, ". . . in a growing number of plans early retirement features have been liberalized to provide a full accrued pension as well, so that the phrase 'normal retirement age' has lost much of its former meaning." (Bankers' Trust, 1975, p. 23) However, 65 is still the stated normal retirement age in most plans even though many or even most beneficiaries retire before this age. Age 65 was also the most usual *compulsory* retirement age when there was one specified. But compulsory retirement before age 70 was made illegal by the 1978 Amendments to the Age Discrimination in Employment Act (ADEA) although 65 may still be the normal retirement age.* In fact, the 1974 pension reform law, the Employee Retirement Income Security Act (ERISA) *requires* that benefits be paid on "the date on which the participant attains the earlier of age 65 or the normal retirement age specified under the plan." (Public

*See Chapter 4 for a discussion of the ADEA.

Law 93–406, Section 206) In addition, the ADEA legislation did *not* require that employers would necessarily have to provide additional retirement benefits (accruals) if employees stay beyond the normal retirement age as set by the pension plan.

The law did not make any changes in Social Security. Full retirement benefits are still available at age 65. Now Social Security provides only a small increase of 1% for covered employees for each year worked beyond age 65 without drawing benefits (delayed retirement credit). The Social Security Financing Amendments of 1977 provided that this credit will increase to 3% beginning in 1982.

Despite the fact that most private pensions are integrated with Social Security, the age 62 Social Security early retirement option has not put a lower limit on private pension eligibility ages. The Bankers Trust study of plan provisions found that some plans provide for retirement as early as age 50, and 55 is common. A U.S. Department of Labor (DOL) 1978 study of 131 plans found that approximately 3 out of 4 plans allowed retirement at age 55 or earlier, compared with 2 out of 3 in 1974. (Frumkin and Schmitt, 1979)

In certain industries, there is no specific age requirement but only the completion of a given period of credited service, usually 30 years (30 and out). The latter provision is found in the steel, aluminum, copper, and automotive industries (Bankers' Trust, 1975).

The United Steelworkers and the United Auto Workers* were the first to negotiate "30 and out" in the 1960s. A special pension supplement is paid to the retirees (they may be in their fifties) until Social Security benefits are available.** The DOL study did not find that these types of special early retirement provisions increased between 1974 and 1978. Those that had such provisions usually increased the supplements.

In testimony before the President's Commission on Pension Policy, representatives from General Motors Corporation addressed the issue of early retirement provisions:

In General Motors, a majority of employees with 30 or more years of service retire in their fifties. Our average retirement age has

---

*International Union, United Automobile, Aerospace and Agricultural Implement Workers of America.
**These benefits are not protected by the Pension Benefit Guaranty Corporation since they are not "basic benefits" as defined by ERISA, the Pension Reform Act.

been as low as 58. This is not a pattern we support. It is not only costly but we lose a large number of employees in the prime of their working lives. However, we must recognize the pressures for early retirement present in our industry. We must also recognize the realities of the negotiation process. In the final analysis, our plans design reflects the concerns of the parties involved. (Olthoff, 1979)

No comprehensive survey of actual retirement ages of beneficiaries of private pension plans exists. But the SSA and other surveys have shown that those with second pensions to supplement Social Security are more likely to be voluntary early retirees. Pension receipt is undoubtedly an economic incentive to early retirement.

Government Employees

The largest group of employees not covered by Social Security consists of federal civilian employees, of whom 2.7 million, or over 90%, are covered by the Civil Service Retirement System (CSRS). Members may retire at age 55 with 30 years' service, age 60 with 20 years' service, and age 62 with 5 years' service. The payment of full benefits at age 55 was established in 1966. Before that time, benefits were reduced 1% for each year below 60.

Until recently, mandatory retirement was at age 70 but was abolished completely by the 1978 ADEA Amendments for this group alone as a compromise by those who wanted to abolish mandatory retirement for *all* covered employees. However, mandatory retirement still exists for small groups of civilian employees including foreign service officers (not included in CSRS) and certain hazardous duty occupations.

Despite the fact that federal civil service employees in the past have not been required to retire until age 70, the average age of retirement has been declining until the average optional age is now about 61. This does not include retirements under disability or involuntary early retirement which are at much earlier average ages—54 and 53. Fifty-five was the single most popular age of retirement for men compared to 62 for women. Of course, these "normal" retirement ages (benefits are unreduced) are much lower than the age 65 Social Security normal retirement.

In the state and local government sector, it is estimated that 85–90% of all employees are covered by a pension plan and the majority are also covered by Social Security. In 1975, about 10.4 million full and part-time state and local employees were in plans. Of these approximately 9.7 million were in occupations other than police work and firefighting and were members of approximately 2230 pension plans. (U.S. Congress, House Committee on Education and Labor, 1978) The large number of plans reflects the fact that very often state and local governments have separate plans for certain categories of employees. Teachers, particularly, are almost always covered by a separate retirement system.

The 1974 amendments to the ADEA specifically included state and local governments under the definition of "employer." Thus, state and local governments are also prohibited from mandatorily retiring employees before age 70. Even before 1978, many state and local governments did not require their employees to retire before age 70. (Waldman, 1968) Recently several states have abolished mandatory retirement altogether.

Normal retirement for state and local government employees is generally either at age 60 or 65 with 5 to 10 years of service or age 55 with 30 years of service. Normal retirement for teachers is usually 65 with 5 years, 60 with 10, or 55 with 20 years of service. Early retirement for state and local governments is usually provided after 20 to 30 years of service, often at age 50 or 55. Although state administered retirement systems generally actuarially reduce benefits provided for early retirement, many large municipal systems do not. (U.S. Congress, House Committee on Education and Labor, 1978, p. 105)

There are no overall statistics on early retirement experience under state and local pension plans largely because of their diversity.

VERY EARLY RETIREMENT

Very early retirement is generally both encouraged and required in public safety occupations in which hazardous duties comprise a significant or potentially significant portion of an employee's responsibilities. In the military, among police and firefighters, airline pilots and air traffic controllers, and certain other hazardous occupations, it is justified by a perceived need to have a younger work force presumably better able to perform the strenuous duties these occupations require.

About 2.5 million people are employed in these occupations which require a high degree of physical and mental stress and involve public safety. On the presumption that qualifications needed to perform the duties deteriorate with age, older workers are required to leave the work force for reasons of public safety and the safety of other workers. It is also generally felt that as the duties required of workers contribute to a decline in physical and mental ability, workers should be adequately compensated at retirement for the arduous services performed while on the job.

In most of these occupations, retirement is mandatory before age 65. The hazardous occupations are generally excepted from the Age Discrimination in Employment Act (ADEA), which prohibits discrimination against workers ages 40–70, by interpretations of the statutory provision which exempt occupations in which age is deemed to be a bona fide occupational qualification (BFOQ). In addition, in the *Massachusetts Board of Retirement et al. v. Robert D. Murgia,* 427 U.S. 307 (1976) the Supreme Court ruled on the constitutionality of a mandatory retirement law, specifically that of Massachusetts requiring police officers to retire at age 50. The Court based its decision on whether Massachusetts' mandatory retirement law was rationally related to a legitimate state interest. Using this standard, the Court found, in essence, that as the purpose of police work was to protect the public safety and as the nature of the occupation was often hazardous, mandatory retirement at age 50 was clearly rationally related to the stated objective, because it "serves to remove from police service those whose fitness for uniformed work presumptively has diminished with age." (*Massachusetts v. Murgia,* p. 315)

Under ADEA, age as a BFOQ must be reasonably necessary to the business being conducted. In hazardous occupations, mandatory retirement age requirements are based on a presumption equating functional capacity with chronological age. Only rarely have courts not upheld mandatory retirement ages for hazardous occupations. Even in such cases, the decisions were based on an employer's failure to provide *any* empirical justification for its retirement age, rather than on a belief that the age was not some indicator of ability.

The age and service at which unreduced "normal" retirement benefits are awarded are considerably lower than the age and service requirements for other occupations and as a rule have higher wage replacement rates for employees in these occupations than for other employees. But there is considerable variation in the age and service requirements for unreduced pension benefits between and within occupations. Some require only a certain number of years of service, generally between 20 and 25 years, while others require, in addition, a minimum age, usually 50 to 55. In those occupations where normal retirement age is lower than mandatory retirement age, such as the military and many police and firefighter retirement systems, employees, on the average, retire before the mandatory retirement age.

The Military

All military employees who have completed 20 years of active service are eligible for a retirement benefit equal to 50% of their terminal basic pay, with semiannual cost-of-living adjustments. No retirement benefits vest before 20 years of service have been completed. For each year of active service completed over 20 years, the annuities increase at the rate of 2.5% of basic pay per year to a maximum of 75%. (President's Commission on Military Compensation, 1978, p. 20) There is no minimum age requirement.

This retirement benefit structure is designed to encourage very early retirement based on a perceived need for "youth and vigor" in the armed services. The specific requirement for youth and vigor is justified by the need to have the military prepared to enter combat in defense of the country and to be able to relocate or accept new assignments when necessary. Another objective is to provide frequent promotion opportunities for younger personnel.

The success of the retirement system in encouraging very early retirement is illustrated by the fact that according to Defense Department statistics about 94% of all 1978 retirees receiving retired pay were below age 50. Of the nondisabled retirees receiving benefits, 98.4% were between ages 35 and 55. The mean age of nondisabled retirees was 42 and more people retired at age 39 than at any other age.

Partially because of the unique nature of the military retirement system, (no vested benefits before 20 years of service when immediate benefits are available) only a portion of those who enter military service ever receive retirement benefits. Data on retention experience between 1973 and 1976 showed only about 11% of all enlisted personnel and 20% of all officers who originally entered military service received retirement benefits.

Mandatory retirement in the military is based on a complex set of rules and varies according to rank, years of service, and branch of the armed services in which an individual is employed. Generally, mandatory retirement is based on an "up-or-out" policy, where the individual is required to reach the next highest grade within a specified period of time or else is forced to retire. This policy is formally applied to officers by statute and, less formally, applied to enlisted personnel by internal policy and regulation.

Most military retirees do not retire from the labor force. In fact, only a small percentage of retirees are not working or looking for work, although the longer an individual has been in the military the less likely it becomes that he or she will be in the labor force after retirement. (President's Commission on Military Compensation, 1978, Tables 3-6) Upon reaching Social Security eligibility ages, military retirees are also eligible for Social Security benefits.

Air Line Pilots and Air Traffic Controllers

The Federal Aviation Administration (FAA) implemented a regulation in 1960 requiring all air line pilots to retire at age 60. This regulation, called the Age 60 Rule, was based on the belief that sudden incapacity due to medical defects become significantly more frequent in any group reaching age 60 and that the possibility of such incapacity cannot be adequately or reliably determined on an individual basis. (O'Donnell, 1979) Although the Air Line Pilot's Association (ALPA) had been opposed to the regulation, efforts in the 1960s and early 1970s to modify or eliminate it were not successful. The FAA had refused ALPA's request to hold evidentiary hearings on the relationship between chronological and functional age, and the Age 60 Rule has been held by the Department of Labor and the courts to be appropriate because age, as a BFOQ, establishes reasonable guidelines necessary to the normal operation of the business.

Only the 35,000 scheduled, commercial airline pilots in the United States are affected by the mandatory age requirements of the Age 60 rule. According to ALPA, very few of the commercial pilots retire for age and service before age 60, although reduced benefits are available to most pilots after 50 years of age and 10 years of service. The great majority of those who do retire before 60 retire on disability. Disability retirement benefits are awarded only when a pilot does not pass the required physical examination, in which case retirement is mandatory.

In 1972, a mandatory retirement age of 55 was enacted for air traffic controllers based on the belief that "because of the natural forces of aging, magnified by the stresses of control functions, the productive and proficient life of a controller is substantially less than that which prevails in most other occupations." (U.S. Department of Transportation. Federal Aviation Administration, 1977) Air traffic controllers may receive an exemption up to age 60, if they are extremely skilled or proficient. The mandatory retirement age only applies to those hired after 1972.

A large proportion of retirees retire as disabled. Only 103 air traffic controllers retired for age and service in 1978, and only 69 in 1977. Those who do retire for age and service do not retire on the average much before age 55 even though they may retire at age 50 with 20 years of service.

The Federal Aviation Administration has a program in operation designed to assist retiring air traffic controllers who wish to start second careers. This program, which was established by Congress and is the only such legislated program, was developed in recognition of the fact that air traffic controllers must retire at an early age and that their skills are not transferable to other occupations. (Batten, 1979)

A retiring air traffic controller may opt for either retirement benefits or the second-career program. The second-career program provides vocational testing and counseling services, full salary for two years during retraining, tuition support, and other related expenses. In spite of the benefits provided by this program, it has been found that only a small percentage of retiring employees choose to complete the program. Because most retiring air traffic controllers qualify for special disability allowances, the benefits awarded disabled retirees act as a disincentive for completing the second-career program. (Batten, 1979)

Police and Firefighters

Police and firefighter retirement plans, which are usually separate from other state and municipal plans, constitute nearly two-thirds of all public employee retirement plans, but cover only 6.7% of the public sector work force. (U.S. Congress, House Committee on Education and Labor, 1978, p. 57.)

A major feature distinguishing these plans from those for other state and local employees is the more liberal age and service requirement for these two occupations. In a typical police and fire retirement system, retirement benefits are computed at a rate of 2 to 2.5% for the first 20 to 25 years of service, when unreduced benefits are available. (U.S. Congress, House Committee on Governmental Affairs, 1978, p. 45–53) Many systems require, in addition to length of service, that an employee reach age 50 to 55 to be eligible for unreduced retirement benefits. Earlier retirement is often provided with actuarially reduced benefits. (U.S. Congress, House Committee on Education and Labor, 1978, p. 105)

Because of the large number of police and firefighter retirement systems, it is difficult to obtain information on the age employees retire. Table 2-4 shows the average age of retirement for police and firefighters for four large geographically separated systems—Los Angeles, Houston, New York State, and Chicago—for fiscal year 1977.

EARLY RETIREMENT COSTS

Age of retirement under the various pension systems is only one factor, of course, in pension costs. Funding costs of Social Security, other public pension programs, and private pension plans have in-

Table 2-4. Average Age for Retirement for Police and Firefighters in Selected Jurisdictions, 1977.

	Police	Fire
Los Angeles	48	53
Houston	59	54
Chicago	NA	58
New York State	49	NA

Source: Retirement ages given by Pension Board in each jurisdiction.

creased greatly in recent years. As the systems have matured more persons have become eligible for benefits and benefits have been made more adequate, particularly under Social Security.

The trend toward retirement below age 65 is one source of concern over the present and future system costs of providing an adequate retirement income. Individuals are retiring earlier yet living longer which means that there is a greater period of time over which retirement benefits will have to be paid. This retirement trend adds to the cost of retirement systems and magnifies the effects of other costly factors such as inflation and demographic trends.

The impact of earlier retirement on retirement costs is not uniform because of the diversity of pension systems and experience. Financial effects of an increased retirement period on a pension system depend on such factors as whether the early retirement benefit is actuarially reduced, how the system is funded, maturity of the system, and whether the cost-of-living increases are added to retirees' benefits.

In the private sector, the effect of the retirement age on any given private pension plan depends on the factors mentioned above. However, in general an earlier retirement will be more costly. A study for the Business Roundtable states:

The age at which retirement occurs has considerable leverage on the cost of benefits. The present value of a stream of retirement income payments will depend on the age of retirement. Under a reasonable set of assumptions, the present value of each dollar of retirement income beginning at age 60 is about 15% higher than if retirement takes place at age 65; nearly 30% higher if retirement occurs at age 55. The actual cost differences are even greater because of the shorter period over which these amounts must be funded and the consequently smaller investment increment in the fund accumulated. (Towers, Perrin, Forster and Crosby, 1978)

In the case of very early retirement which is not actuarially reduced and may be even supplemented until normal retirement age is reached, costs are much greater. As the study points out:

If further supplementation at early retirement is made in order to make early retirement more attractive to meet a specific employer or industry objective, the cost could be substantial. For instance, if retirement at age 55 is permitted without actuarial reduction in the pension and with a temporary supplement until age 62 equal to anticipated Social Security benefits then payable, the cost of the final pay offset plan could increase to 22.4% of payroll under a representative cost model, nearly doubling the cost of the plan. As a general rule, it cannot be expected that private plans can provide such levels of income prior to age 62. (Towers, Perrin, Forster and Crosby, 1978)

Since retirement ages have been steadily going down in private industry and full actuarial reductions are becoming less common, earlier retirement ages have generally increased pension costs in private industry. They have also increased costs for public employers since state and local government retirement systems generally provide for normal retirement below age 65. In many of these retirement plans, particularly the municipal plans, the early retirement benefit is not actuarially reduced. According to one survey:

(The fact that) public plans permit workers to retire on unreduced pensions at earlier ages than private plans. . . is the primary factor responsible for driving up the cost of public pensions. The desirability of expanding the use of early, unreduced retirement is questionable in light of the recent demographic changes that are taking place. (Leibig and Kalman, 1978)

Although 85% of all state and local government employees contribute to their pension plans, the bulk of the finances are provided by the employers whose contributions ultimately come from tax revenues. Normal retirement at an early age and early retirement with unreduced benefits are a financial burden to the employers and taxpayers. The longer the period of retirement the more revenues will be needed to provide an adequate retirement income. The shorter the employment period, the less time the employer and employee will have to fund the benefits if the pension is to be advance-funded.

Federal Civil Service

The federal civil service has some of the lowest normal and early retirement ages with unreduced benefits available at age 55 after 30 years of service. Age and service retirement ages below age 55 are either hazardous duty retirements or involuntary early retirements which are reduced.

Over 90% of federal civilian employees are covered by the Civil Service Retirement System which includes approximately 2.7 million employees. The system is financed by 7% of pay withheld from federal employees, equal amounts from employer agency contributions and some general Treasury appropriations. According to the Congressional Budget Office (CBO), the trust fund is not self-financing from an accounting perspective. Assets and projected income to the fund will not cover future obligations to current annuitants and active employees resulting in an unfunded liability which is estimated to reach $160 billion by the beginning of 1984 due to anticipated cost-of-living adjustments. (U.S. Congressional Budget Office, 1978)

While projected cost increases and unfunded liabilities can be attributed primarily to inflation and pay increases, early retirement benefit options which are not actuarially reduced or not given a full actuarial reduction are also costly. Not reducing the benefits has two effects: (1) There are additional costs to the system for employees who retire at age 55 because of the longer pay-out period; (2) more employees are encouraged to retire early, thus increasing the numbers with a longer pay-out period. CBO has estimated that if the normal retirement age were moved from 55 to 65, the cumulative number of new civil service retirees during the first five years would be about 21 percent less than under the current program. Annual outlays would be $1.4 billion lower in fiscal year 1984 and $2.9 billion lower in 1994. (U.S. Congressional Budget Office, 1978)

Armed Forces

Because military retirement benefits are available after 20 years of service, many retirees are in their late 30s and early 40s when they begin collecting retirement benefits. Thus, many military retirees receive benefits for a significantly longer period of time than retirees under other retirement systems.

The military retirement system is financed by annual appropriations made by Congress on a pay-as-you-go basis. Military members make no direct contribution to their retirement system. Retirement costs were estimated to amount to 8% of the total Department of Defense budget in 1978, a significant increase from 2% in 1964.

A 1977 Rand Corporation study found that part of the reason for the enormous growth of military retirement costs is the number of years each retiree spends on the retirement rolls.

In contrast to the civilian worker who retires at, say, age 65 and spends about 10 years receiving retirement pay (assuming a life expectancy of 75 years), the average enlisted member serving 20 years spends more than 35 years on the retirement rolls, and the average 20-year officer spends just a little under 35 years. (Cooper, 1977, p. 372)

Social Security

Age of retirement affects the Social Security system, which operates on a pay-as-you-go basis, differently from those plans which are advance-funded and also differently from federal programs financed from Congressional appropriations. Old age benefits are paid out of a trust fund financed by current OASI taxes on employees and employers. Thus the ratio of those working to those retired becomes important. This is referred to as the dependency ratio. Should the numbers of the retired increase dramatically while the number of employees decrease, the dependency ratio would increase and tax rates would also need to increase, perhaps to a level unacceptable to the working population. Current retirement trends plus changing mortality and fertility rates suggest that tax rates may be required to increase to potentially unacceptable levels after the turn of the century, perhaps doubling by 2030. This aspect will be discussed further in connection with long-range considerations.

Retiree Costs

It is generally agreed that early retirement may be costly to the retiree. Inflation, which has a significant impact on retirees' benefits, becomes even more crucial when the length of time over which individuals collect retirement income is prolonged. Further, retirement benefits will often be lower at earlier ages, even when they are not actuarially reduced. Even though a benefit is not reduced for the employee who retires at age 55, for example, ". . . it is applied to a final average salary covering the years of employment ending at age 55, not the higher average salary that could be expected later on at age 65. For this reason, the employee's full-formula age 55-early retirement income will be lower than if he had waited until 65 to retire, assuming a higher pay rate at the later retirement age." (Greenough and King, 1976)

This can be illustrated by the federal civil service retirement system where individuals may retire after 30 years of service at age 55 with a benefit equal to 56.25% of preretirement income. If, however, the individual continues working and retires at age 65 and with 40 years of service, the retirement benefit may equal 76.25% of a higher final three-year salary.

Early retirement is probably more costly for women than for men. Early retirement coupled with a longer life expectancy affects the retirement income of women workers. As has been discussed, a large proportion of women retire with a reduced Social Security benefit and this is a factor in the low incomes of women retirees. Because women have a longer life expectancy than men, these smaller benefits must cover a longer period of time and become more and more inadequate as levels of living rise.

LONG-RANGE ASPECTS

Some of the long-range aspects concerning retirement age and demographic changes after the turn of the century have already been touched on. But it is worthwhile to consider them in more detail because of the potential major impact on the age distribution of the population and thus retirement income programs.

The baby boom generation is now in the under age 35 segment of the labor force. After the turn of the century, the forefront of this large cohort will be reaching age 65 in 2012 and thereafter will cause a shift upward in the aged population. Expanding costs of pay-as-you-go retirement programs for this population can be most easily supported if there is a large work force and/or economic growth. Therefore, projections of people of working age are as important to retirement programs' long-term planning as the projections of people of retirement age.

Between now and the year 2035 the number of people 65 and over is likely to increase by more than 120%. But at the same time the population 18–64 years, from which the bulk of the potential labor force would be drawn, is estimated to increase by only between 8–32% depending on the fertility rate assumption. It is this relative difference in the growth of the aged population and the potential labor force in the 21st century that is of most concern for the pay-as-you-go public retirement systems such as Social Security, which pay benefits out of contributions from the working population. The shifts in demography will be less important for pension systems that are fully funded since the funds for financing the annuities have already been set aside and invested. Demographic shifts, however, will affect to varying extents pension plans that are not fully funded or have not correctly estimated the mortality rate of their annuitants.

Retirement Age and the Dependency Ratios

Figure 2–3 illustrates the growth in the dependency ratio in the next century under the assumption that the early retirement trend has been even more pervasive than it has been in the past and continues in the future. The solid line assumes a single, uniform retirement age of 62 from 1970 through 2050. To be more descriptive the distinct

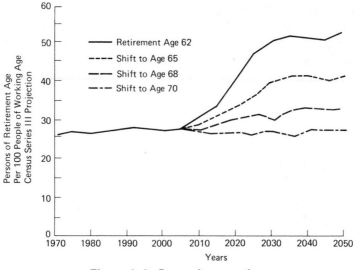

Figure 2-3. Dependency ratios.

Source: Douglas Norwood. *Demographic Trends.* Staff Technical Paper, U.S. Office of Management and Budget, Spring 1979.

lines on the chart should be broad gray areas showing the probable retirement years rather than a single retirement age. The chart also assumes that the population 18–61 is working without taking into consideration disability retirement or other factors which remove younger persons from the labor force. In addition, it assumes that fertility rates continue at about the same low level as is currently the case.

Under the foregoing assumptions, Figure 2–3 shows the steep climb in the dependency ratio that starts at about 2010 and continues upward until there is a ratio of almost one person age 62 and over to two persons in the working population by 2030. The other lines show what could happen if the retirement age were raised. The dependency burden in 2050 is almost halved if the retirement age is 65. A single retirement age between 68 and 70 could dissolve the major increased dependency burden that would exist if everyone retired at 62 in the 21st century. A panel of consultants to the Advisory Council on Social Security came to the same conclusion:

. . . the U.S. economy may find it most difficult to support its aged population after the turn of the century unless the dividing line between the worker and the retired is raised. By 2020, the 'retirement dependency ratio' for retirement age *68* will be about 21 (it is only 15 today). If so, a three-year change in the retirement age will have the effect of restoring the retired/worker ratio to something close to the current level. . . .

. . . the burden borne by workers can be materially alleviated if retirement ages are raised. As one example, the long-term actuarial deficit in the OASDI system, shown in the 1978 Trustees Report as 1.40% of taxable payroll, could be cut in half if the retirement age were raised to 68. . . . (U.S. Department of Health, Education and Welfare. Advisory Council on Social Security, 1979, p. 299-300)

Retirement Income Dependency

In the aggregate, the retired are largely dependent on the working population for their retirement income. Under Social Security, those who are working support all of the financing. Under government employee pension programs (which are usually at least partially funded), the working population provides the financing to varying extents. One of the major implications of an increasing dependency ratio is that a smaller working age population will have to transfer more of its income to a larger retirement age population. Retirement income dependency can be illustrated by examining the proportion of the total income of the entire working age population that must be transferred to the retirement age population in order to maintain the relative per capita income of each population at the 1977 level. They have not been constant in the past and no doubt will fluctuate in the future but for illustrative purposes will be assumed constant.

Figure 2-4 displays the estimates of the proportion of the nonretired population's income that would have to be transferred to the retirees in the 21st century in order to keep their relative per capita incomes the same as in 1977. The estimates of the income transfer includes Social Security, welfare programs such as the supplementary security income program, state, local, and private transfers of income. It does not include the income the elderly get

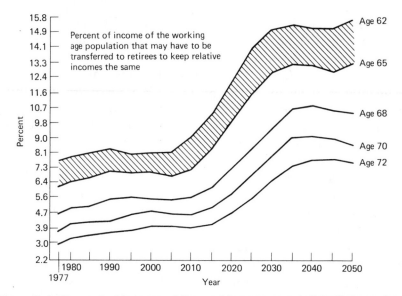

Figure 2-4. Percent of income of the working age population that may have to be transferred to retirees to keep relative incomes the same.

Source: Derived from Richard Lancaster, *Retirement Income Adequacy.* Staff Technical Paper, U.S. Office of Management and Budget, August 1979.

from interest, rent, or assets. It also does not include the income from private pensions, since if they are fully funded the income does not then come directly from the current working population.

It should not be surprising that the shape of the curves in Figure 2-4 are so similar to the dependency ratios illustrated in Figure 2-3. It is the age dependency ratios that largely determine the proportion of income that would have to be transferred between the generations. What is surprising is that by 2030 that proportion of the working age population's income that would have to be transferred to the retired could increase to between 13–16%. This suggests a doubling of the taxes that today help to affect this transfer of income to the retired.

Recent OASDI trustee estimates of old-age, disabled, and survivor benefits as a percent of the taxable payroll of covered workers supports the magnitude of this estimated increase between now and 2030. Under the demographic assumptions, the estimated expenditures more than double as a percent of payroll if there is a fertility rate of 1.7 children per woman; under the fertility assumption of 2.1 children expenditures increase almost 60%

The major transfer of income from the working to the retired population is done by Social Security. But there are also other federal, state, and local programs as well as private transfers that will have to be increased by the same magnitude just to keep the relative per capita incomes of the retired and nonretired as they were in 1977.

Approximately 7% of the income of the nonretired is being transferred to the retired through public programs today. The possibility that the transfer of resources from the working aged population to the retired may have to increase between 60–100% in the next 40 years is important to consider. Limitations on public transfers to the aged could be one reaction to increasing tax rates. This has already happened with regard to other areas of public expenditures. Various limits on the proportion of income of the working population going to support the aged population would decrease the relative income of the aged after the year 2015.

One alternative to limiting transfers for the elderly and the resulting declining benefits is an increase in the retirement age. Just as the dependency ratio is sensitive to different retirement ages, retirement income dependency is also sensitive to different ages as has been shown in Figure 2–3.

There are many uncertainties about the projections which are the core of the future retirement income problem and therefore they should not be interpreted as inevitable. Several factors would help to lighten the potential dependency burden:

- If labor force participation for both young and old increased, then the burden of support of the retired would be spread among relatively more people than at the present time.
- If the number of children declines, the cost of their dependency as a whole would be reduced and it would be easier for the labor force to support the retired.

But there are also several factors that could increase the burden that is already being projected:

- If the recent improvements in mortality for the aged continue then there will be a substantial increase in the number of aged that is not now being projected.
- If the fertility rate continues to fall there will be fewer children to be supported initially but ultimately there will be fewer potential members of the work force.
- As the baby boom generation grows older, the number of the disabled in the preretirement years might increase. This would add to the burden of support that the labor force would have to carry.

Assuming that the projected 21st century financing problems materialize to a greater or lesser extent, they could be solved by a change in retirement ages or an increase in taxes. Other solutions include a combination of the two or, as a last alternative, a decrease in benefits. Although it is too early to accurately predict all of the factors that will determine the extent of the Social Security financing problem in the 21st century, it is not too early to consider the alternatives, especially with retirement ages. Fairness alone would suggest that if eligibility ages for retirement benefits in this country are to be changed that a substantial amount of warning be given to allow for retirement planning.

Transition to older Social Security retirement ages would require careful planning. The 1979 Social Security Advisory Council urged that the normal retirement age be increased 2 months a year beginning in 2000. By 2018 the normal retirement age would be 68. (U.S. Department of Health, Education and Welfare. Advisory Council on Social Security, 1979, p. 177) Other transition schemes could also be devised. Another way of making the transition to later retirement ages could be by providing incentives to remain in the labor force longer and increase annual retirement income. These could include private pension accruals beyond normal retirement ages and additional Social Security retirement credits.

SUMMARY AND CONCLUSION

Since the passage of the Social Security Act in 1935, the predominant normal retirement age has been 65, resulting in a declining proportion of men continuing to work after 65. But superimposed on this trend has been that of early retirement at age 62 which was first enacted under Social Security in 1956 for women and for men in 1961. By the middle of the 1970s, 60% of men and women workers were retiring with Social Security benefits before age 65. At the same time, life expectancy has improved and people are living, on the average, almost 3 years longer after age 65 than they did when the Social Security program began.

Retirement not only before 65 but before 62 has become common policy and practice in pension systems covering private industries and government employees at the federal, state, and local levels. Benefits which are provided at these early retirement ages in the early 60s and 50s are usually liberalized by not being actuarially reduced or only partially reduced which means additional costs to the pension system. Since the normal retirement age is defined as the age when unreduced benefits are paid, the distinction between normal and early retirement ages is becoming blurred when benefits are not reduced and tends to encourage earlier retirement.

Policy rationales for early retirement include long-term unemployment, ill health and the need for youth and vigor in certain occupations. But the prevalence and institutionalization of early retirement raises some questions concerning "old age" retirement at early ages and the consequences. Early retirement provisions in Social Security were enacted in part because of the unemployment problems of older workers and because ". . . the social security system should be flexible enough to take account of this problem." There is some question, however, as to what extent a retirement system should be responsible for combatting problems associated with unemployment, particularly when the result is reduced retirement income over a generally longer retirement period with increased vulnerability to the erosions of inflation. Since women live longer than men and predominate in the very old population cohorts, early retirement may also have long-range adverse economic consequences for women.

Mandatory retirement from hazardous duty occupations is permitted by an exception from the Age Discrimination in Employment Act. But there are wide variations in the mandatory retirement ages in pension systems covering different occupations or the same occupations in different political jurisdictions, ranging from the early 40s to the early 60s. While all mandatory retirement is based on the assumption that physical capacity and thus job performance declines with age, there is no consensus concerning the critical age of decline. Mandatory retirement policies and relatively early normal retirement ages have been used to limit the upper age of the work force in the hazardous occupations. There is some question, however, as to what extent these policies promote the goal of a highly capable work force. Further, there is some question as to what extent the retirement systems should be responsible for this function.

Aside from the current specific and substantial costs of early and very early retirement to individual retirement systems, both public and private, as well as the effect on retirement income, there are the long-range costs of early retirement to Social Security and other public systems which are either wholly or partially supported by taxes paid by the working population. Because of the projected long-range demographic trends, there are projected large increases of the aged population in relation to the working population in the first half of the 21st century. This poses potential problems with regard to maintaining present levels of public income transfers to the aged and present levels of retirement income since a smaller working population would provide the transfers for a larger retired population. Continuance of the early retirement trend of the 1970s into the next century could increase and hasten the financial impact of the retirement of the post-World War II baby boom generation. The future demographic trends that this chapter has speculated about make the consideration of policies which encourage and/or require retirement at later ages compelling.

REFERENCES

Bankers Trust Company. *1975 Study of Corporate Pension Plans.* (10th in a series) New York, 1975.

Batten, Michael D. *Alternatives to Retirement: Policy and Program Considerations.* Statement before the President's Commission on Pension Policy, August 21, 1979.

Cohen, Wilbur and Mitchell, William L. Social security amendments of 1961: Summary and legislative history. *Social Security Bulletin.* September, 1961.

Cooper, Richard V. L. *Military Manpower and the All-Volunteer Force.* Rand: Santa Monica, California, 1977.

Frumkin, Robert and Schmitt, Donald. Pension improvements since 1974 reflect inflation, new U.S. law. *Monthly Labor Review.* April 1979.

Gori, Gio and Brian, Richta. Macro-economics of disease prevention in the United States, *Science.* June 9, 1978.

Greenough, William C. and King, Francis P. *Pension Plans and Public Policy.* Columbia University Press: New York, 1976.

Lancaster, Richard. *The Retirement Income Dependency Problem in the United States, 1980-2050.* Staff Technical Paper, U.S. Office of Management and Budget, Washington, D.C., August 1979.

Leibig, Michael and Kalman, Robert. *Public Pension Crisis, Myth, Reality and Reform.* Unpublished Manuscript, 1978.

Massachusetts Board of Retirement et al. v. Robert D. Murgia, 427 U.S.307 (1976).

Meyer, Mitchell. *The Ban on Mandatory Retirement at 65: Management Responses.* (Information Bulletin No. 46) The Conference Board, New York, October, 1978.

Norwood, Douglas. *Demographic Trends.* Staff Technical Paper, U.S. Office of Management and Budget: Washington, D.C., Spring 1979.

O'Donnell, John J. (President of the Air Line Pilots Association.) *Airlines and Age Discrimination.* Statement before the House Select Committee on Aging. March 21, 1979.

Olthoff, Kenneth. Statement of General Motors Company before the President's Commission on Pension Policy, October 24, 1979.

Parnes, Herbert S. *The Pre-Retirement Years.* Vol. **4,** U.S. Government Printing Office: Washington, D.C., 1975.

Pechman, Joseph A., Aaron, Henry J., and Taussig, Michael K. *Social Security: Perspectives for Reform.* Brookings Institution: Washington, D.C., 1968.

President's Commission on Military Compensation. *Report.* U.S. Government Printing Office: Washington, D.C., April, 1978.

President's Committee on Economic Security. *Social Security in America.* U.S. Government Printing Office, Washington, D.C. 1937.

Reno, Virginia. Chaps. 4, 5 and 7 in *Reaching Retirement Age,* (Research Report No. 47, Social Security Administration) U.S. Government Printing Office, Washington, D.C, 1976.

Sunshine, Jonathan. *Disability.* Staff Technical Paper, U.S. Office of Management and Budget, Washington, D.C., March, 1979.

Towers, Perrin, Forster and Crosby, Inc. *Study of Retirement Benefit Levels, Costs and Issues.* August, 1978 (Unpublished).

U.S. Congress. House Committee on Education and Labor, *Public Employee Retirement Systems,* Pension Task Force Report. 95th Congress, Second Session. March, 1978. U.S. Government Printing Office, Washington, D.C., 1978.

U.S. Congress. House Committee on Ways and Means. *Economic Security Act.* Hearings, 74th Congress First Session, January and February 1935. U.S. Government Printing Office, Washington, D.C. 1935.

U.S. Congress. Senate Committee on Finance. *Economic Security Act.* Hearings,

74th Congress. January and February 1935, U.S. Government Printing Office, Washington, D.C., 1935.

U.S. Congressional Budget Office. *Options for Federal Civil Service Retirement: An Analysis of Costs and Benefit Provisions.* December, 1978. U.S. Government Printing Office, Washington, D.C., 1978.

U.S. Department of Health, Education, and Welfare, Advisory Council on Social Security. *Social Security Financing and Benefits.* Washington, D.C., 1979.

U.S. Department of Transportation, Federal Aviation Administration, *Five Year Report on the Operations Under Public Law 92-297: Air Traffic Controller Career Program.* Washington, D.C., October, 1977.

Waldman, Saul. *Retirement Systems for State and Local Governments. . . 1966.* U,S. Department of Health, Education and Welfare, Social Security Administration, Office of Research and Statistics, Research Report No. 23, U.S. Government Printing Office, Washington, D.C., 1968.

3

CURRENT RETIREMENT TRENDS

Eric R. Kingson, Ph.D.

INTRODUCTION

In this chapter, we examine retirement trends, barriers to the continued employment of older workers and the reasons older people leave the labor force. Special attention is paid to the early labor force withdrawal trend among men because of the particularly important implications of this trend for the future of retirement.

We begin by examining the importance of paid employment to the incomes of older persons and current labor force participation trends.

EMPLOYMENT STATUS OF OLDER PERSONS

Employment Incomes of Older Persons

Retirement benefits under Social Security, private pensions and special public pensions are, to a great degree, related to prior earnings. Persons who make larger contributions from earnings into these systems usually receive larger pension incomes. Consequently, not only are the earnings of older workers an important source of present income, but these earnings may also be an important source of their future income. As a result, the employment status of older people has a particularly important impact on their welfare.

Table 3-1 presents data which emphasize the importance of earnings to the incomes of older persons and their families (when present). The table compares the median incomes in 1978 of all older persons in certain age and family status categories to that of those

Table 3-1. Older Families and Unrelated Individuals: Comparison of Median Incomes in 1978 Between Full-time Year-Round Workers and All Older Persons in Age Cohort.

Age	Percent of Year-Round Full-Time Workers	Median Income For All Members of Cohort	Median Income For Year-Round Full-time Workers
Families (Age of Head)			
45–54	76.1	$22,615	$25,322
55–64	60.9	$19,330	$23,345
65 +	8.8	$10,141	$20,937
Unrelated Individuals			
45–54	58.7	$ 8,624	$12,090
55–64	40.0	$ 6,828	$12,109
65 +	3.5	$ 4,303	$10,128

Source: U.S. Bureau of the Census, *Current Population Reports,* "Money Income and Poverty Status of Families in the United States: 1978 (Advance Report)," Series p–60, No. 120, November 1979, Table 7.

who are year-round full-time workers. The table underestimates the differences between the incomes of year-round full-time workers and those who are not because the incomes of year-round full-time workers are included in the calculation that determines the median income for all members of a cohort. In spite of this limitation, by extrapolating, it is possible to make comparisons between older persons who are year-round full-time employees and those who are either partially or completely retired.

Table 3-1 demonstrates that year-round full-time employment is a major determinant of current incomes of families headed by persons aged 65 and over as well as all cohorts of unrelated older individuals. For example, the table shows that in 1978 the median income of families headed by a year-round full-time worker aged 65 or over was more than $10,000 (or 100 percent) greater than the median incomes of all families headed by like-aged persons. Similar, though less extreme, differences exist among families headed by persons aged 45 to 54 and 55 to 64.

In 1977, 8.6 percent of families headed by persons aged 65 and over and 27.3 percent of unrelated individuals aged 65 and over had incomes below the Social Security Administration's poverty index. However, the percent of persons below poverty declines considerably when earnings of any type are a part of household income—to 4.5

percent for families and to 11.5 percent for unrelated individuals (U.S. Bureau of the Census, 1979a).

Table 3-2 presents data for household units headed by persons aged 65 and over of different racial, sexual, and family status. The table compares the percent of all household units below poverty and within particular categories to the percent of these units that are below poverty when earnings of any type are part of household unit.

The table shows that earnings have strong poverty reducing effects for elder households. The table also suggests that even with the presence of earnings a substantial portion of black households, unrelated individuals and most types of female-headed households are vulnerable to the risk of poverty.

Labor Force Participation Trends

In spite of the importance of earnings to the incomes of older people, there have been dramatic declines in the labor force participation of older men. In 1947, 47.8 percent of men aged 65 and over were in the labor force; by 1978 participation had dropped to only

Table 3-2. Percent of Household Units Aged 65 and Over Below Poverty Level in 1977: Comparisons by Sex, Race and Family Status Between All Units and Units with Earnings.

Type of Unit	Percent of All Units Below Poverty Level[a]	Percent of Units With Earnings Below Poverty Level[a]
Families		
White Male Head	6.2	2.7
White Female Head	7.5	3.0
Black Male Head	28.4	17.6
Black Female Head	38.3	21.1
Unrelated Individuals		
White Male	20.1	14.2
White Female	25.8	9.2
Black Male	39.4	Not available
Black Female	60.8	31.5

Source: U.S. Bureau of the Census, *Current Population Reports,* Series P-60, No. 119, "Characteristics of the Population Below the Poverty Level: 1977," March 1979, Table 38.
[a]Poverty level measure is based on the Social Security Administration poverty index.

20.5 percent. Among men aged 55 to 64 there has also been a significant decline in labor force involvement. Between 1947 and 1978, the
labor force participation of this group dropped over 16 percent,
from 89.6 percent to 73.5 percent.

Although much of the drop in labor force participation is clus-
tered around the age at which men become eligible to receive early
Social Security benefits, there has also been a significant decline
among men below age 62. For example, between August 1967 and
August 1977, labor force participation rates for men aged 55 to 59
fell by 6.4 percent (U.S. Department of Labor, 1977). Similarly, between 1947 and 1978 participation among men aged 45 to 54 has
declined from 95.5 percent to 91.3 percent.

As Table 3-3 illustrates, for the past 25 years the labor force participation patterns of white and nonwhite older male workers have
been similar. However, there is one important difference. The participation rates of nonwhite males aged 45 to 54 and 55 to 64 have
generally trailed that of their white counterparts by 4 to 8 percent;
thus reflecting the relative disadvantage of nonwhite groups in the
labor market and the greater incidence of work-limiting health conditions among older black men.

Table 3-3. Older Male Labor Force Participation Rates[a] by Race and Age: 1954 to 1978.

Year	White			Black and Other		
	45–54	55–64	65+	45–54	55–64	65+
1954	96.8	89.2	40.4	93.2	83.0	41.2
1957	96.6	88.0	37.7	93.5	82.4	35.9
1960	96.1	87.2	33.3	92.3	82.5	31.2
1963	96.2	86.6	28.4	91.1	82.5	27.6
1966	95.8	84.9	27.2	90.7	81.1	25.6
1969	95.1	83.9	27.3	89.5	77.9	26.1
1972	94.0	81.2	24.4	86.1	73.6	23.6
1975	92.9	76.5	21.8	84.6	68.7	20.9
1978	92.1	73.9	20.4	84.5	69.1	21.3
Change between 1954 and 1978	-4.7%	-15.3%	-20.0%	-8.7%	-13.9%	-19.9%

Source: U.S. Department of Labor, *Employment and Training Report of the President,* 1979, Table A-4.

[a]Annual averages based on percent of civilian noninstitutional population in the civilian labor force.

The trends for women are very different. The long-term pattern for women age 65 and over has shown relatively little change. In 1949, 9.6 percent were in the labor force. Participation rose to 10.8 percent in 1956 and by 1978 had declined to 8.4 percent.

Labor force participation trends for women aged 45 to 54 and 55 to 64 are markedly different from those for like-aged men. For example, whereas male labor force participation for the 55- to 64-year-old cohort has declined 16.1 percent between 1947 and 1978, female attachment to the labor force in this age group has increased fully 17.1 percent; from 24.3 percent to 41.4 percent.

The increase in participation among women aged 45 to 64 reflects a trend that has been occurring among all groupings of working age women below age 65. The employment experience of women in defense industries during World War II, changing social attitudes concerning the role of women, the desire for larger family incomes, the availability of labor-saving devices for home management, and smaller family sizes have combined to bring large numbers of women, especially married women, into the labor force. (Clague et al., 1971; Sheppard, 1976).

The participation rates of the 55- to 64-year-old cohort of older women is somewhat less than that of the younger female cohorts. However, as Harold Sheppard has pointed out, the rate of increase participation is greatest for the 55 to 64 age group (Sheppard, 1976). This suggests that labor force participation among the oldest cohorts of women is likely to continue to grow, and retirement, quite naturally, to decline.

There is additional evidence suggesting that the increased labor force participation of older women should continue well into the next century. Since 1949 the largest increases in the labor force participation of women has occurred among cohorts aged 25–34 and 20–24 years of age. These trends seem to be continuing, reflecting both increased labor force involvement of young married women and women with young children, (Moser, 1974) as well as changing family formation patterns which have resulted in later entry into marriage and more employment experience prior to marriage for large numbers of women. A. J. Jaffe and Jeanne Clare Ridley point out that women who work before marriage are most likely to work during marriage (Jaffe & Ridley, 1976). This observation combined with the steady increase in participation of the 20–24 year old cohort leads them to predict very high participation rates (perhaps 75 percent) when these women reach their fifties. Moreover, the slowdown of growth in our standard of living is, for the foreseeable future, likely to provide additional incentive for older women to stay in, enter, or return to the labor force.

Further disaggregation of female cohort aged 55 to 64 shows a very interesting change in labor force participation trends since 1970. While the labor force participation of the 55 to 59 age group has continued to increase, there have been slight declines in participation of both the 60 to 61 (1.7 percent) and the 62 to 64 groups (3.8 percent). Carl Rosenfeld and Scott Campbell Brown suggest that this decline may partially be explained by "the large rise in the number of women age 62 to 64 receiving" Social Security disability and retirement payments (Rosenfeld & Brown, 1979). If this is correct, it seems possible that, as more women become eligible for early retirement and disability benefits in public and private pensions, retirement incentives may lead to an early retirement trend among women. This may partially offset other trends that suggest a growth in the labor force participation of older women.

Examination of Table 3–4 shows that the labor force participation patterns of nonwhite and white older female workers are not the same. Among women aged 65 and over, nonwhites have somewhat higher participation rates, which is probably a reflection of the greater need for earnings of older nonwhites.

More interestingly, the labor force participation trends between nonwhite and white women aged 55–64 are quite different. Whereas the participation rates of the white members of this cohort increased from 29.1 percent in 1954 to 41.2 percent in 1978; the rates for nonwhites have remained relatively stable and relatively high—starting at 41.2 percent in 1954, peaking at 49.1 percent in 1966 and declining to 43.6 percent by 1978. Apparently, the increase in labor force participation of older women aged 55–64 has primarily been a result of increased participation of white women.

This pattern is also reflected among the 45–54 age groups. Although there has been an increase in participation since 1954 among both nonwhites and whites in this age group, by far, the greatest rate of increase occurred among white women.

Table 3-4. Older Female Labor Force Participation Rates[a] by Race and Age: 1954 to 1978.

Year	White			Black and Other		
	45–54	55–64	65 +	45–54	55–64	65 +
1954	39.8	29.1	9.1	53.4	41.2	12.2
1957	45.4	33.7	10.2	56.8	44.3	13.6
1960	48.6	36.2	10.6	60.5	47.3	12.8
1963	49.5	38.9	9.4	60.6	47.3	11.8
1966	50.6	41.1	9.4	61.0	49.1	13.0
1969	53.0	42.6	9.7	60.8	47.5	11.9
1972	53.4	42.0	9.0	57.3	43.9	12.8
1975	54.3	40.7	8.0	56.8	43.8	10.5
1978	56.7	41.2	8.1	59.8	43.6	10.7
Changes between 1954 and 1978	+ 16.9	+ 12.1	-1.0	+ 6.4	+ 2.4	-1.5

Source: U.S. Department of Labor, *Employment and Training Report* of the President, 1979, Table A-4.
[a]Annual averages based on percent of civilian noninstitutional population in the civilian labor force.

While data representative primarily of white and black labor force participation trends are plentiful, there is a scarcity of data on the participation of older persons of different minorities. A recent study by Morris J. Newman profiles the Hispanic populations in the work force. While most of the article allows analysis in terms of the different ethnic identities of Hispanics, the labor force participation trends of older workers are reported for Hispanics as a group. The data show that male participation rates for older Hispanics (45–54, 55–64 and 65 and over) in 1977 closely resembles that of all men. However, the labor force participation of older Hispanic women trails that of all women by 10 percent for cohorts aged 45–54 and 55–64 and by 3 percent for those aged 65 and over (Newman, 1978).

Explanation For Declining Male Labor Force Participation

As the previous discussion suggests, increasingly, men have been withdrawing from the labor force before age 65. This trend, commonly termed the "early retirement phenomenon," has had, and will continue to have, tremendous impact on the institution of retirement. The declining attachment of older male workers to the labor force takes on greater significance in light of current demographic trends showing increasing growth in the over-65 population as well as increasing longevity. The trend towards early labor force withdrawal of men when combined with demographic changes promises to exacerbate already serious problems concerning the adequacy and cost of our public and private pensions.

We will discuss several policy implications of this trend later in this chapter, but first we need to explore explanations of this phenomenon. A better understanding of the cause of this trend will aid us in our analysis of possible policy outcomes.

The increasing incidence of early labor force withdrawal among men has been paralleled and, to a certain extent been preceded by changes in retirement and disability policies in both public and private pensions. Since 1947, early retirement and disability benefits have been included and liberalized in almost all public and private pensions. Most notably, in 1961 the option to receive an actuarially reduced Social Security benefit was extended to men aged 62 to 64. Currently, more than one-half of new male beneficiaries accept reduced benefits.

Is the increased availability of retirement and disability benefits before age 65 the best explanation for the early withdrawal trend? Researchers differ on this point. For example, Social Security Administration (SSA) studies usually conclude that the early retirement of men is not primarily influenced by benefit levels, whereas studies originating outside of the SSA generally find benefit levels to be a major cause of both early and normal retirement (Campbell and Campbell, 1976; Munnell, 1977).

While not dealing directly with early retirement, William G. Bowen's and T. Aldrich Finegan's research suggests that the increased availability of nonwork income explains about three-fifths of the decline in labor force participation among men aged 65 and over between 1947 and 1965. They attribute the changed participation primarily to the income effect* of benefit increases, although they note that the earnings test and institutional effects such as com-

---

*Given additional income in the form of retirement benefits, the worker can afford to purchase more leisure.

pulsory retirement policies also have an influence. (Bowen and Finegan, 1969).

Analysis of cross-sectional data by Joseph A. Pechman, Henry J. Aaron, and Michael K. Taussig also presents information supporting a causal relationship between the availability of early retirement benefits under Social Security as of 1961 and decreased labor force participation of men. They show that "participation rates for men aged 60–61 and 65–68 changed very little between 1961 and 1966, while those in the age bracket 62–64 dropped sharply" (Pechman et al., 1968). A more recent study that uses a national sample of 5,000 men concludes, similarly, that the income effect of Social Security benefits is the most powerful inducement to the retirement of workers aged 62 and over as well as the best explanation of the decreased labor force participation of men aged 55 and over (Boskin, 1977).

The increased coverage and liberalization of early retirement and disability benefits can also be seen as leading to decreased labor force participation through formal and informal institutional channels. The existence of early retirement benefits in some plans has created pressures to establish these benefits in other plans. Similarly, special early retirement benefits in some private pensions provide examples of how the "dovetailing" of private benefits with the onset of Social Security benefits can create formal institutional pressures for labor force departure before age 65. As a result of these special benefits, some workers are able to retire early, receive their expected level of normal retirement benefits and not lose Social Security benefits through an actuarial reduction.

The availability of early retirement benefits can lead to informal early retirement pressures in the workplace. For example employers can use these benefits to "weed out" workers judged to be inefficient. Fellow employees may use the availability of these benefits as a means of placing pressure on older workers with seniority to retire.

The availability of early retirement benefits legitimizes labor force exit before age 65. Changes in such social expectations could explain some of the decreased participation of older men in the workforce.

Many recent studies suggest that health is the major reason that men leave work before age 65 (Andrisani, 1977; Bixby, 1976; Kingson, 1979; Parnes & Meyers, 1972; Parnes & Nestel, 1975; Reno, 1971; Schwab, 1976; Sheppard, 1977). While this may be true for individuals, it is difficult to view the health factor as the major reason for the early retirement trend.

Recent advances in medicine may have enabled some men with severe disabilities to live. Previously, these men would have died and, therefore, would not have been counted in the labor force statistics. However, the net effect of such medical advances has probably increased the ability of many persons to work. In any event, it seems very unlikely that the health status of recent cohorts of older male workers has undergone such great declines as to depress the labor force participation rates.

There are other factors that help explain the recent decline in labor force participation of men. Competition over existing employment opportunities, the increased labor force participation of women, and the entrance of the "war babies" into the labor force may have "crowded out" some older male workers. Changing social attitudes and the growing affluence throughout most of the post-World War II period seems to have resulted in a more leisure-oriented society.

It is tempting to assign causality for the early labor force withdrawal trend primarily to the growth of early retirement benefits. It is difficult to defend the proposition that shifts in the health status of recent cohorts of older workers have caused declines in labor force participation. The combined impact of Social Security and second pension early retirement benefits appears to provide a good explanation for the very large decline in labor force participation among men aged 62 to 64. The singular impact of second pension early retirement benefits and the increased availability of disability benefits could also explain the significant, but considerably smaller declines in participation among older men below age 62.

But, unfortunately (from a conceptual point of view), the real world is considerably more complicated. In fact, we are dealing with somewhat of a "chicken-egg" question. Not only can the existence of early retirement benefits be interpreted as causing the decline in participation of older men, but the decline, itself, can be interpreted as stimulating the growth and expansion of early retirement benefits. Moreover, it is possible that the growth in benefits and the lowered participation are related, but not in terms of cause and effect.

Rather, both may be the effect of other factors such as the long-term trend of economic growth and the long-term problem of unemployment. Examination of these possibilities results in a more fundamental explanation of the phenomenon.

Societies capable of producing at beyond subsistence levels choose between additional production of goods and services and foregoing some or all of the potential production, in exchange for leisure. Continued economic growth results in ongoing opportunities to choose between increased output and added leisure. Once a society creates leisure, the opportunity exists to develop retirement institutions. As pointed out by Juanita M. Kreps and Joseph J. Spengler, until 1946 reductions in the number of hours worked per week were the major form to which leisure was allocated. Since that time there has been "rapid growth in free time in the form of vacations, early retirement, etc." (Kreps and Spengler, 1966).

The 1961 amendments to the Social Security Act reduced the eligibility age for men to 62 and provided men the opportunity to receive actuarially reduced benefits. It was assumed that the early retirement option would help reduce the unemployment problem (Kreps, 1963). As Congressman Vanik stated during the debate, "If 2 million male workers eventually retire under this program, 2 million job opportunities will be created, and unemployment will be reduced" (Social Security Administration, 1961).

Unions and firms also use early retirement policies as mechanisms for the regulation of the supply and demand for labor. Companies and unions use early retirement inducements to encourage early labor force withdrawal during periods of high unemployment (Davis, 1973).

No doubt, the increased availability of public and private pension income to men before age 65 is a major cause of the early retirement trend. However, the inability of the economy to provide jobs for all persons willing and able to work is a more important prior cause. Chronic unemployment directly affects the labor force participation of older workers, particularly marginal ones with health problems, as a result of the limits on employment opportunities that it imposes. Chronic unemployment indirectly affects their participation because it results in political pressures to redefine unwanted leisure as "early retirement" rather than "unemployment." The government and industrial policies that result from these pressures provide pension incentives for people to retire early.

EMPLOYMENT BARRIERS

Retirement as a modern institution has evolved as part of a larger social and economic system. As such, it serves a variety of functions for this larger system. For example, we have discussed how certain retirement policies exist to ration scarce employment opportunities and promote the orderly turnover of personnel. In a slightly different vein, private pensions are often an important tool that management uses to maintain a trained workforce.

In discussing barriers to the employment of older workers as well as the reasons that older people withdraw from work, it is important to remember that, as the needs of the economy change, so does the institution of retirement. Depending on the needs of the economy, employment barriers are liable to be raised or lowered. Similarly, the decisions (or lack thereof) confronting different types and classes of workers on the threshold of retirement are also subject to societal modification.

This section discusses four institutional barriers to the employment of older workers: (1) Unemployment and discouragement; (2) age discrimination; (3) social attitudes and expectations; (4) lack of flexibility in employment conditions.

Unemployment and Discouragement

A glance at the unemployment rates for different age groups in 1978 (see Table 3-5) leads to the reasonable conclusion that relative to other age groups, unemployment is not a serious problem for older workers. However, this is simply not the case. Macrounemployment operates indirectly through the creation of pension incentives and directly through the process of job loss, limited employment opportunity and discouragement to bring about the labor force withdrawal of older workers who, given the option, would otherwise be employed. Further, the impact of unemployment on older cohorts of workers who often contribute to the support of other family

Table 3-5. Average Unemployment Rates in 1978 by Age and Sex.

Age	Unemployment Rate in 1978	
	Female	Male
16 and 17	19.5	19.2
18 and 19	15.3	13.2
20 to 24	10.1	9.1
25 to 34	6.7	4.3
35 to 44	5.0	2.8
45 to 54	4.0	2.8
55 to 64	3.2	2.7
65 and over	3.8	4.2
Total, 16 and over	7.2%	5.2%

Source: U.S. Department of Labor, *Employment and Training Report of the President,* 1979, Table A-20.

members may be more severe than the impact on the younger cohorts.

The reason that unemployment does not appear to be a significant problem for older workers is a result of the manner in which official unemployment statistics are developed. To be counted among the unemployed, one must first be defined as being part of the labor force; that is, as working or actively seeking work.

As Sheppard has observed, once unemployed, older workers tend to remain unemployed longer than younger ones. Consequently, there is greater likelihood that a process of discouragement and labor force withdrawal will occur. He further notes that a "large portion of applicants for retirement benefits—especially those before the age of 65—consist of men and women who have undergone this process" (Sheppard, 1976). The discouraged worker is not considered part of the labor force and, therefore, not counted among the unemployed. In terms of older workers, this serves to underestimate the extent of their employment problems by labeling a significant amount of their "unemployment" as "retirement."

There is evidence suggesting that the retirement rates of older workers are sensitive to national and area rates of unemployment. The decline in labor force participation rates among men has generally been greatest during periods of high unemployment (Rosenfeld and Brown, 1979). Joseph Quinn finds less early retirement in labor markets experiencing a shortage of workers (Quinn, 1978).

High levels of unemployment do not impact on all classes of older workers in the same way. Evidence suggests that low income older workers and persons with health problems are more vulnerable to loss of employment during recessions. Findings by Sheppard suggest that the negative long-term effect of area unemployment falls disproportionately on older male workers who had previously reported health-induced work limitations as opposed to men who had not. He also finds a strong interaction between health, race, and unemployment; with healthy employed whites being the least likely, and unhealthy, unemployed blacks being the most likely to withdraw from the labor force (Sheppard, 1977).

Age Discrimination in Employment

Age discrimination in employment refers to the restriction or denial of employment, training, compensation, or advancement opportunities on the basis of age. It is often justified by stereotypes that hold older workers to be less capable, less competent, less trainable, less productive, and less reliable in comparison to younger workers. These attitudes persist in the face of research that generally shows older workers, as a group, comparing quite satisfactorily with younger workers. Where differences do exist, these differences are often desirable from the point of view of an employer. For example, a recent review of the literature by Elizabeth L. Meier and Elizabeth A. Kerr discusses findings which suggest that older workers tend to experience less absenteeism, fewer (but longer) injuries, longer job tenure after training and equal, if not better supervisor ratings (Meier and Kerr, 1976).

Moreover, differences in functioning between groups of older and younger people (whether favorable or unfavorable to older workers) cannot really provide adequate rationale for discriminating between individuals on the basis of age. The reason is quite simple. There is far more variation in ability, attitudes, performance, etc., within age categories than between categories. Similarly, the costs of group health and life insurance plans are greater for an older work force. Finally, in some circumstances there is an incentive for employers to replace older workers receiving relatively high wages with new employees entering at lower wage levels. However, this can only be accomplished if the positions of older and younger workers are similar. Such circumstances may not be frequent.

Older workers have limited protection against age discrimination through the Age Discrimination in Employment Act (ADEA). A 1965 report issued by the Department of Labor documented widespread age discrimination in employment—estimating, for example, that one-half of all job openings were closed to workers over age 55 and one-quarter to workers over age 45 (U.S. Department of Labor, 1965). The passage of the ADEA in 1967 provided protection against some of the most blatant forms of discrimination for workers aged 40 to 65. However, the more subtle forms of age discrimination in employment often remain difficult to document and prevent.

In 1978, amendments to ADEA abolished mandatory retirement for most federal employees and raised the allowable age for the mandatory retirement of most workers in the private sector to 70. The immediate impact of this legislation on retirement trends is likely to be quite limited. Prior to the passage, relatively few older workers appear to have been forced to retire at a set age. Using data from the 1969 Survey of New Beneficiaries, James H. Schulz estimates that only about 10 percent of the retired men studied who were willing and able to work were forced to retire due to mandatory retirement rules. (Schulz, 1974).

The long-term impact of this legislation and future efforts to totally abolish mandatory retirement may be of much greater import. Faced with projections for increased pension costs, longer life-spans, and future declines in the number of younger workers relative to older workers, there is a clear need to begin to readjust our expectations concerning retirement age. The passage of this legislation may well be the beginning of the legitimization of later retirement (or, to put it another way, the beginning of the "delegitimization" of early retirement).

Shirley Campbell suggests that the reform or elimination of mandatory retirement may have a special impact on older women workers. By expanding the accepted period of work, there may be less pressure for women workers seeking to re-enter the labor force in their forties or fifties (Campbell, 1979).

The passage of this legislation combined with high rates of inflation may also enable some workers to continue to work well past previously established age limits who, in a noninflationary economy, would otherwise have retired voluntarily at or before the mandatory age. Finally, it needs to be mentioned that beyond any impact on retirement, the passage of this legislation is important because it represents a restoration, albeit somewhat compromised, of important civil liberties for older people.

Research has documented systematic biases in government employment programs detrimental to the interests of older workers. For instance, based on U.S. Employment Service data from 50 states, Charles E. McConnell found that relative to workers under age 45, older cohorts of workers received proportionally less counseling or training services (McConnell, 1977). Similarly, relatively few older persons are served by programs funded under the Comprehensive Employment and Training Act (CETA). There is a systematic bias towards providing service to youth in this program based, in part, on concern to reduce official rates of unemployment (Schram & Osten, 1978) and, partially, it would seem from attitudes that view the young unemployed as "more salvageable."

No doubt, age discrimination in employment does not effect all older workers equally. Certain workers, for example self-employed persons, are plainly protected from it. Although the direct effects of age discrimination are often difficult to trace, it is reasonable to speculate that its greatest impact falls on older workers who are likely to be in the most economically vulnerable positions—those in ill health, the long-term unemployed, minorities, and older women who are re-entering the labor force.

Social Attitudes and Expectations

The attitudes and expectations that exist regarding the abilities of older workers present a particularly insidious barrier to their employment. Not only does the older worker have to deal with obstacles to employment as a result of some employer's or potential employer's attitudes, but through the process of internalization the older worker may share these negative stereotypes (Fogarty, 1975).

Lawrence Haber has suggested that as a result of age-related capacity devaluation, "a substantial proportion of older men become severely disabled who might otherwise make a more productive adjustment to disability" (Haber, 1972). This devaluation of ability is related to the limited societal mechanisms for the rehabilitation of older workers as well as the greater negative self-evaluations of capacity by disabled older workers. So, not only do the negative stereotypes create external obstacles, but they also create internal obstacles to the employment of older workers.

Lack of Flexibility in Employment and Retirement Conditions

There is a general lack of flexibility in the way most jobs are structured. Job requirements of hours and tasks are rarely subject to modification. As a result, most employees at the threshold of retirement who are fortunate to be in a position to choose between continued work and retirement are presented with an all or nothing choice—a full-time work week or loss of their job.

The introduction of flexible employment conditions can be accomplished in a number of ways. The option of participating in phased retirement programs, can be extended to older workers thereby enabling older workers to slowly reduce the number of hours worked in a week, take longer vacations and, if desired, continue in employment on a part-time basis. Opportunities for job redesign and retraining could be developed to enable persons to remain employed even though their ability to function in their regular job is changing due to health problems. Private pension plans could encourage flexible employment by providing increased benefits for employment after the normal retirement age (Morrison, 1979).

A small number of private and government employers have instituted limited flexible employment programs. Given the aging of the work force, it seems likely that the future will bring increased flexibility of employment conditions for many older workers. This is especially likely if labor shortages materialize in subsequent years. For now, however, the general lack of flexibility of employment and retirement conditions represents a significant barrier to the continued employment of many older people.

THE RETIREMENT "DECISION"

The quality and degree of choice at the threshold of retirement concerning continued work and labor force withdrawal varies greatly among workers. Workers who have good health, employment opportunities, and adequate retirement income expectations experience a high degree of choice. Of course, for most workers constraining factors impose limitations on their freedom of choice; and, for some experiencing, for instance, a combination of ill health and no employment opportunities, there is simply no choice. For this latter group, the use of the term "retirement decision" is an inappropriate euphemism since these workers have no control over their labor force exit.

The retirement decision literature generally concludes that health problems as well as the availability and magnitude of retirement income are the major determinants for the labor force withdrawal of individuals. This literature is first reviewed; then, limitations and criticisms are discussed along with the implications of the different quality of decision often experienced by classifications of older workers.

Influential Factors

Available pension income is the principal component of retirement finances that influences the retirement decision. Pension income is discussed in the retirement decision literature usually in terms of absolute dollars and replacement rates (the proportion of previous earnings replaced by pension benefits). Personal savings, homeownership (Parnes and Nestel, 1975), other assets and the presence of dependents (Parnes and Nestel, 1975; Schwab, 1976; Sheppard, 1977) appear to exert limited influence.

Retirement finances seem to exert the most influence on the retirement decision when pension income replaces large proportions of average earnings before retirement—high replacement rates. Studies based on data collected in 1967 and again in 1969 to 1970 found replacement rates to be, by far, the most powerful predictor of the early retirement of auto workers (Barfield & Morgan, 1975). However, findings from the Social Security Administration's 1968 to 1970 Survey of Newly Entitled Beneficiaries (SNEB) show that only 2 percent of the nonworking men entitled to Social Security benefits at age 62 view pension benefits as the main reason for leaving work (Reno, 1971).

At first glance, such findings seem contradictory to the auto worker study. However, it should be kept in mind that auto workers represent a special group that have excellent benefits from their second pensions, (pensions in addition to Social Security), whereas most Social Security recipients do not have second pensions. In fact, SNEB findings of men covered by second pensions are consistent with the auto worker study. The rate at which men retire willingly is reported to increase "from 15 percent of those with less than $1000 to about three-fourths of those with retirement benefits exceeding $5000" (Reno, 1971). The availability of second pensions lowers the cost of retirement and increases the likelihood that workers will want to retire. The expectation of early retirement is also especially high among men with second pensions (Andrisani & Parnes, 1977). Similarly, SNEB findings show that among nonmarried women accepting Social Security benefits at age 62, 75 percent with second pensions retired willingly, compared to only 25 percent of those without second pensions (Reno, 1976b).

Persons with second pensions (and hence greater replacement rates) represent a relatively advantaged group of retirees. It is these people who are most likely to retire willingly or expect to retire early in response to pension incentives. Economic incentives do not seem to play as strong a role in the retirement behavior of less fortunate retirees. SNEB findings suggest that the early acceptance of Social Security benefits with its accompanying actuarial reduction is primarily motivated by economic survival for this group (Lauriat and Rabin, 1975); three-fifths of beneficiaries entitled at age 62 having been unemployed for at least three months. For example, in 1969, 48 percent of white men and 83 percent black men taking reduced benefits at age 62 were entitled to poverty level benefits (Reno, 1976a). So, in terms of analyzing the retirement decision of less advantaged retirees, it is important to look at other factors, especially health.

As previously mentioned, many recent studies suggest that health is the major reason that men leave work before age 65 (Andrisani, 1977; Bixby, 1976; Kingson, 1979; Parnes and Meyers, 1972; Reno, 1971; Schwab, 1976; Sheppard, 1977). "Poor health" is considered an acceptable reason for leaving work. Consequently, there is an incentive to mask other reasons for leaving work by claiming health problems and so questions regarding the reliability of self-reported health problems have been raised.

In spite of this qualification, Parnes and Nestel (1975) have been able to suggest with some confidence that poor health is the major determinant of early withdrawal. This finding was particularly important, because the longitudinal nature of the data, allowed these researchers to measure health before and after retirement. This approach provided a very effective control for distortions that could result from self-reported explanations after the fact of labor force withdrawal. Karen Schwab's analysis of the Retirement History Study data found that 65 percent of the men aged 58 to 63 who were out of the labor force in 1969 cited health as the main reason for their withdrawal. Subsequent analysis by Lenore Bixby of the data when these men were 62 to 65 found that nonemployment in 1973 of men who worked in 1969 "was influenced much more by self-assessment of health-related work limitations than any of the other seven factors" employed in the analysis. Health also seems to be a major determinant of whether older women are in the labor force (Sherman, 1976). The SNEB data shows that health is the single most important reason given by women who left work within three years of accepting Social Security pensions. This was especially true for unmarried women who were far less likely to refer to family or personal reasons for retirement. Parenthetically, for women aged 65 and over, compulsory retirement was the major reason given with health being the second most important (Reno, 1976b).

Using data from the 1969 Retirement History Study (RHS), Joseph Quinn found an interesting interaction between health and retirement finances for white married men, such that men in poor health are more likely to take advantage of pension incentives to retire early (Quinn, 1978). A slightly different relationship results from analysis of NLS data for men who leave work before age 62. Health limitations reported at withdrawal may be more severe for men expecting to receive smaller retirement pensions than for those expecting larger incomes; thereby suggesting that a "rich" man's reported work-limiting health condition has a tendency to be less severe than a "poor" man's (Kingson, 1979).

There are more interesting interactions between health and other factors. Quinn also found that undesirable job characteristics by themselves had very little effect on the early retirement of men. However, when health was taken into consideration, the effect of job satisfaction is fairly strong on persons in poor health (Quinn, 1978). RHS data suggest that if manual and blue-collar workers have health limitations, then they are more likely to retire early (Schwab, 1976). This may be because the job demands of manual workers require greater exertion and because the job demands of manual workers subject them to greater risk of disability. Andrisani finds that the effects of health on labor force participation vary considerably by occupational category, such that the effects are greatest among operatives and laborers and smallest among professionals (Andrisani, 1977).

There are other factors besides health and retirement finances which influence the retirement decisions of individuals. For any one individual, these factors may be of greater importance than health and finances. However, in terms of retirement patterns they are not as influential. We will briefly discuss the impact of unemployment, occupation, industry, marriage, education, and racial discrimination.

Previous discussion suggests that retirement rates are sensitive to levels of unemployment. In terms of the retirement decision, here it is only necessary to remind ourselves that the impact of unemployment seems greatest among the more marginal members of the older work force—those with health problems, in low paying, unsteady unemployment and the like.

As factors influencing the retirement decision, both occupation and industry are associated with other influences such as the availability of second pension income, levels of education and unemployment. It is, therefore, difficult to interpret the effects of occupation and industry on the retirement decision separate from these other factors.

Based on data from a nationwide survey conducted in 1974 by Louis Harris and Associates, Elizabeth Meier reports that workers over age 65 are more likely than the population at large to be employed in managerial or service positions (Meier, 1975). Rones reports greater representation in 1977 of men over age 60 in the farming, services, sales, and managerial occupations and less representation "in operatives, crafts, laborers, and professional, and technical occupations" (Rones, 1978).

The physical demands of an occupation and the availability of part-time work within occupations help explain why certain occupations have greater concentrations of older workers. Occupations requiring relatively greater physical exertion limit the likelihood of participation by workers with health problems. Occupations such as sales provide greater part-time opportunities and do not present significant health barriers to older workers.

Self-employment is also an important factor. Self-employed older workers are in an excellent position to choose the terms of their work—hours, season, and the like. Self-employed men are less likely to be out of the labor force, but more likely to be part-time workers than other older men (Reno, 1971). Occupations with high rates of self-employment (e.g., medical doctors, lawyers) afford greater control over the retirement decision.

As Sheppard has pointed out, "retirement rates vary by industry" and within each industry the self-employed and people with high skill levels are "in a better position of autonomy concerning the option to retire or continue working" (Sheppard, 1976). Relative to younger workers, Rones found that men aged 65 and over in 1977 were most likely to be employed in finance, insurance and real estate, trade and miscellaneous service industries and least likely in transportation, communication and public utilities, manufacturing, construction, and mining (Rones, 1978). Unionized and capital-intensive industries such as the ones in which men are least likely to work after age 65 are also the ones that tend to have the greatest pension coverage.

The opportunity for pension income and associated mandatory

coverage policies are the most important reasons for greater retirement rates within these industries. Rones points out that finance, insurance, and real estate industries also have high rates of private pension coverage. However, he suggests that the impact of these pensions on retirement rates is offset by the opportunities these industries provide for self-employment, and therefore greater control over the retirement decision (Rones, 1978).

The marital status of older workers does seem to influence the retirement decision. Again, it is important to note that this factor is associated with other influences, such as health and level of education; thereby making it difficult to interpret the direct effect of marital status. Parnes and Nestel found that married men living with their wives were less likely to expect to retire (Parnes and Nestel, 1975). The reason for less early retirement among married men seems to be that they are more likely to be responsible for the support of others (Schwab, 1976). Analysis of NLS data suggests that the wives of men who left the labor force before age 62 with reported health problems were far more likely to work than healthy retirees. This was especially true of the wives of men who did not receive Social Security disability benefits (Kingson, 1979). This suggests that under certain circumstances marital status may increase the likelihood of male retirement.

SNEB data suggests that married older women are more likely to report voluntary reasons for retirement than nonmarried women. Married women were more likely to be out of the labor force than nonmarried ones, and were more likely to have greater pension incomes. Of the unmarried women in the study, those who were formerly married were more likely to be working, less likely to receive a second pension, and more likely to report leaving work for involuntary reasons (Reno, 1976b).

Amount of education seems to effect the retirement decision primarily because it is associated with factors such as expected retirement income and occupation. Persons with more education are more likely to work in higher paying occupations with second pension coverage. Consequently, these persons are more likely to be in a position to choose between work and retirement. Carl Rosenfeld and Scott Campbell Brown state that the ''decrease in labor force participation of men has been relatively greater for the least educated than for those who attended college'' (Rosenfeld and Brown, 1979). The data they present also shows greater labor force participation among both male and female cohorts of older workers who have completed high school as opposed to those who have not (See Table 3-6). Their findings are consistent with earlier studies showing men without high school diplomas (Parnes and Meyers, 1972) and men aged 58 to 63 with little schooling (Schwab, 1976) more likely to be early labor force withdrawees than men with more schooling.

Findings concerning socioeconomic status (SES), a combined measure of education, income, and occupation, are similar to those concerning education. A. J. Jaffe reports that each cohort of older men with high SES's between 1950 and 1960 had less retirement probability than cohorts with low SES's (Jaffe, 1972). Sheppard reports that early labor force withdrawals for reasons of death, inability to work, and retirement are ''over-represented among men

Table 3-6. Civilian Labor Force Participation Rates of the Population 45 and Over, by Age, Sex and Years of School Completed, March 1978.

Sex and Years of School Completed	45 to 54 years	March 1978 55 to 64 years	66 years and over
Men			
Total.	91.3	72.7	19.6
Elementary: 8 years or less	82.4	62.4	14.6
High school: 1 to 3 years	89.7	66.5	19.8
High school: 4 years	93.3	75.9	23.6
College: 1 to 3 years	94.1	81.6	25.6
College: 4 years or more	96.5	87.1	32.0
Women			
Total.	56.7	41.7	8.4
Elementary: 8 years or less	45.9	29.7	5.5
High school: 1 to 3 years	49.8	38.3	8.2
High school: 4 years	59.0	47.2	11.9
College: 1 to 3 years	60.0	46.7	11.6
College: 4 years or more	72.0	52.2	11.3

Source: Rosenfeld, Carl & Brown, Scott Campbell, ''The Labor Force Status of Older Workers,'' *Monthly Labor Review,* (November, 1979), Table 6.

with the lowest Duncan SES scores; and that early withdrawals among the lower SES groups, as opposed to the higher ones, have the smallest proportion attributable to retirement (Sheppard, 1977).

There are obvious differences between the retirement circumstances of blacks and whites. As a glance back at Table 3-2 shows, the percentage of household units aged 65 and over in poverty in 1977 is greater for all types of black households when compared to white ones regardless of the sex or family status of the household. Similarly, analysis of SNEB data shows that 35 percent of black men as opposed to 30 percent of white men were entitled to Social Security benefits at the earliest age, 62. More significantly, 83 percent of these blacks compared to 48 percent of these whites were receiving poverty level benefits (Reno, 1976a).

The decreased likelihood of second pension income experienced by blacks combined with greater rates of work-limiting health conditions means that, on the average, blacks experience less control over retirement than whites. For example, a recent study of male labor force withdrawals before age 62 found that in practically every occupational and industrial category allowing for reasonable comparisons, blacks were more likely than whites to leave the labor force for involuntary reasons, primarily health problems (Kingson, 1979).

The impact of racial discrimination on the retirement decision is primarily indirect. The major effects of discrimination are manifest throughout the life cycle resulting in differences between blacks and whites in educational, employment, health, and income opportunities. The clear differences in the quality of the retirement decision experienced by blacks is a result of the longterm impact of these and other inequities.

Criticism of the Retirement Decision Literature

The retirement decision literature is ahistorical in two respects. The history of individuals is not examined to explain their withdrawal behavior, and the potential of historical trends to shape and constrain the type of choice (or lack thereof) confronting people at the moment of labor force withdrawal is rarely more than recognized.

By analyzing retirement as a momentary event, the research bypasses a chain of events occurring throughout life that may be casually linked to health, financial, and other circumstances confronting an individual at the moment of labor force exit. It is not enough to identify health and retirement finances as the prime determinants of the retirement decision. It is important to look behind these variables and ask "What factors operate throughout the life cycle to cause some people to face favorable and others unfavorable retirement circumstances?"

This type of question requires not only that we examine the history of the individual, but that we also examine the influence of the historical and institutional setting on older workers. That some workers have favorable labor market experiences with good pension benefits attached is indisputable. That these circumstances affect the quality of choice facing workers at the threshold of retirement is also obvious. However, we do not know the extent to which the labor market experience and retirement choices presented workers are socially determined. Are the different circumstances of retirees simply a function of individual differences in ability and luck? Or, are they a result of socially sanctioned differences in the distribution of employment and income opportunities that operate throughout the life of workers—one manifestation being different levels of retirement income? Retirement research needs to take more cognizance of the influence of the societal context on the retirement process.

Who Gets to Choose?

Freedom of choice is an important societal value. Retirement as a social institution provides a good example of how this value is operationalized. Our examination of the retirement decision literature suggests that workers experiencing good health, employment opportunities, and favorable retirement income expectations are in the enviable position of being able to exercise great control over the retirement process. Who are these workers?

Generally speaking, these are the same workers who have experienced relatively stable and well paid employment throughout their lives. As a group, they are far more likely to be male, white and middle class than those persons with less control over retirement. The passage of the 1978 amendments to the Age Discrimination in

Employment Act means that the retirement decision of all but an extremely small portion of this group is no longer constricted by mandatory retirement policies. Even among those with health problems, their freedom of choice is greater because they are better able to afford retirement than less advantaged workers with health problems. So, like educational, employment, and income opportunities, freedom of choice over retirement is distributed somewhat unequally to the disadvantage of groups that traditionally lose out in the allocative process.

RETIREMENT TRENDS: IMPLICATIONS FOR THE FUTURE

We have discussed labor force trends that show a long-term decline in older male participation and an opposite trend among women. We have also seen that the quality of the retirement decision and the impact of barriers to the continued employment of older workers vary in ways unfavorable to those workers who can be termed disadvantaged. Finally, we have emphasized that retirement as an institution has changed and will continue to change in response to social and economic needs. In this concluding section, we will discuss possible changes in the institution of retirement in light of demographic and economic trends.

Two Early Retirement Trends: Voluntary and Involuntary

Early retirement has been the dominant retirement trend of the past thirty years. Older male labor force participation has declined dramatically during this period. Also, data showing a slight decline in the labor force participation rates of women aged 60 to 64 suggest that we may be seeing the beginning of this trend among women.

Will the early retirement trend continue into the future? To answer this question, we must first understand who the early retirees are.

Studies show early retirees to be distributed primarily into two groups—an economically advantaged group and a larger, disadvantaged group. In contrast to the advantaged group, the members of the disadvantaged group rarely receive private or special public employee pension benefits, usually receive smaller Social Security benefits and usually withdraw from the labor force involuntarily, often as a result of health problems combined with limited employment opportunity. In analyzing NLS data, Herbert Parnes and Gilbert Nestel dichotomize the distribution of male early retirees:

> . . .The more fortunate are those for whom the decision to retire is in a real sense voluntary. Their health is reasonably good, they are attracted by the freedom from regular work and they believe that their financial resources are sufficient to permit them this freedom. . .
> In the other category are those for whom the term retirement, with its usual connotations, is really a misnomer.
> These are the men who are really forced out of the labor market by disability that may be quite sudden. . . (Parnes and Nestel, 1975)

Even though most involuntary early retirees leave work primarily as a result of health problems, their disabilities often do not qualify them for disability from either the Social Security or SSI disability programs. Consequently, the income situation for these retirees who usually lack private benefits or sufficient assets can be quite severe.

If these early retirees are age 62 to 64, then they are usually eligible to receive Social Security retirement benefits on an actuarially reduced basis. If below age 62, they are only eligible for benefits from disability programs. Many, of course, do not receive disability benefits because they are unable to meet the strict eligibility requirements.

The inability of involuntary early retirees to hold or find employment means that those who eventually receive Social Security retirement benefits will experience permanently reduced pensions. First, their time out of the labor force will lower the normal retirement benefit (the Primary Insurance Amount) to which they are entitled at age 65. The structure of the Social Security benefit formula leads to this arithmetic reduction. Second, if they accept early retirement benefits at or after age 62, they will experience a permanent actuarial reduction at the rate of 5/9 of a percent per month of retirement before age 65. So, not only do involuntary early retirees experience a loss of earnings, but (as a result of the arithmetic reduction) this group is also likely to lose a portion of the Social Security retirement benefits they would otherwise have received, had they remained in the labor force.

In seeking to answer whether the early retirement trend will continue into the future, it is important to recognize that there are two distinct trends—voluntary and involuntary early retirement. It seems highly likely that demographic and economic trends will lead to a reversal of the voluntary early retirement phenomenon. However, there is every possibility that the involuntary early retirement phenomenon will expand. We can explore the reasoning behind these positions by briefly summarizing current demographic and economic trends and their likely impact on retirement age policies.

Socioeconomic Trends and Retirement Age Policy

Age 65 is generally considered normal retirement age in the Social Security, special public and private pension systems. However, the widespread availability of early retirement and disability options within pension systems has made it increasingly difficult to defend age 65 as the "normal retirement age." For example, the 1975 Bankers Trust Company Study of Corporate Pension Plans shows that these plans provided early retirement options to 92 percent of covered employees in 1974 (Bankers Trust Company, 1975). Evan L. Hodgens' study of changes in 149 plans between 1970 and 1975 shows that "77 plans made retirement with full normal benefits before age 65 available to at least some of their employees" and further states that plans permitting early retirement at any age after 30 years service are the norm for the "major automobile, truck, farm and construction equipment manufacturers" (Hodgens, 1975). Similarly, we know that over half of all new beneficiaries in the Social Security system accept benefits before age 65.

In the preface to their book entitled *The Graying of Working America,* Harold Sheppard and Sara Rix list the major trends that are resulting in a reassessment of retirement age policy. These trends are:

1. The trend toward more and more persons retiring at earlier and earlier ages.

2. The increased population of retired persons, and the apparent increase in the number of years they live in retirement.
3. The current downward trend in fertility rates, producing a zero population growth and a smaller number of persons eventually moving into the work force to support the increasing non-working older population.
4. Biomedical progress toward increasing the death age.
5. Rising expectations and demands for a better retirement income.
6. Changes in energy and resource base that might negatively affect the productivity levels needed to support the nonworking population.
7. A continuation of inflation rates above those of the past few decades (Sheppard and Rix, 1977).

Current retirement age policies are expensive and will become more so in the future. The long-range financing problems of the Social Security system are well known. Projected declines in the number of retirees, expectations of longer life-spans and the possibility of limited economic growth means that the future cost to the working age population will be much greater than it is presently, especially as the "baby boom" generation moves into retirement—roughly during the years of 2012 to 2025. There are also significant short-range financing problems. For example, continued high rates of inflation threaten the short-run stability of the system because taxable wages generally do not increase at the rate of inflation whereas benefit payments do. Similarly, a recession with high rates of unemployment threatens the short-term stability of the system by also reducing income from taxable wages and increasing the outgo from the system because more people apply for and receive benefits during periods of high unemployment. Our private and other public pension systems are also subject to similar problems.

The financial pressures generated by current demographic and economic trends can be relieved by changes in funding and taxation mechanisms, limitations in the type and magnitude of benefits and increases in retirement age. While changing retirement age policy is plainly not the only means of adjustment; it is almost inevitable that these trends will lead to increases in the average age of retirement.

The important questions seem to be not whether this change will occur, but how it will occur, and in what ways will people be affected.

Changes in retirement age policies will arise principally from adjustments (1) in the expectations and desires of workers, (2) in the terms of employment and retirement incentives offered by employers, and (3) in Social Security retirement incentives and the defined age of normal retirement.

The retirement expectations and the desires of older workers for continued employment are subject to change. Retirement is partially an economic decision. Older workers expecting to finance their retirement, in part, by private pension income (which generally does not adjust for inflation) and/or savings are likely to postpone their retirement in view of today's high rates of inflation. Similarly, a protracted slowdown in economic growth is likely to make it more difficult for future cohorts of older workers to save for retirement. Should the trends of high inflation and slowed economic growth continue into the future, then we can expect less voluntary early and normal retirement and increased desire on the part of older workers to work past what are now considered normal retirement ages.

Of course, there is the possibility that slowed economic growth (unless accompanied by significant shifts towards more labor intensive modes of production) will result in fewer job opportunities. Just as is currently the case, constrictions in the demand for labor could thwart some of the employment desires of future older workers. The outcome of this type of situation would probably be similar to our current situation with regard to the work/leisure choice. Our older workers occupying advantaged labor market positions would have more choice than those in more marginal positions.

There are other ways that retirement expectations and desires may change. First, these attitudes are socially determined and, therefore, subject to change as our institutions change. Should later retirement dates be established within Social Security and other pension systems, then social expectations will adjust. Second, changes in the conditions of labor (better wages, more flexible work) might change these attitudes.

It has been suggested that labor shortages, brought about by declining fertility rates (the "baby bust"), and the eventual retirement of the "baby boom" generation since 1960, might develop in

the late 1980s and, again, around 2015. Such shortages would provide the private sector with strong motive to encourage the continued
employment of older workers. In fact, as a result of the growing expense of private pension benefits (especially early retirement provisions), such motivation exists without the materialization of labor
shortages.

So, even without labor shortages, it may be in the private sector's
interest to develop disincentives to early retirement or, to put it
another way, incentives for continued employment of workers
covered by their pension plans. To a certain extent, such disincentives to voluntary retirement have begun to emerge as a result of current high levels of inflation. Positive pension incentives for continued employment are also likely to be developed. Incentives for
continued employment may also result in changes in the structure of
work that are favorable to older workers—more training opportunities, job sharing, flexible work, and phased retirement options.

Should labor shortages materialize, then it is likely that one
response of industry will be to bid up wages in an effort to attract
and maintain employees. This would increase the cost of retirement
to older workers since they would be trading off larger amounts of
income for their retirement leisure. Greater incentive would exist for
continuing to work. Also, under these circumstances it is possible
that some older workers who are not competitive in today's labor
market would be able to find work. Consequently, the implications
of such shortages would be both a decline in retirement and the
discouraged worker rates.

Changes in the Social Security retirement age can take two forms:
the creation of incentives for later retirement or legislative enactment
of a later normal retirement age. In fact, the 1977 Amendments to
the Social Security Act, legislated a delayed retirement credit of 3
percent for each year that workers postpone the acceptance of
benefits between ages 65 and 70. This creates an incentive for later
retirement and effectively broadens the systems definition of ''normal'' retirement age:

. . . Although age 65 is now referred to as the ''normal'' retirement age, age 65 is actually only a benchmark on a continuum of
retirement ages that ranges from age 62 to 70. Those retiring

before age 65 receive benefits up to 20 percent lower than those retiring at age 65; those retiring after 65 will receive benefits up to 15 percent higher than they would have received had they retired at age 65. The benefit of a worker retiring at age 70 will be 144 percent of the benefit received by a worker with the same average indexed monthly earnings (AIME) retiring at age 62—that is 115 percent of PIA compared to 80 percent (Advisory Council on Social Security, 1979).

The delayed retirement credit will probably have its greatest impact on and be of greatest benefit to a relatively advantaged group of older workers—those who are in a position to choose between continued work and retirement such as voluntary early retirees. It should be recognized, however, that delayed retirement credits of greater than 3 percent now offered in European Social Security programs have not resulted in delaying the retirement of many workers.

The 1975 and 1979 Advisory Councils on Social Security have recommended that consideration be given to a gradual increase in the retirement age after the turn of the century. Most proposals for increasing retirement age suggest age 68.

There is some disagreement as to whether a legislated increase in normal retirement age is necessary or desirable to deal with the long-run financing of the system. Some argue that it is possible to achieve the same results through incentives in Social Security and other pension systems that encourage later retirement and that legislated increases in retirement age will be superfluous if labor shortages materialize. Perhaps, most importantly, "opponents point out that raising retirement age is simply a reduction in the retirement benefits all workers expect to receive because the actuarial reduction would be applied to beneficiaries age 62 through 68" (Advisory Council on Social Security, 1979). This suggests that the persons potentially hurt the most would be older workers who are unable to find or keep work until age 68. Those who choose to retire before age 68 would lose some benefits, but it is fair to assume that since it would be their choice, they can afford the loss.

It seems likely that one very important way in which the institution of retirement will respond to current demographic and economic challenges is by the gradual legitimization of later retirement ages.

The exact nature of the changes in retirement age policy is not clear at this juncture.

In terms of encouraging the labor force participation of older workers, we should expect changes in retirement age policy to have the greatest impact on healthy older workers. This means that we can expect a decrease in voluntary early retirements and some voluntary normal retirements. The increased labor force participation of these older workers should, at a minimum, slow down the decline in labor force participation among older men and could, perhaps, lead to a significant growth in participation. For older women, it may prevent the emergence of a significant early retirement trend and contribute to the general trend of increased labor force participation.

However, changes in retirement age policy hold the potential of being disasterous for large groups of older workers in the future.

Caught between a Rock and a Hard Place

As discussion of the involuntary early retirement trend has shown, there is presently a significant income inadequacy problem among many persons who leave work before age 65. Many involuntary early retirees are unable to work, yet not disabled enough to qualify for disability benefits. Some are not old enough to receive Social Security retirement benefits. In short, many are caught between the proverbial "rock and a hard place"; with little option, but to wait it out as best they can. When they receive benefits, their pensions are permanently reduced even though their labor force exit was involuntary. These people and their families are among the most economically disadvantaged Social Security recipients.

Raising the Social Security normal retirement age either by incentive or gradual increases to age 68 may greatly exacerbate the problems of involuntary early retirees. Even if increases in retirement age are accompanied by labor shortages and more flexible work opportunities, there will still be many older workers whose health problems will not allow them full participation in the labor force.

Assuming normal retirement age becomes institutionalized at age 68, then not only will persons retiring before age 65 be considered early retirees; but so will persons retiring between ages 65 and 67. They too will be subject to actuarial reductions. Further, the actuarial reductions will be greater for the earliest retirees. In fact, this seems to be happening already. One way of looking at the delayed retirement credit is that it represents a 35 percent reduction in benefits for all persons retiring at age 62—20 percent for retiring before age 65 plus 15 percent for not working until 70.

In raising the retirement age there is great potential for creating a larger group of disadvantaged retirees than currently exists. If the present is a good predictor of the future, then it is reasonable to assume that the increase in retirement age is unlikely to be accompanied by special programs for workers who would be caught involuntarily "betwixt and between" the early and the new "normal retirement age." These economically disadvantaged retirees would probably resemble the older workers of today whose retirement choices are restricted by health problems and limited employment opportunities. That is, the population would be overrepresentative of workers who filled the "less desirable jobs" in the labor force, minorities and widows.

Another group that may lose from upward drifts in the retirement age is workers who face occupational hazards. In certain occupations, such as mining, the early retirement option is a negotiated benefit for risky and often life-shortening health hazards present on the job.

In seeking solutions to the demographic and economic challenges confronting the institution of retirement, we must be careful to avoid defining this challenge only in terms of pension costs. It must also be seen as a challenge to strengthen an institution which has yet to meet the goal of providing adequate protection against the risk of income losses confronting all Americans. Only by viewing the future of retirement as both an income adequacy and pension cost challenge, can we avoid silently authoring social policies that disregard the needs of disadvantaged retirees while creating newly disadvantaged groups.

REFERENCES

Advisory Council on Social Security. 1979. Social security financing and benefits— Reports of the 1979 advisory council on social security. Washington, D.C.: U.S. Government Printing Office.

Andrisani, Paul J. 1977. Effects of health problems on the work experience of middle-aged men. *Industrial Gerontology* (Spring): 97-112.

Andrisani, Paul J. and Parnes, Herbert S. Five years in the work lives of middle-aged men: Findings from the national longitudinal surveys. Presented at the Aspen Institute for Humanistic Studies Conference on Major Transitions in the Human Life Cycle. Aspen, Colorado (August).

Bankers Trust Company. 1975. *The 1975 Study of Corporate Pension Plans.* New York: Banker's Trust Company.

Barfield, Richard E. and Morgan, James N. 1975. *Early Retirement: The Decision and the Experience and a Second Look.* Ann Arbor, Michigan: University of Michigan Press.

Bixby, Lenore E. 1976. Retirement patterns in the United States research and policy interaction. *Social Security Bulletin* (August): 3-19.

Boskin, Michael Jay. 1977. Social security and retirement decisions. *Economic Inquiry* (January): 1-23.

Bowen, William G. and Finegan, T. Aldrich. 1969. *The Economics of Labor Force Participation.* Princeton: Princeton University Press.

Campbell, Colin D. and Campbell, Rosemary G. 1976. Conflicting views on the effect of old-age and survivors insurance on retirement. *Economic Inquiry* (Fall): 369-388.

Campbell, Shirley. 1979. Delayed mandatory retirement and the working women. *Gerontologist.* (June): 257-263.

Clague, Ewan Balraj, Pahli, and Kramer, Leo. 1971. *The Aging Worker and the Union.* New York, N. Y.: Praeger Press.

Davis, Harry E. 1973. Pension provisions affecting the employment of older workers. *Monthly Labor Review* (April): 41-45.

Fogarty, Michael P. 1975. *Forty to Sixty: How We Waste the Middle Aged.* London: International Publication Service.

Haber, Lawrence D. 1972. Age and capacity devaluation, in *Employment and the Middle-Aged.* (Gloria M. Shattox, Ed.) Springfield, Illinois: Charles C. Thomas.

Hodgens, Evan L. 1975. Key changes in major pension plans. *Monthly Labor Review* (July): 22-26.

Jaffe, A. J. and Ridley, Jeanne Clare. 1976. The extent of lifetime employment of women in the United States. *Industrial Gerontology.* (Winter): 25-36.

Jaffe, A. J. 1972. The retirement dilemma. *Industrial Gerontology.* (Summer): 1-88.

Kingson, Eric R. 1979. Men who leave work before age 62: A study of advantaged and disadvantaged very early labor force withdrawal. Dissertation. Florence Heller School, Brandeis University. In mimeo. Ann Arbor Michigan: University Microfilms International.

Kreps, Juanita M. ed. 1963. *Employment, Income and Retirement Problems of the Aged.* Durham, N.C.: Duke University Press.

Kreps, Juanita M. and Spengler, Joseph S. The leisure component of economic growth in *National Commission on Technology, Automation and Economic Progress: Technology and the Economy, Appendix 2-The Employed Impact of*

Technological Change: Washington, D.C., U.S. Government Printing Office, 1966.

Lauriat, Patience and Rabin, William. 1976. Characteristics of newly entitled beneficiaries by age at entitlement, in *Reaching Retirement Age.* Social Security Administration. Washington, D.C.: U.S. Government Printing Office.

McConnell, Charles E. 1977. Age discrimination and the employment service—Another look. *Industrial Gerontology* (Summer): 167-172.

Meier, Elizabeth L. 1975. Over 65: Expectations and realities of work and retirement. *Industrial Gerontology* (Spring): 95-109.

Meier, Elizabeth L., and Kerr, Elizabeth, A. 1976. Capabilities of middle aged and older workers: A survey of the literature, *Industrial Gerontology,* Summer.

Morrison, Malcolm H. 1979. International developments in retirement flexibility. *Aging and Work* (Fall): 221-234.

Moser, Collette H. 1974. Mature women—The new labor force. *Industrial Gerontology* (Spring): 14-25.

Munnell, Alicia H. 1977. *The Future of Social Security.* Washington, D.C.: The Brookings Institution.

Newman, Morris J. 1978. A profile of hispanics in the U.S. work force. *Monthly Labor Review* (December): 3-14.

Parnes, Herbert S. and Meyer, Jack A. 1972. "Withdrawal from the labor force by middle aged men, 1966-1967, in *Employment* of Middle Aged Men. *op. cit.*

Parnes, Herbert S. and Nestel, Gilbert. 1975. Early retirement, in *The Pre-Retirement Years—Vol. 4.* U.S. Department of Labor. Washington, D.C.: Government Printing Office.

Pechman, Joseph A., Aaron, Henry J., and Taussig, Michael K. 1968. *Social Security: Perspectives for Reform.* Washington, D.C.: The Brookings Institution.

Quinn, Joseph F. 1978. The early retirement decisions: Evidence from the 1969 retirement history study. Social Security Administration: Staff Paper No. 29.

Reno, Virginia. 1976, 1976a. Background of the survey and summary of findings, in *Reaching Retirement Age. . . . op. cit.*

Reno, Virginia. 1976, 1976b. Retired women workers, in *Reaching Retirement Age. . . . op cit.*

Reno, Virginia P. 1971. Why men stop working at or before age 65: Findings from the survey of new beneficiaries. *Social Security Bulletin* (June): 3-14.

Rones, Philip L. 1978. Older men—the choice between work and retirement. *Monthly Labor Review* (November): 3-10.

Rosenfeld, Carl and Scott Campbell Brown. 1979. The labor force status of older workers. *Monthly Labor Review* (November): 12-18.

Schulz, James H. 1974. The economics of mandatory retirement. *Industrial Gerontology* (Winter): 1-22.

Schulz, James H. 1980. *The Economics of Aging.* Belmont, California: Wadsworth Publishing Company.

Schwab, Karen. 1976. Early labor force withdrawal of men: Participants and nonparticipants aged 58-63, in *Almost 65: Baseline Data from the Retirement History Study. op. cit.*

Sheppard, Harold L. 1977. Factors associated with early withdrawal from the labor force, in *Men in the Pre-Retirement Years* (Seymour L. Wolfbein, Ed.) Philadelphia, PA.: Temple University.

Sheppard,tHarold L. 1976. Work and retirement, in *The Handbook of Aging and the Social Sciences*. (Robert H. Binstock and Ethel Shanas, Ed.) New York: Van Nostrand Reinhold Company.

Sheppard, Harold L. and Rix, Sara E. 1977. *The Graying of Working America*. New York: The Free Press.

Sherman, Sally R. 1976. Labor-force status of nonmarried women on the threshold of retirement in *Almost 65:. . . . op. cit.*

Social Security Administration, 1961. *Social Security Amendments of 1961: Reports, Bills, Desates and Acts.* Washington, D.C.: U.S. Government Printing Office.

U.S. Bureau of the Census. 1979. Characteristics of the population below the poverty level: 1977. *Current Population Reports* (March): Series P-60, No. 119. Washington, D.C.: U.S. Government Printing Office.

U.S. Bureau of the Census. 1979. Money income and poverty status of families in the United States: 1978 (Advance Report). Current Population Reports (November). Series P-60, No. 120. Washington, D.C.: U.S. Government Printing Office.

U.S. Department of Labor, 1977. *Employment and Earnings.* Washington, D.C.: U.S. Government Printing Office.

U.S. Department of Labor. 1965. *The Older American Worker: Age Discrimination in Employment.* Washington, D.C.: U.S. Government Printing Office.

U.S. Department of Labor and U.S. Department of HEW. 1979. *Employment and Training Report of the President.* Washington, D.C.: U.S. Government Printing Office.

4

ECONOMICS OF RETIREMENT

Gary Hendricks and James R. Storey

INTRODUCTION

The economics of retirement is the study of the financial alternatives to work as one grows older and approaches pensionable age. Included in the area are two fundamental sets of issues. From the individual worker's perspective, the issue is the trade-off in economic well-being associated with maintaining the usual level of labor force participation versus the attractiveness of withdrawing in large part from the labor force. From a broader social perspective the issue is how retirement is to be financed—what choices individual workers are to have in providing financially for their retirement, what responsibilities employers have in providing for their employees' retirement, and how much of a worker's retirement will be financed by society at large.

The purpose of this chapter is to give the reader an overview of the field. The overview begins with a general description of the current system for providing income in retirement. This description includes an enumeration of the major pension systems, who these systems cover, and the relative importance of the retirement programs. Following the general discussion of the retirement system are descriptions of the major programs within the system. These descriptions detail who can participate in each program, the criteria for becoming eligible for a benefit under the program, the formulas determining the amount of a worker's benefit, and the proportion of earnings workers can expect to have replaced by the program's pension at retirement. Such detailed knowledge is important to an evaluation of the system and to an understanding of its problems.

The ultimate criteria for judging the efficacy, equity, and efficiency of any national pension system is the outcomes it produces. The outcomes of the retirement system for current retirees is the topic of the third major section of this chapter. This section presents the distribution of income among the current aged, the sources of this income, and how it measures up to the expectations implicit in current retirement programs.

Discussions of systems and their outcomes inevitably lead to discussions of their problems. The basic problems of the current structure and mix of retirement programs in the U.S. are outlined in the fourth section.

The discussion in the fourth section is followed by a discussion of a set of particular historical and demographic forces which are likely to compel reform of the current system. Some of these forces are a natural outgrowth of the current system for providing income in retirement. Others result from trends and developments outside the current system for providing income to the retired.

Because historical circumstances have changed and, in some ways, the overall system for providing income in old age in the U.S. has failed, change is inevitable. However, before this change can occur, it is necessary to answer a number of key policy questions. These questions are as diverse as: At what age should workers be considered pensionable and to what extent should real benefit levels be maintained after retirement? Strictly speaking, these questions are not directly a part of the study of the economics of retirement. However, their answers will shape policy for many years to come and are essential to the framework within which policy in this important area will develop. These questions are the subject of the fifth section.

The concluding section of this chapter presents the authors' suggestions for future directions retirement policy should take in this country. Although these suggestions are tentative and incomplete, they are important to a survey of the field. Hopefully they will prove provocative and inspire others to explore in depth issues which are only touched upon in this chapter but will undoubtedly have significant impacts on economic growth, the future distribution of income in our society, and the economic security of workers—both as workers and as retirees.

THE OVERALL RETIREMENT INCOME SYSTEM

The development of the retirement system as we know it today dates back to 1935 when the first Social Security Act was passed by Congress. Since 1935 the Social Security Old-Age, Survivors, and Disability Insurance (OASDI) programs have expanded steadily until today Social Security is the backbone of the retirement system in this country. The program is the most nearly universal program in the country, covering more than 90 percent of all employment outside the federal government. Moreover, it is the most portable pension program in the country. Workers who remain within the private sector job market are virtually assured of retaining coverage when they change jobs and of continuing to acquire Social Security retirement credits in their new job. In order to qualify for a retirement benefit it is necessary to contribute to the program during at least ten years at anytime during one's work life.

The Social Security program is financed primarily through contributions from employees and employers. These are paid through a payroll tax (FICA). In 1980 the combined tax rate for retirement, survivors, and disability insurance is 5.08 percent of earnings up to $25,900. The tax rate is scheduled to rise and will reach 6.2 percent of earnings by 1990. The tax rate and actual contributions made are independent of the worker's retirement benefit. Benefits are based on the amount of wages on which taxes are paid rather than the tax rate or contributions *per se*.

Since the inception of Social Security in 1935, a large number of other retirement programs have been established to supplement Social Security's retirement benefits. Among these, private pension plans are the most important.

By the mid-1970s, 40 percent or more of private sector jobs were covered by private pension plans. Generally these plans are intended to be established by an individual employer, a group of employers in the same industry, or negotiated union plans. Currently, there are tens of thousands of distinct private pension plans.

Unlike Social Security, credits toward retirement benefits under private pension plans are generally not transferable between plans. Thus, when a worker leaves a job covered by a particular plan, the worker either forfeits all future claims to benefits under the plan or, if vested, has benefits under the plan frozen. For younger workers or during times of rapid inflation, fixed dollar amounts of vested benefits quickly lose their value as a real retirement asset. Moreover, since private pensions, though prevalent, are far from universal, a worker who leaves a job covered by a private plan is not assured of moving on to a job with another plan unless the worker makes some special effort to do so.

The level of benefits provided by private pension plans vary greatly. However, they are generally lower than Social Security benefits since private benefits are intended to supplement the Social Security benefits to which the worker will be entitled. Unlike Social Security, most private pension plans do not require employee contributions.

Many public employee pension plans are also designed to supplement Social Security. State and local governments operate nearly 6000 separate employee pension systems covering about 85 percent of state and local workers. These systems, at their option, can join the Social Security system. Currently, about 70 percent of state and local employees are covered by Social Security. In addition, most of these employees have a separate state or local retirement plan to supplement Social Security. These plans, like private pension plans, vary greatly in the level of benefits provided. Some of the larger state and local plans are very generous while smaller plans often provide only minimal supplementation. Unlike private pension plans, which are largely noncontributory, many state and local plans require the employee to contribute (via a payroll deduction) to the supplemental pension.

The federal government, which has over 60 different pension plans for its employees, also covers some of its employees under Social Security. All members of the armed forces are covered under Social Security. In addition, there is a generous program to supplement retirement income for the career military.

About 10 percent of civilian federal employees are covered under Social Security. Generally, civilian federal employees covered by Social Security also have supplementary federal pension programs.

In addition to retirement programs intended to supplement Social Security, a number of major retirement programs operate totally outside the Social Security system. With few exceptions these are public employee programs.

As many as 30 percent of state and local employees are not covered by Social Security. The vast majority of these employees, however, are covered by a separate state or local plan. Most of these plans are contributory, and most long-service employees covered receive generous retirement benefits.

The major federal civil service retirement programs are also not part of the Social Security system. The single most important of these, the Civil Service Retirement System, covers almost 90 percent of all civilian federal employees. The program is designed to provide, without supplementation, adequate retirement incomes to long-service employees. Employees are required to contribute 7 percent of gross earnings toward their retirement, survivor, and disability benefits. These benefits currently cost about 30 percent of payroll.

Retirement pensions are not the only source of retirement income. The major federal welfare programs are another important source of income in retirement. These include the Supplemental Security Income (SSI) program and state SSI supplemental benefits, pensions for needy veterans (Veterans Pensions), and food stamps. Although these are not intended to be retirement programs, they are an important source of retirement income for the most disadvantaged in the labor force. In March of 1979, for example, almost 2 million aged persons received SSI payments, and about 1 million received food stamps. About 70 percent of SSI recipients also received social security benefits.

The tax system also indirectly provides important benefits to retired workers. While labor income is taxable as personal income, many forms of retirement income are taxed less heavily or not taxed at all. No taxes are paid on Social Security, and a part of private pension benefits may be nontaxable. Persons age 65 or older are given double personal exemptions on their federal income tax, and a special retirement income credit can reduce the tax liability of the aged who do not receive Social Security.

A final source of retirement income is private savings. Private sector employees who are not covered under a company pension plan may establish Individual Retirement Accounts (IRA's) or, if self-employed, Keogh accounts. Amounts set aside in these accounts receive favored tax treatment similar to that for contributions to company pension plans. Individuals may also provide for retirement through private savings in the form of savings accounts, ordinary life insurance, tax-deferred annuities, and investments in other financial assets. Persons aged 65 and over currently receive more than $80 billion a year in income from private investments.

Investments in homes and consumer durables are also important sources of indirect retirement income. Among couples headed by a person 65 years and over, 82 percent owned their own home in 1975 and of these only 16 percent had any mortgage. Among aged individuals living alone, 56 percent of men and 59 percent of women owned a home. Only 9 percent of the owners still had a mortgage.

Because of the threat of major illness as one grows older, health care and health insurance not paid for directly by the worker is an important component of economic security in retirement. Benefits here include Medicare, health insurance provided by employers and unions to their employees after retirement, and Medicaid.

Everyone who is eligible for an immediate retirement benefit under Social Security is covered by Medicare even if working and not collecting the Social Security benefit. Aged survivors of retired workers under Social Security are also eligible for Medicare. Overall, more than 90 percent of all persons over 65 in the country qualify for Medicare.

Unlike Medicare, Medicaid is a means-tested program. All aged SSI recipients are eligible for Medicaid health care benefits. In addition, anyone who can pass the asset and income means tests for the program can receive benefits. A special provision in the program allows persons with very large medical expenses to deduct a large portion of these from current income in determining eligibility.

Strictly speaking, social services to care for the aged who for health reasons can no longer care for some of their own needs are directed toward an involuntary condition and are not part of the study of the economics of retirement. In some localities services are provided to all aged, however, and senior citizens, discounts for transportation and other municipal services can increase the disposable income of the aged. To the extent that these services decrease the need for cash income after a certain age, they should be considered a part of the economics of retirement. These are a minor part of the study of the economics of retirement and are not considered further here.

The relative importance of the various retirement programs is shown in Table 4-1. The estimates of the percent of the work force covered are based on data for 1975; the percent of aged receiving benefits is from 1976 data. These years were selected because for some programs more recent data are not available. However, no major changes in the percents should have occurred since the mid-1970s. As the table shows, Social Security is by far the most important retirement program in the country. An estimated 93 percent of the work force is covered by the program, and 90 percent of persons 65 and older receive benefits. An even larger percent of the aged are eligible for benefits but earn more than is permissible under the program. It is clear from the percent of the aged receiving benefits from other programs that for almost half of the aged Social Security is the only formal pension income received.

Table 4-1. The Relative Importance of Retirement and Related Programs.[1]

Retirement and Related Programs	Percent of Work force Covered in 1975	Percent of Persons Age 65 and over Receiving Benefits in 1976
Social Security (OASI)	93	90
Railroad Retirement		3
State and Local Pension Plans	11	7
Federal Civil Service Retirement Programs	3	3
Career Military Service Retirement	2	2
Private Pensions	32	31
Supplemental Security Income	——	10
Veterans Pensions	——	8
Food Stamps	——	5
Medicare[2]	——	96
Medicaid	——	10

1. The estimates were developed from a large number of sources which are listed in th bibliography.
2. Ninety-six is the percent of the aged population who were covered by Medicare in the event of illnes Only a small fraction of this group actually had claims for benefits in 1976.

INDIVIDUAL RETIREMENT PROGRAMS

An understanding of the economics of retirement and the major issues surrounding the development of future retirement policy requires specific knowledge of the individual programs which in large part determine a worker's potential income in retirement. This section describes in some detail the old age component of Social Security. It also describes the general structure of an individual private pension plan and tries to give the reader some sense of the diversity of these plans. The public employee retirement systems are discussed in more depth than above as are the tax advantages afforded retired workers under the federal and state personal income tax programs.

Social Security

Eligibility for retirement (OAI) benefits under Social Security is based on the number of calendar quarters in which a worker has covered wages. Beginning in 1978, a worker was credited with one quarter of coverage (up to a total of four during the year) for each $250 of annual wages, salaries or self-employment income on which Social Security (FICA) taxes were paid. Thus, $1000 of earnings on which FICA taxes were paid sometime during 1978 were sufficient for four quarters of coverage. The $250 is automatically increased each year to take account of increases in average wages. Thus, in 1979, a worker received a quarter of coverage for each $260 on which taxes were paid. In 1980 a worker will need $290 of earnings to receive a quarter of coverage.

In order to qualify for a retirement benefit under Social Security's Old-Age Insurance (OAI) provisions, a worker must have one quarter of coverage for every year since 1951, or age 22 if later. By 1991, all workers will need 40 quarters of coverage to qualify for a retirement benefit.

For workers who qualify for a benefit, the amount of the benefit is determined by average indexed monthly covered earnings (i.e., those earnings on which FICA taxes were paid). There are several steps necessary to compute average indexed monthly earnings (AIME). First, earnings on which taxes have been paid are updated (indexed) for changes in average annual earnings that have occurred between the time the earnings were received and the second year prior to the worker's 62nd birthday. This updating is done by multiplying past earnings by the ratio of average earnings in the year the worker was age 60 to average earnings in the year in question. Thus, a worker who turned age 62 in 1979 would have any covered earnings in 1951 multiplied by 3.532 to update those earnings to 1977 average wage levels.[1] Earnings after age 60 are not indexed. They are counted at actual dollar value.

After earnings for each year have been indexed, indexed earnings are summed over all years from 1951 (or after age 21, if later) up to the year the worker reached age 62, excluding the 5 lowest years of indexed earnings.[2] Earnings outside the years between ages 22 and 62 can be substituted for lower years of earnings within the period if they raise the worker's AIME.

To compute final average monthly indexed earnings, the total indexed earnings minus the 5 lowest years is divided by the number of months between 1951 and the year the worker turns age 62 minus 60 months (5 lowest years times 12 months). For workers who turned 62 in 1979, this divisor is 276 months. For workers who turn 62 in 1991 and later years, this number will always be 420 months.

The final benefit is computed by applying a step-formula to the AIME. For those turning 62 in 1979, the benefit formula was 90 percent of the first $180 of AIME, plus 32 percent of the AIME between $181 and $1085, plus 15 percent of the AIME over $1085. The dollar amounts in the formula are adjusted each year to reflect increases in average earnings levels. Thus, the relative weighting of the formula is maintained over time, and the rates at which benefits replace earnings will remain constant.

Several other provisions are important in determining the final retirement benefit and replacement rate under the Social Security OAI program. First, even for those on jobs covered under Social Security, not all wages may be covered. There is a maximum amount of earnings in a year covered by Social Security. In 1979, maximum

---

1. Average annual wages were $9,779 in 1977 and $2,769 in 1951. Thus, the indexing factor is $9,779 divided by $2,769, or 3.532. An earner with covered wages of $3,000 in 1951 would have $10,596 credited to his or her total indexed earnings.
2. These may be years of zero covered earnings if the worker was not in the labor force or worked in employment not covered by Social Security.

covered earnings were $22,900. Any earnings in excess of $22,900 were not taxed and not credited to the worker's Social Security earnings record. Thus, any earnings above the taxable maximum will have no effect on a worker's ultimate Social Security benefit. The tax base will be raised to $29,700 by 1981 and thereafter automatically adjusted upward as average wages rise. It is estimated that nearly 95 percent of all covered workers will have their full earnings covered under Social Security by 1981.

A major adjustment is made to Social Security OAI benefits for early retirement. Workers receive the full benefit described above only if they retire and apply for their benefits at age 65. However, workers may opt to begin receiving retirement benefits as early as 62. About half of retired workers currently accept benefits before age 65. Workers who opt for early retirement benefits have their benefits reduced by 20/36 of a percent for each month they are under age 65 when retiring. Thus, workers who accept benefits at age 62 have their benefit reduced by 20 percent (3 years x 12 months x 20/36 percent).

Workers can also increase their benefits if they choose to delay retirement until after age 65. Workers who postpone retirement (receipt of Social Security) receive a delayed retirement credit which increases their basic benefit by one quarter of 1 percent for each month (3 percent for each year) retirement is delayed after reaching age 65. Workers cannot get delayed retirement credits after age 70. Therefore, the maximum delayed retirement credit a worker can receive is 15 percent.

Once a benefit is received, it is adjusted annually for increases in the Consumer Price Index. The adjustments occur in June of each year and are reflected in July Social Security checks. An adjustment occurs if the Consumer Price Index for the first quarter of the year is at least 3 percent over its level in the first quarter of the year that last triggered a benefit increase.

Workers receiving old-age benefits are not precluded from some active labor force participation. Under the 1977 revisions to the law, workers age 65 to 70 in 1978 could earn up to $4000 and receive their full Social Security benefit. The law provides that, in 1982, workers in this age group can earn up to $6000 without any loss in Social Security benefits. If workers earn more than the exempt amount, their Social Security benefit is reduced by 50 cents for each dollar of earnings in excess of the exempt amount. Thus, in 1982, workers between 65 and 70 can earn up to $6000 plus twice their annual Social Security benefit before losing their entire old-age benefit.

Workers under age 65 have lower exempt amounts for earnings. For workers 62 but under 65, the exempt earnings amount was $3240 in 1978. This exemption is adjusted each year for increases in average wages. Workers 70 and over can earn any amount and receive their full Social Security benefits.

In addition to benefits paid to the retired worker, the law provides for extra benefits to dependents. In general, aged spouses receive half the amount of the worker's benefit as long as the worker is alive. When the worker dies, the aged widow(er) receives the worker's full benefit. In cases where a spouse qualifies for a benefit on the basis of his or her own quarters of coverage and covered earnings, the spouse receives his or her own retired-worker benefit unless it is less than one-half the other spouse's benefit, in which case the spouse still receives half of the primary worker's benefit.

Dependent children's benefits are also provided. However most retired workers do not have dependent children. The child's benefit is 50 percent of the worker's benefit.

From the worker's perspective one of the most important characteristics of any retirement program is the proportion of earnings immediately prior to retirement that the program benefits will replace after retirement. This proportion is referred to as the replacement rate.

Estimates of Social Security replacement rates published by the Social Security Advisory Council are reproduced in Table 4-2. Because the step-rate benefit formula provides higher percents of benefits for lower amounts of average indexed monthly earnings, replacement rates are higher for lower income workers. Thus, a minimum wage earner, as defined in Table 4-2, is expected to have a replacement rate of 57 percent if he is the only beneficiary, while a maximum wage earner will only have 25 percent of his gross earnings replaced at retirement. Because the dependent's benefit is 50 percent of the worker's, workers with dependent spouses have replacement rates that are 50 percent higher.

Table 4-2. Relation Between Pre-retirement Income and Social Security Benefits For 65-Year-Old Workers at Different Earnings Levels.

	Replacement Rate (in Percent) for:	
Pre-Retirement Earnings[2]	Worker Only	Worker and a Dependent Spouse[1]
Maximum Earner ($29,700)	25	38
Average Earner ($13,548)	44	65
Full-time Minimum Wage Earner ($6,972)	57	85

1. A dependent spouse is defined as one who is not eligible for a Social Security retirement benefit except as a dependent.
2. The numbers in parentheses are earnings in the last year before retirement. The three earners are defined as: (1) worker has always earned maximum level taxable under Social Security; (2) worker has always earned average earnings in employment covered by Social Security; and (3) worker has always worked full-time at the federal minimum wage.

Private Pensions

The second most prevalent type of retirement benefit is a private pension. The basic types of plans vary greatly from employer to employer, and within plan types specific provisions also vary greatly.

There are two major types of pension plans: defined benefit plans, and defined contribution plans. Defined benefit plans base benefits on a known, predetermined formula. Virtually all such plans make benefits a function of years of service and use years of service in combination with either a flat dollar amount of benefit per year of service or a percent of earnings. In 1974 about 80 percent of workers covered by private pensions were covered under defined benefit plans.

Defined contribution plans do not have a specified benefit formula. Rather the contribution rate is defined by the plan. Usually both employee and employer make contributions. These contributions are accumulated and invested. At retirement the worker's benefit is defined by the annuity the contributions plus interest can purchase. In 1974, about 20 percent of covered workers were covered under defined contribution plans.

In addition to defined benefit and defined contribution plans, there are several other types of plans employers establish to assist workers to save for retirement. The most common of these are profit sharing, thrift, and stock ownership plans. Except for profit-sharing plans, these types of plans are not widespread and are often optional programs employees may use to supplement the employer's major defined benefit or defined contribution retirement plan. These types of plans are not discussed further here, but several references to their structure are included in the bibliography.

Regardless of the basic plan type, all private pension plans have a common set of characteristics which affect whether a worker receives a benefit and the amount of the benefit received. These characteristics are :

- Participation requirements
- Vesting requirements
- Break-in-service rules
- Eligibility rules for normal retirement
- Early retirement provisions
- Benefit formulas
- Postretirement adjustments in benefits
- Survivor's provisions

Each of these characteristics is discussed briefly below.

Many plans still have years of service and age requirements before permitting a worker to participate—i.e., begin accumulating benefits. However, in 1974 the Employee Retirement Income Security Act, which set minimum standards for many types of private pension provisions, greatly reduced the impact on workers of participation requirements. In general, the age at which employees become eligible for retirement plan membership cannot be higher than 25 nor can employees be required to have completed more than one year of service for eligibility.

Vesting is the minimum number of years a worker must participate in the plan before being guaranteed a benefit. A worker leaving the plan prior to being vested forfeits all rights to any benefits under the plan.

Vesting provisions vary greatly among private pension plans. Some plans, especially defined contribution plans, begin vesting as soon as the worker begins participating. Under other plans, it may take up to 15 years for a worker to become vested. Prior to 1974, some plans were never fully vested. Under ERISA all employees must be fully vested after 15 years of service. However, if full vesting does not occur until 15 years, workers must be at least partially vested beginning at 5 years of service under the plan.

Although minimum vesting standards ensure that workers with long-term service cannot totally lose their pension rights if they choose or are forced to leave the company, the vested benefit is usually frozen when the worker leaves the employer. Vesting may not be of much value to workers who leave jobs 10 or more years before reaching retirement age if there is erosion of the real value of the vested benefits due to inflation over that length of time.

Break-in-service rules define permissible breaks in the worker's service under the plan. Generally, these rules state a minimum number of hours a worker must be employed under the plan during a given year to be covered. Extended layoffs, a leave of absence or major illness may result in a break in service. A break in service prior to vesting often means that all benefits or years of service under the plan are lost, and the worker must begin acquiring eligibility anew. These rules are most important for workers who experience frequent lay-offs. However, the extent to which workers lose benefits because of these rules is not currently known.

Plans generally specify a normal retirement age at which the worker will receive the full benefit for which he/she is eligible. The normal retirement age under the majority of plans (probably about two-thirds) is 65. The remainder of plans have earlier normal retirement ages. Most plans also specify a minimum years of service for retirement, and many have joint years of service and age requirements for full retirement benefits. Ten years of service is the most common requirement.

Most plans also provide for earlier than normal age retirement with reduced benefits. Rates of reduction vary greatly. Some of the largest plans also have special early retirement provisions for very long-service (30-year) workers.

After vesting provisions, probably the most important aspect of a pension plan from the worker's perspective is the method of computing benefits. Benefits from defined contribution plans are most generally based on the annuity which can be purchased for a worker with the contributions the worker has made plus the employer's contributions plus the interest earned on total contributions. The primary disadvantage of such plans is that it is difficult for either the worker or the plan sponsor to project benefits until the worker is quite near retirement age. Its primary advantage is that no benefits are promised that cannot be paid from the plan's funding arrangement, thus limiting the future fiscal burden on the firm and its workforce.

In 1974 almost half of defined benefit plans had formulas that did not vary by wage but were based on dollar amounts times years of service (Schulz, et al., undated). These dollar amounts varied from $0.90 to $25.00 in 1974. The other half of the plans had wage-related formulas.

The wage-related formulas vary both in structure and in the parameters used in the formula. They are all based on a percent of earnings times years of service. However, some use final earnings, some use the last 5 or last 10 years, average earnings, and some use career earnings with the firm. Some earnings formulas also apply different percentages to earnings above and below specified break points. The higher portion of income is replaced at a higher percentage rate than the lower portion of the income. This in part compensates for the step-rate structure of the social security benefit formula. In 1974 about half of the earnings formulas offset some portion of the worker's estimated social security benefit (Schulz, et al., undated).

In addition to the actual formulas, many plans contain provisions that further complicate benefit computations and may restrict the worker's benefit. Many plans specify maximum years of service on which benefits will be paid. Once a worker passes this maximum his benefits do not increase at all if the formula is not related to wages and will only increase with increases in wages under earnings formulas. Plans may also not provide increases in benefits for years of service and earnings after initial normal retirement age and service eligibility requirements are met. Although there are no representative data for the entire private pension universe, it is generally thought that the majority of plans freeze a worker's benefits at the normal retirement date. Plans may also specify maximum benefit amounts as well as benefit minimums.

In the past, one of the greatest weaknesses of many private pension plans has been the complete lack of provisions for survivor's benefits. Under the ERISA minimum standards a majority of retirement plans must now include a method of payment of benefits that provides automatic death benefit protection for a retired participant. This method, the qualified joint-and-survivor annuity, provides the surviving spouse with a monthly income equal to at least half the amount of the participant's benefit. In return for the death benefit protection, the amount of the participant's benefit usually is reduced when benefits begin.

A final private pension plan feature of utmost importance to the worker is cost-of-living increases or the expectation that benefits will at least be periodically adjusted after retirement. Little is known about the frequency of ad hoc adjustments or the inclusion of limited or regular cost-of-living clauses in private pensions. Regular adjustments are unusual, and ad hoc adjustments probably only occur with any regularity in the major union plans.

Given the complexity and diversity of private pension plans, it is not surprising that they yield a wide range of replacement rates. Using a sample of defined benefit plans in 1974, Schulz, Kelly and Leavitt (1979) estimated replacement rates for median income male workers with 30 years on the job. The results are shown in Table 4-3. On average, single employer plans replaced 24 percent of final earnings and multiemployer plans replaced 16 percent of final earnings. However, many workers fell far outside this range. Ten percent of workers in single employer plans had less than 10 percent of their earnings replaced even after 30 years of service, and 48 percent of workers in multiemployer programs had less than 10 percent of their earnings replaced. At the other extreme, 24 percent and 16 percent of workers under single and multiemployer plans, respectively, had 30 percent or more of their earnings replaced after 30 years.

Table 4-3. Distribution of Workers in Plans [1] with Varying
Replacement Rates for the Median Male Worker. [2]

Replacement Rate (percent)	Single Employer Plans	Multiemployer Plans
Less than 5	4	11
5– 9.99	6	37
10–14.99	13	14
15–19.99	16	7
20–24.99	22	11
25–29.99	15	4
30–34.99	10	8
35–39.99	4	2
40–44.99	4	4
45 or more	6	2
Total	100%	100%
Mean, All Plans	24%	16%

1. Plans where benefits can be calculated by computer (see text), the 1974 BLS survey of defined benefit plans.
2. Assumes final earnings of $12,454 in 1974, normal retirement, 30 years of service, and a 5% average increase in earnings over the working period.

Public Employee Retirement Plans

Both the U.S. Civil Service retirement system and the military retirement system base benefits on years of service and salary. For federal civil servants, the retirement benefit is 1.5 percent of the highest 3 consecutive years' salary for the first 5 years of service, plus 1.75 percent for the next 5 years, plus 2.0 percent for all remaining years. Military retirement benefits are 2.5 percent of highest base pay per year of service. Base pay is generally about 75 percent of gross take home pay.

The vesting provisions under the civil service and military retirement systems differ dramatically. Under the federal civil service system, workers are vested after 5 years' service. Under the military retirement system, 20 years' service is required before any benefit is payable.

Actuarial or other specific reduction rates are not directly applied in setting benefit levels for uniformed servicemen and federal employees who retire before age 65. However, since years of service is a primary factor in the retirement benefit formula, benefits are lower the earlier a person retires. Benefit eligibility is attained when a person completes a minimum duration of 20 years in the military service or a combination of minimum duration and attained age in federal civil service. Almost all military retirees terminate before age 65. Civil servants may draw regular pensions as early as age 55 with 30 years of service. They may also draw benefits at age 60 with 20 years of service or at age 62 with a minimum of 5 years' service.

Unlike Social Security, there is no earnings test applied as a condition of benefit eligibility under the military or federal civil service plans. However, restrictions are imposed on receipt of a pension if the pensioner resumes paid employment with the federal government.

In the U.S. Civil Service, a pensioner may not receive a pension while in regular paid civil service employment. When that employment terminates and pension benefit payments resume, the pension amount is recomputed to take into account the added period of service. A similar provision applies for military duty by military pensioners. However, military retirees may hold civil service jobs while drawing retirement benefits. In addition, since the military, unlike the federal civil service, is covered under Social Security, all military retirees will be eligible for a Social Security benefit at age 62.

Mandatory retirement for federal civil servants was eliminated in 1978, and civil service employees who defer retirement past the normal retirement age of 65 accrue increased retirement credits as a result. However, a maximum limit of the system's wage replacement rate set at 80 percent means that service beyond 43 years will not yield any pension gain other than through salary increases which may occur. The rate of pension increase that results from extending years of service is less than an actuarially fair rate would be. Members of the armed forces must retire from the military after 30 years of service unless granted a special exception. Such exemptions usually occur only in the most senior ranks.

Replacement rates under the two major federal systems are shown for selected years of service below. These replacement rates do not vary by wage level, and, since both systems index benefits for changes in the Consumer Price Index, the real value of replacement rates is retained throughout the duration of retirement.

| | Percent of Wages Replaced for: | |
Years of Service	Civil Service	Military
10	16	N.A.
20	34	50
25	44	62
30	54	75
40	73	75

State and local retirement programs are almost as heterogeneous as private pension plans. About 80 percent of state and local plans are defined benefit plans (as are the federal employee plans). The most common plan sets benefits as a multiple of years of service. Thus, the financial trade-off for most state/local employees with an option to retire early is similar in form to that for federal civil servants, although some plans provide an optional early retirement benefit that is an actuarial reduction of the normal benefit. Eligibility for retirement of vested employees is determined on the basis of age only, years of service only, or a combination of the two factors, depending on the specific plan. For the majority of plans, normal retirement age is set earlier than age 65. As with the federal system, the benefit reduction associated with early retirement typically works out to be much less than that an actuarially fair reduction formula will produce.

State and local governments usually place restrictions on a person's employment in a jurisdiction that is under the same pension plan from which benefits are being drawn. However, no restrictions are applied on hiring pensioners whose prior work was under other pension systems.

State and local governments may still require mandatory retirement, although 1978 legislation raised the permissible age limit from 65 to 70 for most employees. About half of state/local plans set a maximum on benefits that can be paid which may have the effect of curbing added pension credits from deferred retirement. Some plans will not provide added pension benefit amounts for deferred retirement where the normal retirement age is less than 65, and some plans provide added pension credits beyond the normal age but not beyond 65.

Unlike the federal systems, only 4 percent of large state/local plans and 1 percent of other plans provide unlimited cost-of-living benefit adjustments automatically. Over half the large and medium-size plans and three-fourths of the small plans provide no adjustments or make adjustments only on an ad hoc basis. Thus, the real value of wage replacement for state and local retirees typically falls during the retirement period.

Looking at the full spectrum of state and local employee pension plans for age-65 retirees, the replacement rates that result vary among the plans not only by years of service but also by whether employees are covered by Social Security, by the level of government and by plan size. As Table 4-4 indicates, the highest replacement rates are provided by large plans where employees do not have Social Security coverage. The average replacement rate for such state plans for retirees with 40 years' of service is 94 percent, and the corres-

Table 4-4. Average Replacement Rates Under State and Local Retirement Systems.

Years of Service	Employees Covered by Social Security[1]		Employees Not Covered by Social Security	
	State	Local	State	Local
Large Systems				
10	16	15	27	20
20	31	30	51	41
30	47	47	74	61
40	61	60	94	75
Medium and Small Systems				
10	27	13	—	23
20	53	28	50	43
30	65	38	57	64
40	68	49	67	75

1. Replacement rates are for nonintegrated plans.

Source: Derived from *Pension Task Force Report on Public Employee Retirement Systems,* U.S. House of Representatives, Committee on Education and Labor, 95th Congress, 2nd Session, March 15, 1978 (pp. 262-264).

ponding local plan average is 75 percent. While the average replacement rates for state and local plans that are integrated with Social Security were only 61–68 percent and 49–60 percent, respectively, adding in Social Security benefits increases these rates to at least 70 percent and more frequently to just below or just above 100 percent.

The distribution of employees by replacement rate around these average figures is highly concentrated. For most combinations of wage level, years of service, plan size, and Social Security coverage status, at least 60 to 70 percent of state/local employees are in plans with replacement rates that are within 10 percentage points of the average rate.

Tax Subsidies During Retirement

This section describes income taxation at the federal, state, and local levels and how special rules affect the aged and retired.

The federal income tax is a progressive tax which taxes additional dollars of income at increasing rates. The progressive rate structure of the federal income tax yields a marginal tax rate that rises from 14 to 70 percent, although average tax rates are much lower than marginal rates.[1] For example, at an income of $5,000, the average rate for an individual is 5 percent, as compared to the 16 percent marginal rate. At $10,000, the average rate is 11.8 percent; at $20,000, it is 19.1 percent.

Although retired workers face the same general rate structure as the general population, the law provides special exemptions, exclusions and special deductions for the elderly. Taxpayers age 65 and over are entitled to extra personal exemptions. The extra exemption, currently $1000 per person, reduces tax liability by $140 in the lowest tax bracket and by $700 in the highest. The effects of the extra exemption on average tax rates are illustrated in the table above.

Social Security and railroad retirement benefits are excluded from taxable income. Benefits from private pension plans and public employee plans are taxable, however, except for that portion which

---

1. The marginal tax rate is the percent of one *additional* dollar of income that is paid in taxes. Since tax rates are higher on increments of income as income rises, the marginal tax rate is higher than the average tax rate, which is the percent of total taxable income paid in taxes.

Adjusted Gross Income	Average Tax Rate for:			
	Individual		Couple	
	under 65	over 65	under 65	over 65
$ 5,000	5.0	2.0	0.0	0.0
10,000	11.8	9.8	7.1	3.8
20,000	19.1	17.5	13.8	11.4

represents the personal investment the retiree contributed when employed.

Capital gains on the sale of a personal residence may be excluded from taxable income for persons age 55 and over. This once-in-a-lifetime exclusion is limited to $100,000 and can be applied only for property that is used as a principal residence for at least three of the five years preceding the sale. (Persons 65 or older not meeting this test can qualify if the property was their principal residence for at least five out of the eight years preceding a sale occurring before July 26, 1981).

There is also a special tax credit for the elderly. This credit primarily benefits taxpayers age 65 and over who do not receive Social Security or railroad retirement. The credit is 15 percent of a base amount ($2,500 for an aged individual, $3,750 for an aged couple), less Social Security or railroad retirement benefits, and less half of adjusted gross income (AGI) in excess of $7,500 for an individual ($10,000 for a couple). Thus, the maximum value of the credit is $375 for an individual, $562.50 for a couple.

For taxpayers over age 65 whose AGI exceeds the exempt levels, an additional dollar of earnings reduces the credit base by 50 cents, thereby reducing the credit by 7.5 cents (15 percent of 50 cents). Thus, an extra dollar earned by credit eligibles serves to increase income tax liability by 7.5 cents in addition to whatever other tax effects might result.

Persons under age 65 may be eligible for the credit if they receive public employee retirement benefits. The maximum credit amount is the same as above, but it is reduced not only by tax-free pension income but also by a percentage of earned income. If under age 62, each dollar above $900 reduces the base, thereby reducing the credit by 15 cents. For those over age 62, earnings between $1,200 and $1,700 reduce the base by 50 cents on the dollar; earnings over $1,700 reduce the base dollar by dollar.

All states except six (Florida, Nevada, South Dakota, Texas, Washington and Wyoming) tax individual income, but only a small proportion of local governments (New York City; Baltimore; Kansas City and St. Louis, Missouri; Wilmington, Delaware; Birmingham and Gadsden, Alabama; cities in Kentucky, Michigan, Ohio and Pennsylvania; and counties in Indiana and Maryland) apply income taxes independent of the state system. Most local income tax rates are between 1 and 2 percent, although New York City's progressive rate structure reaches 4.3 percent and Philadelphia's rate is 4.3125 percent.

Most state systems have progressive rate structures. The highest marginal rates are 19.8 percent (income over $100,000) in Delaware, 17.0 percent (over $40,000) in Minnesota, 15.0 percent (over $30,000) in New York, and 14.5 percent (over $200,000) in Alaska. Twenty-one states have progressive structures with maximum rates less than 10 percent. Most often the maximum rate begins to be applied at taxable income brackets between $5,000 and $10,000. The majority of progressive rate systems have minimum rates of 2 percent or less. Eight states have flat rate tax systems, the rates ranging from 2.0 percent in Indiana to 6.0 percent in Tennessee. Three states with income taxes tax only investment income (Connecticut, New Hampshire, and Tennessee).

Almost all states follow the lead of the federal government and allow extra exemptions for the aged. The normal exemptions for a single nonaged taxpayer range from $100 to $4,500 with the majority of states having personal exemptions between $600 and $1,000. Personal exemptions for couples are twice the exemption for a single person in all but two states. The personal exemptions for aged single and married couples are twice the exemption for their nonaged counterparts.

State income taxes exclude Social Security and railroad retirement benefits from taxation. In many instances, they also exclude pension benefits from their own state and local government pension systems.

Twenty-one states provide income tax credits to the aged to offset property taxes. Another seven states and the District of Columbia provide such tax relief to all age groups. The rules for eligibility and the credit amounts vary a great deal among the states. All states, however, have now legislated some form of property tax relief for the aged.

The impact of income tax systems on post- and preretirement income differentials can be substantial. For an unmarried person with an earned income of $20,000 at age 64 and no earnings at age 65 but a Social Security benefit of $6,000 and a private pension of $3,000, age 65 pension income is only 45 percent of age 64 earned income before taxes. After taxes, age 65 pension income is 63 percent of age 64 earned income. For a married couple the before tax retirement income is 60 percent of age 64 earnings, but after taxes it is 78.5 percent of age 64 earnings.[1] For an individual or couple with earnings of $10,000 at age 64, a 35 percent Social Security replacement rate and a private pension of 15 percent of earnings, the before-and-after tax post- and preretirement income ratios would be:

Pension Benefits	Ratio of Post- to Preretirement Income	
	Before Taxes	After Taxes
Unmarried Individual		
Social Security only	.35	.45
Social Security plus a		
Private Pension	.50	.64
Married Couple		
Social Security only	.52	.63
Social Security plus a		
Private Pension	.67	.81

INCOME OF CURRENT RETIREES

The ultimate test of the overall retirement system is the outcomes it produces. One of the most important of these outcomes is the amount and distribution of income generated for retirees.

1. This example assumes the standard deduction is taken for the federal income tax and that the entire private pension is taxable. The state tax rate used was 5 percent of income after deducting a per person personal exemption of $800 before age 65 and $1600 per person after age 65 and a 10 percent standard deduction. The amount of the FICA tax was deducted from earned income in deriving after tax income at age 64.

As one moves from being primarily a worker to primarily a retiree, the composition and relative importance of income from various sources change. Table 4-5 shows the percent of units with various types of income at different ages. In the table a unit is defined either as a married couple or an unmarried individual. Among units age 55-61, 83 percent have some earned income. However, by age 65 only 25 percent have earned income.

At the same time that the percent of units with earnings is declining, the percent with retirement benefits is increasing. At age 55-61 only 23 percent of the units have retirement benefits—mostly disability benefits from Social Security or early retirement benefits from a private or government employee pension program. By age 65, 92 percent of the units receive retirement benefits. Eighty-nine percent are receiving Social Security; 13 percent, other public pensions (including federal, state, and local pensions and railroad retirement); and 20 percent, private pensions.

Although the differences in sources of income observed in 1976 between units 55 to 61 and older units are not surprising, they represent a marked shift in the income sources of the aged over the past 30 years and even the past 15 years. In 1951 less than a third of aged units were receiving any retirement benefits (Schulz, August 1979). By 1962 a little over three-quarters received retirement benefits. However, in 1962 retirement benefits were predominately only Social Security benefits. A maximum of 10 percent received government

Table 4-5. Percent of Aged Units with Various Types of Income in 1976 By Age.

| | Age | | |
Percent with:	55-61	62-64	65 and older
Earnings	83	67	25
Retirement Benefits	23	56	92
Social Security	13	49	89
Other Public Pensions	6	10	13
Private Pensions	6	13	20
Public Assistance	5	7	11

Source: Susan Grad and Karen Foster, "Income of the Population Aged 55 and Older, 1976," *Social Security Bulletin,* Vol. 42, no. 57, July 1979.

pensions, and only 10 to 11 percent received private pensions. Fifteen years later in 1976, the receipt of Social Security benefits by the aged had gone from under 75 percent to almost 90 percent; 30 percent more aged units were receiving government pensions; and the percent of aged units with private pensions doubled.

The substantial changes in sources of income as one reaches retirement age are accompanied by equally substantial changes in the level of total money income. According to tabulations reported from the March 1977 Current Population Survey (Grad and Foster, 1979), the distribution of total money income in 1976 among groups of aged units was as follows:

	Percent Distribution of Units/Age:		
Total Money Income	55–61	62–64	65 and older
Under $5,000	22	31	53
$ 5,000– 9,999	20	24	28
$10,000–14,999	17	17	10
$15,000–19,999	16	13	4
$20,000 or more	24	15	4
Total	100	100	100
Median	$12,100	$8,830	$4,700

The income brackets selected here divide units aged 55 to 61 roughly into quintiles. The quintile distribution degenerated dramatically for the older age groups, and for units age 65 and older over half are in the lowest income bracket, which is occupied by only 22 percent of the units aged 55 to 61. Such a dramatic downward shift seems startling in light of the replacement rates most often presented for average wage earners.

Using the Advisory Council's Social Security replacement rates for the average earner implies a replacement rate of 44 percent for an unmarried worker and 65 percent for a couple with a dependent spouse. The concept of the average earner is highly deceptive, however. As pointed out by Schulz (1980):

The "average earner" designation implies that replacement rates are being measured for retiring workers in the approximate middle of the earnings distribution for all retiring workers. In fact, this is not the case. The earnings before retirement used for the hypothetical "average earner" calculations are a hodgepodge of earnings for part-time and full-time workers, part-year and full-year workers, men and women workers, and workers at *all* stages of their earnings careers (i.e., and average of anybody at any age with any earnings). This average does not accurately reflect the earnings of retiring workers who typically earn much more than their younger counterparts.

Schulz continues his argument by pointing out that:

> In 1975, average earnings for all workers were about $8,000. In contrast the average earnings of full-time men and women workers in their fifties who were close to retirement were $10,200 and for full-time men alone were $13,500. Defining the average worker this way results in a replacement rate about 10 percentage points lower. The replacement rate for a single worker drops from 44 percent to roughly a third.

Even though gross Social Security replacement rates may be lower than the hypothetical cases most frequently presented, the situation may not be as bad as it first appears. As shown above, after-tax replacement rates are likely to be 10 percentage points higher than before taxes both because Social Security benefits are not taxed and because of preferential tax treatment of the aged. Moreover, large numbers of the aged own their own home outright and receive some property tax relief. Other demands on income, especially those associated with work, fall at retirement, and the need for some major expenditure items, such as a second car, become less pressing. Relocating from a colder to a warmer climate or to a smaller, more cheaply maintained house may also reduce expenditure needs. Eligibility for Medicare may also reduce out-of-pocket medical expenses and relieves many workers of paying for some portion of group health insurance through an employer. As evidenced by the almost 50 percent of units who accept reduced Social Security benefits prior to age 65, these factors must be somewhat important and must make current replacement rates adequate enough to entice many to accept even lower replacement rates than necessary.

Despite the general leveling of the distribution of income for the 65 and older group and a decline of almost 50 percent in median income, some aged units are clearly much better off than others. To a large extent, this is the result of the source of the pension income and whether the unit qualifies for more than one pension.

As shown in the first column of Table 4-6, 65 percent of units 65 and older receive pension income from only one source; 27 percent receive pension income from more than one source; and 8 percent receive no pension benefit. Units with benefits from two pension systems have a median income about twice that of units with a pension from only one source. This is true whether the unit does or does not have any earnings.

The pension program from which the pension is derived affects

Table 4-6. Percent of Units Aged 65 and Older in 1967 Receiving Different Combinations of Pension Income and the Median Income of These Units by Earnings Status.

		Median Total Income		
Pension Receipt	Percent of All Units	All Units	Those with Earnings	Those with No Earnings
No Benefit	8	$3,180	$12,650	$1,780
One Benefit	65	3,740	6,710	3,290
Social Security	62	3,660	6,550	3,210
Private Pensions and Annuities	1	a	a	a
Government Pension	1	8,970	a	7,910
Railroad Retirement	1	4,830	a	4,640
More Than One Benefit	27	7,800	11,480	7,060
Social Security and Federal Civil Service Pension	2	8,360	a	8,020
Social Security and Other Public Pension	6	7,210	11,880	6,510
Social Security and Private Pension	19	7,840	11,100	7,120
Total	100	4,700	8,560	3,860

[a] Too few cases.

Source: Susan Grad and Karen Foster, "Income of the Population Aged 55 and Older, 1976," *Social Security Bulletin,* Vol. **42**, no. 57, July 1979.

retirement income, as well as the number of systems from which benefits are received. Among those with only one benefit, government employees have median incomes of $8,970 compared with $3,660 for units with Social Security only. Indeed, government employees with no other pension have higher median incomes than units with two benefits, regardless of the source of the benefits.

Only 8 percent of units age 65 or older receive no pension benefit. These are about equally divided between units with and units without earnings. The median incomes of units with and without earnings are $12,650 and $1,780, respectively. Thus, a large proportion of units with earnings and no benefits are probably forfeiting benefits in order to continue working.

Not surprisingly the incidence of poverty among the aged is highly correlated with the number and source of pension benefits. The percent of units age 65 or older in poverty by pension receipt is shown below:

Percent of Units in Poverty

Pension Receipt	All Units	Those with Earnings	Those with No Earnings
No Benefit	49	13	83
One Benefit	32	10	39
Social Security	33	11	40
Government Pension	10	—	13
Railroad Retirement	12	—	13
More than one Benefit	3	1	3
Total	25	8	31

The most striking number in this display is the 25 percent of all units who were below the poverty line in 1976. Since 40 percent of the units are married couples, who have a much lower incidence of poverty, the poor units contain only 15 percent of all persons age 65 or older in 1976. Nonetheless, these persons were living on cash incomes below $2,730 in 1976 if unmarried and a joint income of under $3,445 if married.

Almost equally striking is the 33 percent of units whose only pension benefit is Social Security who are poor. Eighty-seven percent of these units are unmarried persons—mostly widows.

Very few units—3 percent—with more than one pension benefit are in poverty.

BASIC PROBLEMS OF THE CURRENT SYSTEM

In many ways the current system for providing for retirement in the U.S. has been very successful. Over the past 30 years poverty among the aged has been greatly reduced, and at the same time many who formerly would never have been able to retire now retire as early as age 62. However, many difficult problems remain.

Several problems arise because we have not one but many retirement systems in the United States. With little careful planning to integrate these systems, they often produce outcomes that are irrational, socially undesirable, politically unacceptable, and out of the control of any one factor in the process. The interaction of the different retirement systems produces "windfall" benefits for some and quite generous retirement income for a relatively few fortunate people. For example, among federal civil service annuitants in 1975 who received civil service annuities of $14,000 a year or more, 17 percent also qualified for Social Security benefits and many more will qualify for Social Security retirement benefits when they are old enough (Price and Novotny, 1977). Moreover, of those 17 percent who qualified for both civil service pensions and Social Security, 10 percent were eligible for Social Security benefits of $3,000 a year or more (an amount slightly higher than the average annual Social Security benefits for retired workers in 1975). Both of these pensions are adjusted for inflation.

In other instances, workers with certain career patterns can find themselves even better off after retirement than while working. A career military officer could retire with a full pension at age 45, work 10 years in a private job and draw a private pension at age 55, become a civil servant for five years and receive a pension at age 62, and begin drawing Social Security retirement benefits at age 62. This retiree would receive four pensions that might add up to more than final earnings. Three of these pensions would be adjusted automatically for inflation, and total retirement benefits would bear little relation to the individual's past contributions.

Other workers, despite long working careers, may find themselves without substantial replacement income when they retire. A study of males and unmarried females age 58 to 63 in 1969 showed that over 30 percent of the males had tenures on the longest job they had held in their careers of fewer than 15 years, and 17 percent of the workers had tenures of fewer than 10 years. It is not surprising, then, that another recent study (Fox, 1979) found that only half of recent Social Security retirees had any pension income other than Social Security and a fifth of *age-65* retirees have less than 40 percent of final earnings replaced by pensions.

Thus, without sufficient integration pension outcomes can easily become irrational and inequitable. Some patterns of job mobility produce windfall benefits unintended by the designers of any one component of the system. Other patterns of job mobility lead to large losses of benefits through the lack of pension portability or insufficient tenure to build up significant benefits under any one pension program, except perhaps Social Security.

A second fundamental problem with current retirement systems is that outcomes are so unpredictable and individual pension programs so complicated that careful planning for retirement is not easily done. Social Security policies depend on legislation that is often enacted rapidly at the end of a congressional session without much thought or debate about possible impacts on personal savings or the private pension industry. Private pension offerings are determined in part by the structure of the Social Security system but mainly by a company's or industry's business outlook, by the competition for labor and the organization of labor, by tax incentives established by the Internal Revenue Code, and by government pension regulations. Pension plans for public employees respond to analogous forces in the public sector, plus the important factor of the political influence of different public employee groups on legislatures. Individual savings and investment decisions, while in part influenced by Social Security, the income tax, and employers' pension policies, generally are made in ignorance of benefits likely to be available upon retirement and under conditions of extreme uncertainty concerning future inflation, real wage growth, time of retirement, and future family responsibilities.

Thus, each of the major factors—governments, pension managers, labor organizations, and individual workers—makes policy decisions without adequate knowledge of likely future directions the other parties may take and largely in ignorance of how the various components of retirement income fit together, a vital piece of information in a highly mobile society where most workers will have held at least three different jobs before they retire and many will have held a government job as well as one or more private jobs.

A third problem is that the system is not neutral with regard to when workers chose to retire. A well-designed system would offer workers the option of retiring at a wide range of ages without penalizing the worker unduly for his or her choice. Currently this is not true. Pension plans frequently pay higher total lifetime benefits to workers who retire early because benefits are not reduced by enough to compensate for the large number of years early retirees will receive them. The same is true of Social Security where the 20 percent reduction in benefits is an actuarial bargain for many groups of workers and, if it is not accepted, the worker's lifetime Social Security benefits will be lower.

At the same time that early retirement is encouraged, delaying retirement beyond age 65 is generally heavily penalized because lifetime benefits will be much lower. This is particularly true for private pension programs which often do not permit the amount of benefits to rise after a worker becomes eligible for normal retirement. In addition, many private sector workers are mandatorily retired from their companies at age 70—as of 1979 the earliest legal age that retirement can be compelled for most employees.

Delayed retirement also includes a financial penalty under Social Security. The delayed retirement credit is far less than the amount of benefit increase that would make total lifetime benefits for workers who retire later equal to those who retire earlier.

Finally, poverty among the aged remains a problem. Much of the incentive for the development of the myriad of public and private programs providing income in retirement was to eliminate poverty in old age and to offer long-service workers the opportunity of financial security in old age. Despite federal spending on retirement, welfare programs, and direct tax relief to assist the aged of up to $200 billion in 1979 (almost $9000 per aged person), substantial poverty among the aged remains. In 1977, 14 percent of all aged persons lived in poverty and an additional 11 percent had incomes less than 25 percent above the poverty line; 25 percent of the aged were near or in poverty. Only 17 percent of all persons were in or near poverty. Clearly, poverty remains a problem, even though not as serious as in 1959 when 35 percent rather than 14 percent of aged persons had cash incomes below the poverty level.

FORCES FOR CHANGE

The retirement institutions and the retirement behavior patterns that have developed over the last four decades may be entering an era of unusually rapid change. Several factors will make a continuation of past policies and trends increasingly difficult and will force a rethinking of work/retirement patterns and the provision of retirement income. The single most significant factor is the likely escalation of public and private pension costs over the next several decades because of the changing age structure of the population. The aging of the post-World War II baby crop, combined with anticipated low fertility rates, improved mortality rates and restricted legal immigration, will reduce the ratio of working-age (22–64) to retirement-age adults (65 and over) from 5.0 in 1975 to 3.0 in 2025. Thus, there is a potential for fewer people to be paying for retirement benefits relative to the number drawing them than ever before.

How is the Population Changing?

What are the population trends that demographers foresee for the rest of this century and the beginning of the next? The predicted "graying of society" is a shift in the age distribution of the population to the older age groups, a virtually inevitable change that will result mainly from three factors:

- The unusually large number of post-World War II babies, who will start reaching age 65 in 2010;

- The low birth rate prevalent since 1960, continuing a long history of declining fertility in the U.S., interrupted only occasionally by such events as the post-World War II rise in fertility;
- Continuing reductions in death rates, a trend that now serves mainly to prolong old age since very little room is left for improvement in mortality at younger ages.

Our society has been getting older since the founding of the nation. The median age has risen in each decennial census since 1790 with only two exceptions—1960 and 1970 (Figure 4-1). These exceptions reflect the presence of the huge post-World War II baby crop, the progress of which has already impacted elementary schools, secondary schools, colleges, housing, and the criminal justice system. After 2010, the influx of this unusually large age cohort into senior citizenry will greatly increase the proportion of the population over age 65, while simultaneously making the elderly a "younger" group (i.e., relatively fewer will be over 75 since so many will be 65-75).

The most commonly used Census Bureau projections may prove to be conservative in the degree of aging they portray since they assume a replacement fertility of 2.1 births per woman (the current rate is 1.8 and has been below 2.1 since 1970). The projections assume mortality rate reductions that are less dramatic than the actual experience of the past few years. On the other hand, the projec-

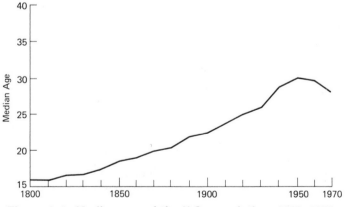

Figure 4-1. Median age of the U.S. population, 1800-1970.

tions make no allowance for the possibility that the official annual immigration of 400,000 people is being increased illegally by a large influx of young workers, some of whom may become permanent additions to the population.

The percentage of the total population age 65 and over, now 10.7 percent, is projected to rise only to 12.2 percent by the year 2000 but will zoom up to 15.5 percent in 2020 (Figure 4-2). The full range of official Census projections is from 12.7 to 17.8 percent in 2020, but if the 1976 death rate were reduced by half over a 75-year period, the higher estimate would rise to 19.6 percent.

Much of the concern over the graying of society has to do with the reduced number of workers per retiree that is expected and the implications of that growing cost of dependency for taxpayers. It is often mentioned that the ratio of Social Security contributors to beneficiaries (now a little over 3:1) will decline to nearly 2:1 in 50 years. These ratios are somewhat misleading, since 16 percent of beneficiaries are under age 21 and 2 percent of retired beneficiaries have reduced benefits because they continue to work.

However, looking at changes in young and old dependents collectively, the picture is different. The total dependency ratio—the ratio of children under age 18 plus senior citizens over age 64 to working-age adults—actually declines until the next century and only exceeds the 1976 level of about 7 "dependents" per ten working-age people

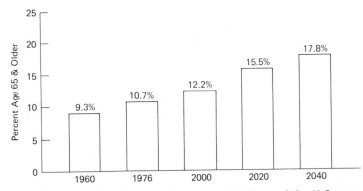

Figure 4-2. Intermediate Census Bureau projections of the U.S. population age 65 and older as a percent of the total population.

Table 4-7. Projected Ratios of Children Under Age 18 and Adults over Age 64 to Working-Age Adults 18-64, 1976-2050 (Intermediate Projections).

Year	(1) Ratio of Children (Ages 0-17) to Working-Age Adults (Ages 18-64)	(2) Ratio of Aged (Ages 65 and over) to Working-Age Adults (Ages 18-64)	(3) Total Dependency Ratio (sum of Columns 1 and 2)
1976	.513	.181	.694
1985	.435	.191	.626
2000	.432	.200	.632
2010	.392	.202	.594
2015	.398	.227	.625
2025	.421	.296	.717
2050	.417	.302	.719

well after the "senior boom" of 2010 (Table 4-7). This decline in dependency will result from a sharp drop in the relative number of children between 1976 and 2010. If the normal retirement age were to rise from 65 to 70, the total dependency ratio in 2025 would be close to the 1976 level. However, public costs to support an aged person exceed that for a dependent child, and the costs are concentrated at different levels of government. (Programs for the aged are primarily federally financed, those for children are primarily financed by state and local governments.)

One aspect of an older population which has received less attention than the cost of supporting aged dependents is the changing ages of the workers who will be supporting them. The working-age population will be older in the next century in two respects. There will be relatively few new labor force entrants in the 18-to-24 age group and relatively more older workers in the 55-to-64 age group (Table 4-8). Thus, the social tension generated in recent years by large numbers of unemployed youth should be diminished, with retraining for older workers becoming a more dominant concern of efforts to prevent structural unemployment.

Concern is often expressed about the growing number of the very old and the greater cost of supporting them for ever lengthening lifetimes. Particularly worrisome is the prospect of a much greater

Table 4-8. Projected Age Composition of Working-Age Adults, 1976-2050 (Intermediate Projections).

	Composition of Working-Age Adults by Age Group		
Year	Percentage Age 18-24	Percentage Age 25-54	Percentage Age 55-64
1976	22	62	16
1985	19	66	15
2000	15	70	15
2010	16	65	19
2025	16	64	20
2050	16	64	20

caseload for the costly and much-maligned long-term care facilities. While the number of people over age 75 will continue to grow in absolute numbers, the very old will actually decline as a share of the elderly population after 2010 due to the large number of persons reaching age 65 in 2010 and immediately thereafter. Of course, the very old will become a much larger segment of the aged population after 2025 as the baby-boom cohort moves across the age-75 threshold (Table 4-9). Demographers expect the very old population to remain heavily female; the minority representation among the very old may rise as minority groups benefit more from future mortality reductions and experience higher fertility rates. Those trends may also have cost implications, since women and minority groups will more likely need welfare-type assistance in old age.

Table 4-9. Projected Age Composition of Adults, Age 65 and Over, 1976-2050 (Intermediate Projections)

	Composition of Aged by Age Group		
Year	Percentage Age 65-74	Percentage Age 75-84	Percentage Age 85 and Over
1976	62	29	9
1985	61	29	10
2000	55	33	12
2010	57	30	13
2025	61	29	10
2050	52	31	17

Will the Budget be "Busted?"

Given these demographic trends and forecasts, it is easy to see that continuing "business as usual" with respect to retirement policy and health care financing could have an enormous impact on the federal budget. June O'Neill, now an Urban Institute economist, estimated while on the Congressional Budget Office staff that about a quarter of FY 1979 federal outlays directly benefited the aged through Social Security, medicare, federal employee retirement, and various welfare programs. If one simply projects these current programs and assumes that overall federal spending returns to the "historic" level of 20 percent of GNP (it is now at 22.5 percent), then the elderly's share of the federal budget will rise slowly during this century to 32 percent, then leap upward by another 10 percentage points in the next 15 years, and soar to 63 percent by 2025 (Table 4–10). As a share of labor income, aged benefits will remain fairly stable at 9 to 10 percent until the 2010 "senior boom," the share then rising to 19 percent by 2025.

Several factors could, of course, mitigate the problems of the impact of an aging society on pension costs. These include lower public expenditures related to a declining proportion of youth in the population, more women workers expanding the labor force, and more public and private pension plans accumulating reserves to cover all future liabilities.

Table 4-10. Projected Benefits for the Aged as a Share of Total Federal Spending under Current Policy, 1979-2050 (Intermediate Projections)

Fiscal Year	Aged Benefits[1] ($ trillions)	Percentage of Total Federal Outlays[2]
1979	0.1	26
2000	0.7	32
2015	2.3	42
2025	5.9	63

1. Includes benefits to persons age 65 and over from social security, medicare, SSI, civil service retirement, VA pensions, and railroad retirement. Projections are in current dollars and assume price inflation of 4%, health care price inflation of 7%, and real wage growth of 1.75%.
2. Total federal spending assumed to be 20% of GNP for years after 1979.

Another contingency which could prove very important is if more people choose to work past age 65. This issue of retirement age has already been publicly addressed, but for another reason. Interest groups representing the elderly have successfully challenged policies that force retirement at age 65, and job discrimination on account of age may come under increasing attack. However, should larger numbers of people elect to work past age 65, they will nonetheless resist any effort to raise the age of Social Security or other pension benefit entitlement but will exert pressure to liberalize further the Social Security retirement test. Without the former type of change to accompany the latter, there may still be strong financial incentives to retire early, especially for people with good opportunities to work in jobs that will earn them second pensions under other systems.

Other Pressures for Changes in Policies

A greater number of working women raises other concerns that are likely to exert substantial pressure for changes in retirement programs. Already the higher labor force participation rate for women and the accelerating divorce rate have highlighted the equity problems of a Social Security system built to serve a more traditional population of intact, one-earner families. Working women often earn little more in Social Security benefits than they would have received anyway as nonworking wives (who receive 50 percent of the amount of their husbands' retirement benefits). Unhappiness with the original allocation of spouses' Social Security benefits to current instead of former spouses has prompted two liberalizations of the old rule that denied spouse benefits to divorced spouses, but there will no doubt be continued pressure for more generous treatment of former spouses. There is also likely to be increased pressure to provide benefit entitlements for nonworking wives with small children independent of Social Security entitlements accrued by their working husbands. All these initiatives could increase pension costs unless other benefits are trimmed back.

Another major element in the uncertain future of retirement systems is the current inflation. Continued high inflation without effective price controls, an occurrence unknown in the U.S. since the 1920s, prior to the Social Security Act, means escalating costs for pension systems that adjust benefits for inflation and drastic reductions in real income for beneficiaries of systems that do not keep up with inflation. Inflation averaged 2.2 percent a year in the 1950s, 2.6 percent in the 1960s, but rose to 9.8 percent annually over the 1970s; the 1980's have begun with double-digit inflation. A 5-percent annual inflation rate reduces the real value of a $1000 pension to only $614 over a 10-year period. If a fixed pension replaces 60 percent of final wages, the replacement ratio will fall to 37 percent of the real value of those wages after 10 years of 5-percent annual inflation. An inflationary psychology may cause today's workers to rely on the indexed Social Security system more and private pensions and savings less in planning for their retirement years.

Past failures to coordinate the various retirement systems may also generate change through public pressure to correct the inequities produced by the existence of many separate and ill-coordinated pension plans and programs. Some mobile workers in private jobs receive little or no private pension due to the lack of portability of contributions among most pension funds. Even a break in service with the same employer sometimes results in a loss of pension rights. Other retirees pyramid military, public employee, Social Security, and private pensions into handsome sums largely financed by the contributions of others.

The pressures of increasing costs may prompt further examination of another coordination problem, namely the overlaps between Social Security and welfare programs. Past growth and reforms in welfare programs have rendered anachronistic such Social Security provisions as the minimum benefit floor and students' benefits. Other provisions, such as the extreme weighting of the benefit formula to favor low earnings levels, may now be less important features from a welfare standpoint. These features of the system were intended to help the needy at a time when welfare aid was quite limited, but they can be a more costly means of putting a floor under income than are programs that base the amount of aid explicitly on income. These provisions of Social Security require the government to redistribute more income for a given level of income protection. For example, Social Security dependents' benefits to college students aid both the well-to-do and those in need of help. But education opportunity grants to low- and moderate-income students required

$2.3 billion from federal general revenues in 1978, with very little in offsets realized in the grants that go to students who also receive Social Security benefits. In effect, payroll taxes are financing income protection under Social Security that could be paid for, at least partially, at less cost by general revenue assistance programs.

Cost pressures associated with retirement affect not only pensions per se but also health and disability benefits. Health care costs have risen faster than consumer prices generally for more than a decade and have a particularly heavy impact on the aged. Efforts to control hospital charges, reform health care financing, and reduce the extent of institutional care will affect payroll taxation, the need for retirement income, and the ability of employers to fund pension benefits. With respect to disability, there has been a cost explosion associated with higher than anticipated Social Security disability claims (up 523 percent since 1967) and evident abuse of disability retirement provisions under public employee systems. To cite an extreme case, 80 percent of retired police and fire personnel in the District of Columbia receive disability benefits which are more generous than regular pensions, a situation Congress has moved to correct.

Future cost increases will only add to fiscal problems that are already apparent. The inadequate funding of many pension systems, often disguised in prior years by rapid growth, has now been exposed for all levels of government, for private pension funds, and for Social Security as well. A study by the Pension Benefit Guaranty Corporation (PBGC) found that 40 private multiemployer plans are in danger of collapse within five years, and another 200 are financially troubled. It is feared that the cost of meeting ERISA's rules may precipitate plan terminations, with the PBGC proving incapable of meeting the liabilities that would result. State and local taxpayer resistance has prompted numerous efforts to curtail the cost of public employee plans. Congress enacted Social Security tax increases and benefit reductions two years ago that will greatly reduce a projected trust fund deficit, but taxpayer grumbling has sparked a search for financing alternatives.

The rapid increase in wages covered by Social Security that Congress enacted in December 1977 may prompt a re-examination of the structure of a great many public and private employee pension plans. Those that were integrated with Social Security will have to re-evaluate the way in which the integration was designed, since the ceiling on wages subject to Social Security taxation will rise by 144 percent over the next nine years. Plans which were never integrated may find it necessary to seek a closer coordination by revising existing contribution and/or benefit rules.

In summary, a continuation of past practices with respect to retirement policies and pension plans could have disastrous social and financial consequences. However, the combination of demographic and social changes, high rates of inflation, pressures to control costs and to correct inequities, and the impacts of each component of retirement income on the others is likely to produce widespread change in retirement plans and policies over the next few years. Already, some signs of this likelihood are apparent in the increased focus of both government and the private sector on policy studies and research directed at finding solutions to the problems just enumerated. The crises that may develop will not occur overnight, so efforts now to improve our fund of knowledge, generate new ideas, and build public understanding and support for change will leave plenty of time for fashioning and implementing new policies to avert these evident pitfalls.

KEY RETIREMENT POLICY QUESTIONS

The fundamental problems facing the current retirement system in the United States seem clear. They are:

- Further reducing poverty among the aged.
- Removing inequities in coverage and benefits for various groups.
- Integrating the many systems and plans to prevent irrational outcomes.
- Providing mechanisms that allow workers to plan carefully and systematically for retirement.
- Reducing disincentives for continued work among older Americans.
- Avoiding the potential financial crisis that may await current programs.

However, before solutions to these problems can be discussed, it is necessary to consider systematically a number of key questions:

- When should nondisabled workers retire?
- What proportion of a worker's former earnings should be replaced in retirement?
- How should retirement benefits be adjusted for inflation or for economic growth?
- How should the financing of retirement benefits be shared?
- How should the various retirement systems be coordinated?
- How should retirement and social welfare needs be rationalized?

These six questions constitute the major policy questions the answers to which will guide policymakers and pension plan managers on specific issues. Without answers to these questions, planning future retirement policy will be haphazard, determined largely by the uncoordinated interaction of specific policy decisions rather than by a social consensus of what retirement should mean in our changed society and how it should be paid for. Each of these major policy questions is discussed.

When Should Nondisabled Workers Retire?

The selection of age 65 as the normal retirement age for Social Security and for a large number of private pension plans occurred at a time when relatively few people lived to be much older than that. This policy should be questioned today for at least five reasons:

1. More and more people should experience good health for long periods past age 65 and will be better able to continue working than was the case 45 years ago;
2. Many people want to work longer, or need to work to make up for inadequate retirement income, but have been prohibited from doing so by laws just now amended—future aged workers will not only have broader legal rights to continue work, but their greater levels of education compared to today's retirees and the decreased physical demands of many jobs may stimulate more work activity as well;

3. The prospects for a tight labor market if low fertility rates continue calls into question the economic wisdom of encouraging healthy, productive 55-, 62-, or even 65-year-olds to retire;
4. The tremendous cost increases associated with the aging of the U.S. population can be offset by a lengthening of the traditional working life. For instance, the ratio of people in dependent age groups (children and the aged) to working age people would be about the same in 2025 as today if the normal retirement age were raised to 70;
5. People have been encouraged to retire early (age 62 with actuarial reductions under Social Security, age 55 with 30 years in the federal civil service, any age with 20 years of military service, age 55 with 25 years of service for white-collar employees in New York City), and many people have responded to these incentives (over half the new Social Security beneficiaries in recent years have retired early). Yet many early "retirees" keep working and continually exert pressure to liberalize the retirement test that reduces Social Security benefits by 50 cents for each dollar earned over a modest exempt amount.

The retirement-age question involves at least three major issues of system design—whether encouragement of early retirement should continue; how employee pension and Social Security benefits should be integrated for those who retire from more than one career; and the extent to which Social Security and pension benefits should be reduced for beneficiaries who still work, or increased for those who defer retirement past the normal age. Also, a larger social question is raised of whether the traditional pattern of labor force participation will continue. That is, will the predominant model of full-time work followed by full-time leisure give way to some other sequencing or mixing of work and leisure over a lifetime?

What Proportion of a Worker's Former Earnings Should be Replaced in Retirement?

A pension may be designed to replace a substantial part of earnings over the last few years before retirement, since a 70- to 80- percent replacement rate is usually needed to maintain preretirement disposable income. At the other extreme, a pension may be related to an employee's lifetime contributions to a retirement fund to max-imize equity among all contributors. Many public employee pension plans reflect the former philosophy, while Social Security embodies the latter, and private pension plans are well represented in both camps.

The more closely a pension benefit is related to final earnings, the more it is subject to abuse through manipulation of the earnings level just prior to retirement and the less protection it affords workers who leave jobs before retirement age. On the other hand, Social Security's method yields low wage-replacement rates for those who had relatively low earnings early in their careers or who were out of the labor force for long periods. Social Security compensates such workers for the effects of averaging by replacing a much higher proportion of low average earnings than of higher amounts. Added benefits for spouses and dependents raise replacement rates for retirees who claim them. On average, Social Security now replaces about 43 percent of final wages, but this rate is 73 percent, for exam-ple, for a low-wage married worker. A high-wage single worker has a replacement rate near 20 percent. Recent legislation to correct a flaw in benefit indexing will keep replacement rates near their present levels (they would have risen under the old law).

The level of wage replacement for retirees involves aspects of retirement systems other than benefit formulas and requires tradeoffs with other goals. Liberal vesting and portability rules result in higher total replacement rates, for example, but also encourage labor mobility. Benefits for dependents and survivors increase replacement for some retirees but at the cost of lower replacement rates for others, particularly working women under Social Security. SSI benefits have the effect of increasing replacement for persons with very low wages, but SSI levels out Social Security benefit dif-ferentials based on past earnings, thereby negating Social Security's wage replacement for this group (about 8 percent of Social Security beneficiaries age 65 or older).

Coordination of credits and benefits among Social Security and public employee systems is also a factor. For example, retirees eli-gible for more than one pension could be much better off, or much worse off, than the less mobile retiree, depending on the particular sequences and timing of the different spells of employment under separate systems. The wide variations in wage replacement that now result raise an overall equity issue in regard to the fairness of retirement programs for different groups of people.

The desirable level of wage replacement depends on what we are willing to pay in foregone spending by those currently working to assure a given standard of living in retirement. However, the level raises social as well as economic issues, since higher replacement levels mean more independent living for retirees, more mobility, and more separation of the generations.

How Should Benefits be Adjusted for Inflation and Economic Growth?

Benefits paid by Social Security, federal employee systems, railroad retirement, and a few state and local pension systems are adjusted automatically for price increases. Some state and local systems want to end automatic adjustments as a cost-saving measure. Few private pension plans make adjustments tied directly to inflation, although many have increased benefits somewhat in recent years (about two-thirds of the plans in one survey did so between 1969 and 1975).

The extent and nature of inflation adjustments will be a crucial issue for some time to come, for we are in an era where workers and retirees may face high inflation rates for an indefinite period without price controls. Such a situation has not occurred since the boom of the 1920s, before Social Security was enacted. Thus, a significant impact on attitudes of current workers toward retirement seems probable. The prospect of high inflation rates can affect drastically decisions on where to work, for how long, how much to save, and in what forms.

Inflation will also determine the generosity of the initial retirement benefits set by systems saddled with the tremendous costs of maintaining the real value of those benefits, and continued inflation will shift the relative importance of retirement income sources. For example, the average married man retiring in 1968–70 received 56 percent of his retirement income in Social Security benefits. Assuming an annual inflation rate of 5 percent, after a normal life expectancy of 14 years his Social Security would rise to 72 percent of his retirement income if other pension benefits were not adjusted.

Thus, continued high inflation would probably have the following effects: (1) It would increase Social Security's importance as a source of retirement income; (2) it would prompt governments to retreat from past practices (Illinois is now experimenting with "inflation insurance" bought by higher employee contributions); (3) it would reduce the attractiveness of fixed annuity plans as a part of retirement planning; (4) it would discourage traditional forms of saving at fixed interest rates; and (5) it would spur more people of retirement age to continue working as a hedge against inflationary erosion of living standards. Clearly, adequate initial wage-replacement rates will be a hollow achievement for retirees if they live longer than prior generations and experience greater price increases over their longer retirement periods.

A related issue is whether retirement benefits should be adjusted to reflect real economic growth occurring after retirement. That is, should living standards for retirees be maintained relative to their position in the income distribution prior to retirement. Simply indexing benefits for price increases results in an unintended redistribution of real income to beneficiaries of indexed systems during recessions, but such beneficiaries sink to lower relative living standards during periods of real growth.

How Should the Financing of Retirement Benefits be Shared?

Except for benefits earned under annuity contracts purchased by employees and/or employers, retirement benefits are, in large part, intergenerational transfers from current workers to current retirees, institutionalizing transfers that once took place mainly within families. The extent of these transfers is inversely related to the extent a plan is "funded" (i.e., the extent that a reserve fund can cover all accrued pension benefit liabilities). The source of the funds, of course, also determines a plan's mix between personal saving and transfer payments.

Social Security benefits are almost entirely transfer payments, with current reserves adequate to pay only 3¼ months' benefits. The civil service retirement fund can cover 5.2 years of benefits, but only 17 percent of annual fund receipts is contributed directly by covered workers. Private pension plans vary widely in the extent of fund accumulation to pay future liabilities.

The less the degree of prior funding, the greater the danger that future retirement income may be jeopardized by faulty management planning or unforeseen events (e.g., a decline in an industry's work force, or a prolonged period of slow economic growth). On the other hand, large fund accumulations have significant implications for consumption versus investment activity and for the control of capital markets, the fluidity of capital, and the availability of venture capital. For example, restraints some state and local governments and unions want to apply to the use of their pension fund assets would result in restrictions on capital flows among geographic areas, among industries, and between public works and private initiatives.

Different sources of funds for income transfers may have different economic impacts as well. A payroll tax or an employer pension contribution is a direct cost of producing a good or service and will add to the cost, and therefore the price, of that product and retard aggregate demand. Transfers funded through income taxes have no such direct link to prices or employment but help determine how governmental fiscal policy affects the economy as a whole.

The basic components of retirement costs to society overall include the amount that society in the aggregate should be encouraged or compelled to save for workers' retirement years and the amount that should be transferred to current retirees. How the financial burden of these savings and transfer payments are allocated among employees, employers, consumers, and taxpayers will have much to do politically with the aggregate costs society is willing to bear. The choices made will be reflected not only in aggregate financial data but in the individual household's consumption, investment, and work behavior as well.

How Should the Various Retirement Systems be Coordinated?

Since Social Security taxes and benefits apply for only a portion of the taxable wages, it has been customary for many private pension plans to supplement Social Security by concentrating contributions and/or benefits above the taxable wage ceiling. Such "integrated" plans must meet certain tests of fairness in order to qualify for tax exemptions under the Internal Revenue Code. The Bankers Trust 1975 study of 271 major pension plans found that 65 percent of them were integrated with Social Security.

The rapid increase recently enacted in the Social Security wage base, from $16,500 in 1977 to $29,700 in 1981, will force many of these pension plans to re-evaluate the methods used to coordinate their benefits and contributions with those for Social Security, since Social Security taxes will apply to total wages for 9 percent more workers in 1986 than was the case in 1977. The rising base means that the maximum Social Security retirement benefit will be much higher in the long run. For example, using constant 1976 dollars and a real economic growth rate of 1.8 percent, the maximum benefit in 1988 will be 1.7 times the 1978 maximum in constant dollars; the maximum in 2008 will be 2.3 times the 1978 maximum, rising to 5.2 times the 1978 maximum by 2035.

Federal employee retirement systems have never been coordinated with Social Security, but such coordination will be necessary if the strong congressional sentiment to extend social security coverage to all federal employees leads to action.

Although the majority of state and local employees have Social Security coverage, about 85 percent of state/local plans either are not integrated with Social Security at all or are coordinated in ways that do not meet the standards applied to private plans under the Internal Revenue Code. State and local plans must cope not only with rising Social Security wage coverage in any future modifications, but they also may encounter: (1) A congressional effort to legislate ERISA-type regulations for their plans; and (2) an IRS effort to apply the same tax code treatment to state/local pension contributions and earnings as now apply to private plans. All of these factors will affect how they realign themselves vis-à-vis Social Security. Of course, states and localities currently have the option of withdrawing entirely from Social Security.

Obviously, changes in the coordination of public and private employee plans with Social Security could have a profound impact on the private pension industry and will be a major determinant of how retirement income is provided and financed.

How Should Retirement and Social Welfare Needs be Rationalized?

Social Security benefits became available to a broad spectrum of people at a time when federal efforts to alleviate poverty were minimal. There was no federal aid to low-income, aged, blind and disabled through SSI, no medicaid or medicare, no food stamps, far less was spent on subsidized housing, and federally aided state welfare payments to families were much more limited. Thus, given the widespread need and the limited public benefits available, Social Security was used as a vehicle to reach many low-income people, and the "social insurance approach" of income support, whereby all persons in a given risk group were aided without regard to income, became a popular tool for achievement of social progress through the mid-1960s.

However, the War on Poverty focus of that decade led to a proliferation and expansion of needs-tested benefits that caused renewed questioning of the social welfare tilt that the Social Security system had acquired over its first 30 years. The fiscal squeeze that became apparent in the 1970s added to the concern that overlaps between welfare programs and welfare-related features of Social Security should be rationalized to reduce the total amount of tax dollars necessary to assure a given level of minimum income protection throughout society or for selected groups. A reduction in total federal benefit costs would leave more funds available for private initiatives, including expansion of pension coverage or increased pension benefits.

To make Social Security more purely related to wage replacement raises numerous issues, many of which are closely connected to the issues discussed under the other key questions raised in this section. For example:

● A Social Security benefit formula more closely related to past earnings would result in lower wage replacement rates for persons with histories of low earnings, many of whom have low total incomes as well, and such a benefit formula would destroy the basic factor upon which private pension plans have based their coordination with Social Security benefits (i.e., that low-wage workers will have high replacement rates independent of private pension benefits);

• Greater equity under Social Security for working women, if achieved at the expense of unpaid married homemakers, could have deleterious effects on the financial well-being of low-income families where one spouse has had little work experience;

• A trimming of certain welfare aspects of the Social Security system (e.g., in disability benefits, students' benefits, and other survivors' benefits) would adversely impact on some needy individuals who would fail to qualify for welfare benefits given the inequities and gaps in existing federal, state, and local welfare programs; and

• Improvements in welfare aid for the aged, blind, and disabled under SSI as part of a reorientation of Social Security away from welfare goals would further exacerbate the preferred treatment already accorded those groups compared to other needy individuals and families.

Thus, consideration of how retirement behavior and pension plans should develop in the future must address welfare concerns and the welfare system as well.

POLICY DIRECTIONS FOR THE FUTURE

Devising a fully detailed legislative plan to resolve the various problems identified herein is beyond the scope of this chapter, since a complex and costly analysis of costs and benefits of each program change would be necessary to arrive at a satisfactory comprehensive reform package. However, it is feasible to suggest the directions policy change should take in response to the six questions as framed above:

• *Retirement age*—The age at which pensions are taken should increase over time, and one approach is to slowly raise the normal retirement age of Social Security and employer pension plans over several decades. However, as an independent and more immediate measure, the financial incentives to retire early can be lessened and to delay retirement improved. This approach could involve not only changes in Social Security benefit computation for early and late retirees but also ERISA requirements regarding such computations for private plans, new regulations for government plans, elimination of the Social Security retirement test, and prohibition of mandatory retirement age limits.

- *Wage replacement*—We should move to eliminate poverty among the aged as soon as possible. Social Security should be improved as needed to replace 70 to 75 percent of wages for workers at or below the median wage. This same level of replacement should be achieved from the sum of Social Security and employer pensions for higher wage workers, a step which will require improvements in pension coverage, especially for mobile workers. Liberalized rules for IRAs could be a part of this approach.

- *Indexing*—Greater protection against inflation is needed for employer pension plans, but it is possible that federal benefits are over-adjusted for inflation due to fallacies in the logic of the CPI-based method. Alternative methods for indexing should be explored. Also, capping inflation increases to avoid exceeding average wage growth should be considered. Longevity bonuses under Social Security could be used to reduce the gaps in real living standards that develop over a long time period for the very old due to real economic growth.

- *Financing*—The Social Security payroll tax should be retained to fund retirement benefits related to earnings; general revenues should be used to fund aged benefits that are related to need either explicitly or implicitly. Government employee pension plans should move toward a fully funded status.

- *Pension plan coordination*—Social Security coverage should be extended to all jobs, and requirements for integration of employer plans with Social Security should be updated periodically. A method to ensure portability of pension credits among plans should be pursued.

- *Social Security/welfare relationship*—The welfare aspects of the Social Security system should be eliminated, with an expanded SSI program or system of per capita "old age grants" relied upon instead. Social Security should be redesigned to resemble an individual annuity in terms of how benefits are related to earnings histories.

Finally, a problem with the current system or any reformed system lies in the lack of planning individuals undertake for their own retirement. The federal government, through the Social Security Administration and the Department of Labor, should undertake a substantial public education campaign to facilitate the understanding of workers about their present and future coverages for retirement, disability and survivorship and the income needed to maintain a given real level of living throughout their retirement years.

BIBLIOGRAPHY

Ball, Robert M. *Social Security Today and Tomorrow,* Columbia University Press: New York, 1978

Bankers Trust Company. *1975 Study of Corporate Pension Plans,* New York, 1975.

Burke, Vee. *Cash and Non-Cash Benefits for Persons with Limited Income: Eligibility Rules, Recipient and Expenditure Data,* FY 1976–78, Congressional Research Service: Washington, D.C., October 1, 1979.

Commerce Clearing House, Inc. *ERISA and Its Interpretations until May 30, 1976,* Chicago, Illinois, 1976.

Congressional Budget Office. *Poverty Status of Families Under Alternative Definitions of Income,* Background Paper No. 17 (Revised), Washington, D.C., June 1977.

Council of Economic Advisors. *Economic Report of the President,* Washington, D.C., January 1978.

Doty, Robert. Oral presentation to the National Association of Counties Public Pension Roundtable, March 14, 1978.

Employee Benefit Research Institute. *The Employee Retirement Income Security Act,* Washington, D.C., undated.

_____. *The Employee Stock Ownership Plan,* Washington, D.C., undated.

_____. *The Pension Plan,* Washington, D.C., undated.

_____. *The Profit Sharing Plan,* Washington, D.C., undated.

_____. *The Thrift Plan,* Washington, D.C., undated.

Executive Office of the President. *Budget of the United States Government, Fiscal Year 1979, Special Analyses,* Washington, D.C., 1978.

Foster, Karen, and Grad, Susan. Income of the population aged 55 and older, 1976, *Social Security Bulletin,* **42** (57), Washington, D.C., July 1979.

Fox, Alan. Earnings replacement rates of retired couples: Findings from the retirement history survey, *Social Security Bulletin,* **42** (1), Washington, D.C., January 1979.

Gordon, Nancy M. The treatment of women under Social Security, in *Consultation on Discrimination Against Minorities and Women in Pensions and Health, Life and Disability Insurance,* U.S. Commission on Civil Rights, Washington, D.C., April 25, 1978.

Harris, Robert. Welfare reform and social insurance: Program issues and budget impacts, testimony and prepared statement before the Committee on the Budget, United States Senate, Washington, D.C., April 9, 1977.

Hendricks, Gary and Peters, Elizabeth. Social security coverage of government workers, in *Policy Analysis with Social Security Research Files,* Proceedings of a workshop held March 1978 at Williamsburg, Virginia, U.S. Department of Health, Education and Welfare, Washington, D.C., 1978.

Myers, Robert J. *Social Security,* McCahan Foundation Book Series, Richard D. Irwin, Homewood, Illinois, 1975.

O'Neill, June. Income differentials among the aged, written statement for hearings on *Retirement Income and Coverage of Women and Minorities,* President's Commission on Pension Policy, Washington, D.C., Number 30, 1979.

Price, Daniel N. and Novotny, Andrea. Federal civil-service annuitants and Social Security, December 1975, *Social Security Bulletin,* **40** (11), Washington, D.C., November 1977.

Samuelson, Robert J. The arithmetic doesn't look good for industry-wide pension plans, *National Journal,* **9** (51), Washington, D.C., December 17, 1977.

Schulz, J. H. et al. *Private Pension Policy Simulations,* Draft Final Report to the U.S. Department of Labor, Washington, D.C., August 1979.

Schulz, James H., Kelly, Leslie C., and Leavitt, Thomas D. Private pensions fall far short of pre-retirement income levels, *Monthly Labor Review,* **102** (2), Washington, D.C., February 1979.

Schulz, James H. Assessing the adequacy of pension income, prepared statement for hearings of the President's Commission on Pension Policy, Washington, D.C., January 11, 1980.

Schulz, James H., et al. *The Economic Impact of Private Pensions on Retirement Income,* research report to the National Science Foundation, Washington, D.C., undated.

Siegel, Jacob S. Prospective trends in the size and structure of the elderly population, impact of mortality trends, and some implications, prepared statement for the Select Committees on Aging and Population, U.S. House of Representatives, Washington, D.C., May 24, 1978.

Snee, John, and Ross, Mary. Social security amendments of 1977: Legislative history and summary of provisions, *Social Security Bulletin,* **41** (3), Washington, D.C., March 1978.

Storey, James R., Hendricks, Gary, and Vaughn-Cooke, Denys. Disincentives for continued work among older Americans: Interim report on individual program disincentives, Working paper 1394–01, The Urban Institute, Washington, D.C., February 1980.

Ture, Norman B., and Fields, Barbara A. *The Future of Private Pension Plans,* American Enterprise Institute for Public Policy Research, Washington, D.C., 1976.

U.S. Bureau of the Census, *Statistical Abstract of the United States,* 1979, Washington, D.C., 1979.

_____. Social and economic characteristics of the older population: 1978, *Current Population Reports,* Series P–23, Number 85, Washington, D.C., August 1979.

_____. Projections of population of the United States: 1977 to 2050, *Current Population Reports,* Series P–25, Number 704, Washington, D.C., July 1977.

U.S. Department of Health, Education and Welfare. *The Desirability and Feasibility of Social Security Coverage of Federal, State and Local Governments and Private, Nonprofit Organizations,* Report of the Universal Social Security Coverage Study Group, Washington, D.C., March 1980.

_____. *Social Security Financing and Benefits,* reports of the 1979 Advisory Council on Social Security, Washington, D.C., December 1979.

_____. *Social Security Handbook,* Sixth Edition, Washington, D.C., July 1978.

_____. *Medicaid Statistics,* December 1976, NCSS Report B–1 (12/76), Washington, D.C., April 1977.

_____. Benefits and beneficiaries under public employee retirement systems, Social Security Research and Statistics Note Number 17, Washington, D.C., August 20, 1976.

_____. Annual statistical supplement, 1976, *Social Security Bulletin,* Washington, D.C., undated.

_____. *Reaching retirement age: Findings from a survey of newly entitled workers, 1968–70,* Social Security Research Report No. 47, Washington, D.C., November 1975.

U.S. House of Representatives. *Pension Task Force Report on Public Employee Retirement Systems,* Committee on Education and Labor, 95th Congress, 2nd Session, Washington, D.C., March 15, 1978.

Yohalem, Martha Remy. Employee-benefit plans, 1975, *Social Security Bulletin,* **40** (11), Washington, D.C., November 1977.

5
CURRENT PROGRAMS FOR THE RETIRED

Charles S. Harris and Dorothy Bauer

Preceding chapters have outlined general demographic trends, emerging work life-retirement patterns and trends, and recent legislative responses to the perceived needs of older workers. The themes of identifying needs and describing responses are continued in this chapter.

Our discussion proceeds along three lines. First, the current and projected employment situation for older workers is sketched. The structural and attitudinal factors responsible for the employment problems of older workers are then examined, and finally, the programmatic efforts aimed at ameliorating these problems are described and evaluated.

CURRENT AND PROJECTED EMPLOYMENT SITUATION

Demographic Trends

To have an accurate picture of the potential job market for older workers, it is helpful to briefly recap trends in the employment and the population growth of the elderly. Since the turn of the century, the number of persons continuing to work past age 65 has declined dramatically. In 1900, two out of three males 65 and older were employed; by 1950, the proportion had declined to less than one in two, and in 1976, one in five men over 65 was employed. Currently,

191

less than 2 million of the total elderly male population of 9.2 million are employed (Harris, 1978).

The employment of elderly women is also declining. In 1975, less than 1 in 12 women over 65 was working. While this is the same proportion as was employed in 1900, it is considerably lower than in the intervening years. Black women continue to be employed after age 65 with greater frequency than do white women; however, the difference is growing smaller.

Changes in the employment rate have been taking place against a backdrop of major shifts in the age structure of our population. Middle-aged and older populations are growing, with the elderly population almost doubling in the last 25 years (Harris, 1978). This pattern, coupled with the trend toward progressively earlier retirement and increased life expectancy, foreshadows not only a continued and major decline of middle-aged and elderly people in the work force but also a slackening of labor force growth in the eighties. The projected 1990 labor force participation of elderly males is one in six, a decrease severe enough to have profound implications for individuals and society (Harris, 1978).

Current Employment Categories

Of the 12 percent of Americans 65 years of age and older who are employed, 3 percent hold full time jobs, and 9 percent are employed on a part-time basis (Harris, 1978). These workers occupy a broad spectrum of job types, though they tend to leave occupations which demand physical strength or exacting sensory-motor coordination. A recent study of workers age 65 years and older reveals that 19 percent hold jobs as managers, officials and proprietors, and 17 percent are service workers; unskilled, semiskilled, and skilled positions are held by 11-15 percent of the employed elderly. The remaining workers were in professional, sales and agricultural occupations (Meier and Kerr, 1976). Recent figures from the Bureau of Labor Statistics are presented in Table 5-1.

A study which included an aerospace company's most prevalent occupations (Kunze, 1974) revealed that of 275 office, technical, factory and management jobs, 58 percent were held by workers age 63-68. The results also suggest that there are many older adults in

Table 5-1. Employed Persons by Age. (numbers in thousands) October, 1979

| | | NONAGRICULTURAL INDUSTRIES | | | | |
| | Wage and Salary Workers | | | | | |
	Total	Private Household Workers	Government	Other	Self-Employed	Unpaid Family Workers
Total, 16 years and over	87,542	1,290	15,673	70,579	6,753	396
55 to 64 years	9,835	251	2,058	7,526	1,151	61
65 years and over	2,129	188	345	1,596	516	30

| | AGRICULTURE | | |
	Wage and Salary Workers	Self-Employed	Unpaid Family Workers
Total 16 years and over	1,448	1,677	341
55 to 64 years	126	376	45
65 years and over	77	244	18

U.S. Department of Labor, Bureau of Labor Statistics *Employment and Earnings,* November, 1979 Table A-23

nontraditional, relatively new occupations. For example, adults 55 years of age and over were found in the data-processing, electronics, numerically controlled machine and flight-test fields, performing as analysts, technicians, and engineers.

The percentage of the employed elderly who hold part-time positions is currently quite high, even though the NCOA/Harris survey

Table 5-2. Persons at Work in Nonagricultural Industries by Full- or Part-Time Status and Age. (numbers in thousands) October, 1979

	Total at Work	On Part Time for Economic Reasons	On Voluntary Part Time	On Full-time Schedules			Average Hours Total at Work	Average Hours, Workers on Full-time Schedules
				Total	40 hours or less	41 hours or more		
Total, 16 years and over	90,472	2,979	13,085	74,408	50,124	24,284	38.6	42.8
45 to 64 years	25,310	690	2,496	22,124	14,974	7,150	40.0	42.9
65 years and over	2,430	97	1,147	1,186	819	367	29.9	43.2

U.S. Department of Labor, Bureau of Labor Statistics *Employment and Earnings*, November, 1979 Table A–29.

showed that as age increases, full-time employment declines. The most recent figures from the Bureau of Labor Statistics show that for persons 45–64 years of age the average total hours at work is 40.0 per week; for persons 65 and older, it is only 29.9 (See Table 5–2). Part-time workers represent 12.6 percent of the 45–64-year-old group, but over half (51.2 percent) of the 65 and over group. Older workers often choose part-time work, preferring the reduced hours yet wishing to supplement their Social Security payments. However, the majority of part-time jobs currently available is comprised of low-paying clerical or unskilled positions which are below the appropriate skill level of many retirees.

Future Occupational Opportunities

The job possibilities for the next generation of older workers should include a wide range of occupational categories. In business and industry, technological advances have reduced the level of physical strength necessary to perform most jobs and has reduced the probability of worker error. A recent study by Holly et al., (1978) revealed that persons 57 years of age and older are well-suited for paraprofessional jobs, as this age group received the highest performance evaluation at that occupational level. A study by Thompson and Dalton (1976) indicates that, if sufficiently motivated and updated on current findings in their disciplines, scientists and engineers remain highly suited for their positions in later life. The data suggest that technical obsolescence may actually be caused by the employing firm, since assignments implementing new technology are most often given to younger workers. In addition, in both blue- and white-collar fields, new techniques in job scheduling and job redesign can open many new job possibilities for older workers.

BLOCKS TO EMPLOYMENT

A lack of job and training opportunities is clearly a problem for a substantial number of elderly job seekers, particularly those who are members of minority groups. Among elderly who are unemployed or retired, 25 percent felt that lack of job opportunities was a "very serious" or "somewhat serious" problem; 26 percent of the working elderly shared this view (Harris, 1978).

In 1975, unemployment among workers 45 years of age and older was the highest in the nation's history—almost 28 percent above the figures for the previous year. That meant that nearly 1.6 million persons age 45 and older were unemployed (Harris, 1978). These statistics are considerably underestimated since they do not account for individuals who eventually abandon their hopes and cease to search for employment.

Survey data have shown that among unemployed or retired elderly people, 30 percent (4 million) would like to be employed and 29 percent of people over 65 are willing to learn new job skills or participate in a training program to obtain a job. An additional 15 percent of the elderly already employed also expressed an interest in additional job training, with the goal of a better job (Harris, 1978). These facts bring into question some common notions concerning older workers. The idea that older workers look forward to the time when they no longer have to work is obviously not true in every case. In fact, the data suggest that a considerable number of people 65 and over have an interest in remaining active members of the labor force. Structural and attitudinal factors limiting their options are discussed in this section.

Employer Discrimination

Employment opportunities are often unavailable to older people due to age discrimination and negative employer attitudes toward older workers. These attitudes, coupled with discrimination, create a very real impediment to employment for many competent, valuable workers. In the NCOA/Harris survey, four-fifths of a total public sample agreed either "strongly" or "somewhat" with the statement "most employers discriminate against older people and make it difficult for them to find jobs." During that same survey, an overwhelming majority (87 percent) of the employed respondents who claimed personal responsibility for the hiring and firing of other employees agreed that employers discriminate against older applicants (Meier, 1976). In fact, during fiscal year 1976, the Department of Labor located 13,000 men and women who had been fired, denied jobs, or otherwise illegally discriminated against due to their age (Brown, 1977). There is little doubt that age stereotypes work against the older worker in management decisions regarding training and development, career opportunities, and retirement. Management training programs, created by specialists in the field, can help to change these negative attitudes.

There is also considerable misinformation regarding the possible consequences of hiring and retention of older workers. Two common misconceptions are that such practices would deprive a large number of young people of work and that a higher proportion of older workers would increase labor costs. Many employers mistakenly believe that to hire and retrain older workers is in conflict with affirmative action programs. A concerted effort to merge older workers' placement objectives with affirmative action programs should help clarify this issue. Inasmuch as the Equal Employment Opportunity Commission took on responsibility for enforcing the Age Discrimination in Employment Act (ADEA) in 1979, the impetus for such programs most logically lies with this agency.

Retirement

The widespread general acceptance of the practice of retiring workers at a prescribed age does not alter the fact that mandatory retirement is a form of age bias. In the past, mandatory retirement has been a major and often insurmountable obstacle for elderly people desiring employment. The ADEA Amendments of 1978 (P.L. 95-256) ended mandatory retirement for most federal workers (excepting fire-fighters, law enforcement officers, air traffic controllers, and employees of the CIA, Foreign Service, Panama Canal Zone and Alaska Railroad). In the nonfederal work force, mandatory retirement before age 70 became illegal on January 1, 1979, with three exceptions:

   . . . workers age 65–69 who are covered by collective bargaining agreements in effect on September 1, 1977, were not protected by the ADEA until the agreements terminate or January 1, 1980, whichever came first.
   . . . tenured college or university faculty members can be forced

to retire at age 65 or above until July 1, 1982, when that age limit also becomes 70.

. . . compulsory retirement as early as age 65 will continue to be legal for high-level executives or policymakers who will receive a retirement income of $27,000, excluding Social Security, employee contributions, and contributions of previous employers. The exemption applies only to employees who served in such high-level positions for at least two years prior to retirement.

The purpose of the Amendments was to remove chronological age as the sole criterion for continued employment (Harris et. al., 1978).

It is a common assumption that most older people welcome retirement for the increased leisure time it will afford them. An indication of the reality of this "leisure-time" is given by the results of a life-satisfaction survey of senior citizens. Seventy-two percent of the working elderly stated that they expected something "interesting and pleasant" to happen each day, while only 50 percent of those unemployed felt this way. The attitude of many workers toward retirement is expressed in data from 1971, in which 105,000 Federal workers who could have retired chose not to do so (Butler, 1973). Not all workers have this much influence over their situation, as a 1974 survey of retirees revealed; 37 percent (4.4 million people) did not retire by choice but were forced to do so. In addition, of persons 65 and over who are employed, 73 percent of those 65–69, 85 percent of those 70–79, and 95 percent of those 80 and over reported they did not look forward to retirement (Meier, 1976). These data leave some doubt as to the credibility of the notion that seniors "welcome" or desire retirement.

Another argument used to support the practice of mandatory retirement is the common belief that older workers must be removed from the economy to make room for the young. This rationale assumes that for each older worker leaving the labor force, a new, younger worker takes his or her place. It also assumes that there is a fixed number of jobs to be done. Neither of these assumptions is supported by evidence available to date. In fact, the Congress, in passing the ADEA Amendments, concluded that there was no significant evidence that the amendments would seriously jeopardize employment opportunities of younger workers (Harris, et al. 1978).

Data on the effects of the ADEA Amendments on women workers and job opportunities for younger women are as yet nonexistent. Little is known about the extent of life-time labor force participation among women in the U.S. What is known is that older single women are probably the poorest group in society (Heidbreder, 1972). This is caused by a number of factors—lower earnings during employment, irregular or nonexistent employment, ineligibility for pensions (80 percent as compared to 68.8 percent for men), lower Social Security benefits and frequent ineligibility for unemployment insurance (Harris, et al. 1978). These factors, often coupled with widowhood or divorce, leave older women with a low economic status and a great need to begin or continue working. Any effect the ADEA Amendments might have in meeting this need would clearly be beneficial.

Job Performance

Turning to the third factor that impacts the employment opportunities for older workers' job performance, we find that the increased *possibility* of physical limitations with age, rather than the *actuality* of such limitations, acts as a deterrent to the employment of competent older workers. When asked to assess their own ability to contribute to the community, 40 percent of the persons 65 and older saw themselves as "very useful" and 39 percent saw themselves as "somewhat useful." Research indicates that the decrease in physical ability associated with age generally has no significant effect on job performance. In a study by Richard Arvey and Stephan Mussio involving test discrimination, job performance and age, correlations were made between a combination cognitive clerical test battery and performance ratings of 266 civil service clerical workers. The findings disclosed that parts of the battery would discriminate against younger workers and other parts against older workers, if used without reference to age. Most importantly, they found that in supervisors' ratings of employees' overall job performance "no difference between the two groups was observed in the measure of job performance" (Arvey and Mussio, 1973). In addition, a recent BLS study of 6000 typists, key-punch operators, and general clerical workers in government agencies and the private sector disclosed "no significant production differences associated with age." Other BLS studies of factory workers indicate that both younger and older groups are somewhat lower in production than the group 35–44 years of age. In some cases, differences were significant, and in others they were not.

In fact, the idea of a major decline in productivity with age has been disproven consistently by experimental and survey data, showing older workers to be as productive as their younger counterparts, or only slightly less so (Schwab, 1977). Specific areas of physical and mental change and the nature of those changes are factors unique to the maturation of the individual. In addition, the significance of the change relative to job performance is dependent on the specific demands of each person's job. Therefore, it is more useful to employers to identify workers by ability than by a generally irrelevant characteristic such as age.

Limited Education and Training Opportunities

A low level of education has often been singled out as a major factor in the older job seeker's lack of labor force marketability. Statistics from 1973 show that 15 percent of older Americans are functionally illiterate, and the average urban dweller over age 65 has had only eight years of formal education (Butler, 1973).

Age bias in training and educational programs maintains many older workers in their disadvantaged position by denying them opportunities to enhance their qualifications. A relatively small proportion of national training and retraining efforts reach people 45 and older—the average enrollment is around 10 percent (Butler, 1973). Very few employers are willing to invest in training for older workers (often despite good work records), and many colleges and universities still have age limits on the award of their degrees. These biases are often the result of the erroneous belief that learning ability decreases with age. Studies have shown that between the ages of 20 and 65 there is little, if any, change in the ability to retain new information and learn new skills. It was found that the differences that do exist between age groups are usually the result of differences in perception, attention, motivation, and physiological state, rather than learning capacity. In fact, the older members of this sample proved to be "more intellectually efficient, responsible and tolerant" than the younger ones (Sheppard and Rix, 1977).

In addition, average educational levels of age groups have been changing in recent years. In 1966, the median years of schooling for employed men between the ages of 55 and 64 was only 77.7 percent of that of men 25–34. However, in 1976, the percentage had risen to 94.6, indicating that the overall educational discrepancy between younger and older workers had become negligible. For women, the change from 1966 to 1976 was slight; in 1966 women's median years of schooling were already quite high—11.6 as opposed to 9.7 for men—which explains the difference between male and female employment statistics. Since the educational disadvantage of the elderly as a group has been greatly reduced—particularly for employed males—lack of education can no longer suffice as a blanket excuse for hiring discrimination against older workers (Sheppard and Rix, 1977).

CURRENT PROGRAMS

This section discusses programmatic efforts and legislative mandates which seek to widen job opportunities for older workers, including those persons who are approaching, or who have reached, retirement age.

We usually consider the economics of aging as the need of retirees for income. We can address, as well, the need of the community for retirees to serve as volunteers in small business and economic development, evaluation and improvement of current community services, and as "elder statesmen" advisors to political, educational and other human service groups. To assure an acceptable future in retirement, we need first to take a look at the early development and current status of employment programs, which offer both paid and volunteer opportunities. Some programs are already categorical in nature, i.e., serve specified segments of the work force (youth, older workers, females, blacks and Spanish surname); others need to achieve age equity in their services to older applicants. A third group of programs, differing from the paid work programs in the types of payments and other benefits offered, are thus considered to be "volunteer" in nature. Such programs offer a very positive opportunity for the retired who frequently do not want or need the income, but wish to continue work in some type of community endeavor. The principal emphasis in this chapter, however, will be on paid jobs. (See Table 5–3)

U.S. Employment Service

Setting the stage for employment programs was the passage in 1933 of the Wagner-Peyser Act, which created a federal-state partnership in "a bureau within the Department of Labor (to be) known as the United States Employment Service (USES)." Passed in the midst of the Great Depression, the Act established a network of state run but federally financed employment service offices. These offices were viewed as a labor exchange, offering counseling and placement service, and assisting employers and labor unions in evaluating the cause of inplant manpower problems.

Some years later, after passage of the act, concerned administrators reviewed the USES record of service to older workers. The examination disclosed that older workers were not being served in proportion to their presence in the labor force and in 1956, the Department of Labor conducted a study called the *Older Worker Adjustment to Labor Market Practices: An Analysis of Experiences in Seven Major Labor Markets* which reached the following conclusions, and which have been underscored by subsequent studies:

- Older workers (45 and above) tend to be more stable than younger workers and have lower turnover rates.
- Older workers tend to achieve higher performance ratings from employers than those under 45.
- The older worker is more productive than those under 45.
- Older workers have fewer accidents than younger workers and miss fewer working days per year due to accidents.
- On-the-job morale tends to be higher among middle-aged and older workers than among younger workers.
- Job motivation tends to be higher among older workers than those under 45.

	Executive Agency			
Program	**Equal Employment Opportunity Comm.**	**Employment and Training Adm.**	**ACTION**	**Small Business Administration**
Age Discrimination in Employment (ADEA) 1967 Amended	Investigation of charges of age discrimination in employment by persons between ages 40 to 70.			
Comprehensive Employment & Training Act CETA (1973 Amended)		Prime Sponsors funded by Dept. of Labor to establish community based employment programs.		
Employment Service (ES) Wagner-Peyser Act of 1933-Amended		Federal-State partnership providing employment services.		
Older Americans Community Service Employment Prog. (AoA Title V).		Program to serve older poor (aged 55 and over) by assignment to community service agencies.		
Retired Senior Volunteer Prog. RSVP Domestic Volunteer Services Act of 1973		Program to provide out-of pocket expenses to expand volunteer activities in non-profit agencies.		
Service Corps of Retired Executives (SCORE) Domestic Volunteer Services Act of 1973				Retired professionals and businessmen assist small businesses with management problems.
Foster Grandparents Senior Companion Prog. Domestic Volunteer Services Act of 1973			Creation of volunteer opportunities for older persons 60 and over as companions to children and older persons	

Adapted from Hearings before the Select Committee on Aging House of Representatives Ninety-fourth Congress Second Session page 16

Based on these and other conclusions brought forth by the study, the United States Employment Service called for the budgeting and designation of an Older Worker Specialist (OWS) at the regional, state, and local office level to design and implement special activities in recruitment, counseling, testing, and placement of older workers. With the passage of the Economic Opportunity Act of 1964, setting up the executive Office of Economic Opportunity (OEO) older worker priority in USES was greatly reduced, and the specialists' job became overly burdened with the necessity to serve a variety of applicant categories, as well as to certify enrollees for employment programs mandated by OEO. In the past few years, the OWS designation has been dropped; in some instances the title has been changed to indicate a staff specialty in adult services, with equal emphasis being sought for handicapped, veterans, displaced homemakers, minorities, and older workers. Last amended in 1950, some oversight hearings have been held recently, and others are scheduled for evaluation of Wagner-Peyser to determine whether the Act should be amended or new legislation should be written.

Manpower Development and Training Act

The Manpower Development and Training Act (MDTA) was passed in 1962 in recognition of the "proposition that some measure is needed to match people and jobs." (Wirtz, 1965) The purpose of the legislation was to provide training and related education for youth about to enter the labor force and for those already in it who were unemployed and underemployed. The training was to be backed up by intensive manpower research and job development. Amended in 1963 and 1965, the Act mandated an appraisal of the nation's manpower requirements and resources, and required the Government to develop and apply the information and methods needed to deal with the problems of persistent unemployment. It was under Title I of MDTA that some research and demonstration projects were conducted.

Under the amended Act in 1965, the Secretary of Labor in concert with the Secretary of Commerce, launched a job development program to expand job opportunities in the area of service jobs, which were then growing at three times the rate of other jobs. Title II of

MDTA called for programs to upgrade the skills of the disadvantaged in the work force to help place them in jobs. Under this title, basic education programs and OJT methods were developed; the training of youth was emphasized. Under MDTA programs there was an effective and continuing relationship between DOL, and the Office of Education (OE) in Health, Education and Welfare (HEW). OE provided the classroom facilities and staff for the basic education and skill development for the eligible enrollees in MDTA programs. The Employment Service had the responsibility for recruiting, certifying, testing and counselling the program participants.

An interesting insight into MDTA is offered in *Job Development and Placement* by Miriam Johnson and Marged Sugarman:

The original intent behind the Act had been to train people out of work because of technological change for occupations in which workers were in short supply. The belief that this country was faced with a serious shortage of skilled workers had grown out of an earlier shock given the United States by the Soviet Union's first space launch and theorists demonstrated the need for legislation of this kind by pointing to the putative paradox of swollen pages of help wanted ads appearing at the same time that the employment service offices were burgeoning with jobseekers. The formula for correcting imbalances in the marketplace seemed simple: train the technologically displaced to fill skill shortages.

The record reveals that the formula broke down early in the course of implementation. First then as well as now, there was no workable methodology for defining skill shortage occupations in the local labor market. More importantly, the target population changed from those who had been displaced to those who had never been allowed in, as the fear of being technologically surpassed by foreign powers gave way to the fear of Americans burning their own cities. As experience with MDTA grew, it became obvious that the formula was conceptually faulty. The costs, the restrictions in length of training, the difficulties in obtaining training facilities and instructors for special occupations, the low skill and education levels of the new target population—all worked against the goal of training individuals to approach the level of skill where employers might experience shortages. Thus the goal changed from training for skill shortages to training in occupations in which there was a "reasonable expectation of employment." (Johnson and Sugarman, pp. 7-8, 1978 (revised).

This experience was not universal, however, and to many program operators, MDTA was restricted only by the imagination and initiative of local staff in the adult and vocational education schools. In other localities, classes were greatly restricted by the availability and competence of instructors who were hired to teach the subjects they were qualified to teach, regardless of local labor market requirements. Great discontent ensued when a group of clerical skills instructors operated in an area where tool designers were sorely needed.

One outcome of MDTA was clear and fairly consistent: it did not serve older workers. To address this problem, a demonstration was funded in 1965 geared exclusively to the older worker. A report of the project, prepared by Sarah Leiter, noted that "there was no lack of awareness of older worker job problems, but that relatively little program attention had been focused on the mature, unemployed adult."

Under this grant, thirteen projects with various objectives were undertaken in eleven areas. Seven were under the general sponsorship of the National Council on the Aging (NCOA), a private, non-profit organization concerned with issues on aging. The Council was also responsible for the convening of a three-day National Conference on Manpower Training and the Older Worker in early 1966 in connection with the demonstration. The conference provided a forum at which developments and continuing needs for research and action in the field of older worker training and employment were presented and discussed.

Most of the projects served the retired worker; the rest sought participants 50 years of age and over. Only one served a group under 45 years old. The conclusions and recommendations were objective (and still valid) in several areas which included:

a. The term "older worker" should be restricted to those of retirement age (65 and over);

b. Older worker programs should make use of tools and technical assistance already developed by USES;

c. MDTA should offer a greater variety of courses and provide more training slots (to accommodate older worker entry);

d. Middle-aged and older workers should not have courses specially designed for them. Such a practice would tend to limit training opportunities for older workers and would imply that some occupational fields (usually the less desirable ones) are particularly suited to middle-aged and older workers. Good instructors and efficient training programs can cope with a wide variety of trainees;

e. Older persons must not be limited to restricted occupational areas erroneously considered suitable for them. Their interests and abilities embrace the whole world of work. They should not be "fitted" to jobs which fail to meet their vocational interests or other requirements. Placement must be person oriented rather than job oriented.

The comment (see recommendation "d") that "good instructors and efficient training programs can cope with a wide variety of trainees" is in contrast with the statement by Sugarman and Johnson that the problems occurred because of the low skills and education levels of the new target population.

Only one of the recommendations has been satisfied; that of prohibiting hiring discrimination based on age. The 1967 Age Discrimination in Employment Act (ADEA) is discussed at length in another chapter of this publication. On the whole, the experiment was not viewed as a great success. According to Ms. Leiter, those who directed individual projects were generally dedicated and enthusiastic, but many of them had little manpower expertise. Some observers considered this an advantage, others did not. In a number of sites, the Employment Service was unwilling to help—at others, they hesitated to volunteer their assistance and be unwanted, according to the report.

Operation Mainstream

Originally established in 1968 under Title I of the Economic Opportunity Act, Operation Mainstream was continued under 1969 amended OEO legislation. According to a 1971 evaluation of the program, by Kirschner Associates, Inc., "Operation Mainstream (OM) is not a completely homogeneous program, but consists rather of a collection of programs, including the Green Thumb-Green Light program, and OM projects operated under the auspices of DOL Manpower Administration Regional offices. The various types of OM programs differ from one another in several important respects. . . . The Green Thumb-Green Light program and the Senior Aides Program are administered by DOL under national contracts. The Green Thumb-Green Light program is operated under contract with the National Farmers Union and the Senior Aides Program under four national contractors: National Council of Senior Citizens (NCSC), the National Council on the Aging (NCOA), the National Retired Teachers Association (NRTA), and Virginia State College (VSC)." The program remains in existence under Title V of the amended Older Americans Act as the Senior Community Service Employment Program (SCSEP). Since Operation Mainstream terminated with the passage of the Comprehensive Employment and Training Act in 1973, transition funding for continuation of the Senior Aides program was provided from unallocated Mainstream funds combined with CETA Title III until 1975. The Older Americans legislation then absorbed the national contractors program operations and funding.

Administration of the program continues to be delegated to the Department of Labor, where the funds are currently allocated to national contractors who run SCSEP, and are monitored by DOL. The national contractors are:

1. The National Council on the Aging, Inc. (NCOA)
2. National Council of Senior Citizens (NCSC)
3. American Association of Retired Persons/National Retired Teachers Association (AARP/NRTA)
4. Farmers Union—Green Thumb
5. U.S. Department of Agriculture/U.S. Forest Service
6. National Center on Black Aged
7. National Urban League
8. Associacion Nacional Pro Personas Mayores

Established in 1968 as a demonstration to employ older poor persons, the project was understandably viewed as an income maintenance effort. Its enrollees were assigned to local community service agencies who agreed to expand services or provide new ones with the assistance of the program participants.

There has been no change in enrollment criteria requiring that program participants meet poverty income requirements and be 55 years of age or over, but there has been a gradual reemphasis of goals to those of a job training program, with selective training offered to facilitate placement in unsubsidized employment either in the host agency, in the private or the public sector. Primary emphasis is placed on support mechanisms which expand the older workers' confidence, refurbish old skills or develop new ones; training in job-seeking methods is offered to produce placement in unsubsidized jobs. Learning new skills is assumed to be part of the job experience. The program is an extremely popular one, and even though legislated by the Older Americans Act, is viewed as DOL's one firm "claim to fame" where older worker programs are concerned. The funding has increased from the initial allocation of about $5 million for five national contractors providing nearly 2500 enrollee slots to nearly $267 million in FY '80, supporting 52,250 enrollees.

Comprehensive Employment and Training Act

Frustration with MDTA, general disenchantment with government control of manpower programs and increasing unemployment came at a time when the Administration voiced its desire to take decision-making back to the people. The Comprehensive Employment and Training Act (CETA) of 1973 was a response to the cry of manpower planners and program operators for decentralization, decategorization, and consolidation (Snedeker and Snedeker, 1978).

Decentralization was achieved through transferring authority for manpower program planning and administration from the federal government to state and local governmental units. These units, termed "prime sponsors" became responsible for developing policies and goals reflecting local labor market conditions and needs. Decategorization was achieved through permitting the prime sponsors to allocate manpower funds among a variety of generic services. Consolidation was achieved by combining manpower programs funded under the MDTA and Economic Opportunity Act. Taken together, decentralization, decategorization, and consolidation were designed to improve the efficiency and effectiveness of manpower programs.

Eligibility for prime sponsor status was limited to political jurisdictions with populations of 100,000 or more; allocations went directly to those areas which submitted approved plans. Regulations permitted consortia of areas under 100,000; under a balance-of-state designation, smaller states and in-state units not otherwise eligible received the funds under the same regulations as any other prime sponsor, but the state did not exert control over any other prime sponsors or consortium. The appointment of a manpower advisory council to each prime sponsor was mandated as a means of assuring management and client group input.

CETA absorbed both MDTA and Operation Mainstream, and sought to remove the categorical labels from both programs. There was no mandate to coordinate with the Employment Service. In addition, no informal arrangements were suggested to aid the job training and placement process, even though ES staff had developed valuable skills in recruiting, counseling and placement activities.

In the first years of operation, CETA had a difficult time. Having emerged at a time of extraordinarily high unemployment, it was faced with the problem of implementing public service employment policies, while attempting to carry out its training mission. Even as these first crises were handled with mounting experience by CETA operators, it became clear that once again older workers were not considered a priority and were not included to any appreciable degree in local manpower planning or programs.

It is unfortunate that in the tax-supported employment and training agencies services to applicants continue to decline in direct proportion to age. According to the 1979 Employment and Training Report of the President, less than 4 percent of the applicants served under Title I of CETA were 55 years of age and over; for the older age group in Titles II and VI of the same Act, the ratio was less than 6 percent. An examination of the Employment Service reports indicates a proportionately low record of service to older workers.

Of special interest at this time is the new CETA emphasis on middle-aged and older workers. For the first time, the 1978 amended legislation focuses directly on program development to benefit this age group under Title III. According to a report from the Secretary of Labor to the Select Committee on Aging, in fiscal 1979, $18.6 million was allocated from Title III of CETA: the employment related allocations were $17.9 million to continue the phase-out of the former Commerce Department's Title X, and $678,000 in three other programs, including a $492,000 Green Thumb National On-The-Job-Training Program.

Section 308 of Title III is off to a very slow start, but is strong in its language mandating "the development and establishment. . . . of programs for middle-aged and older workers, which will lead to a more equitable share of employment and training resources for middle-aged and older workers." Definite steps are set out for establishing this objective, including research on the relationship between age and employment, and authority to pay reasonable training costs for participants in second career programs.

Overall, the attention paid to the older worker in the 1978 CETA amendments are heartening, and indicate some progress in correcting the disservice of the past years.

An interesting development has been in the number of private nonprofit agencies which have been established at the local level to fill the employment gap for older workers. Support for their activity comes from a variety of sources or combinations which include United Way, foundations, CETA, political jurisdictions (city and county Commissions), Senior Centers, etc. Some agencies are administered with one or two paid staff and some volunteers; others are solely volunteer.

At the request of some of its members, NCOA is engaged in an effort to provide a national forum for these agencies, has agreed to sponsor and is organizing a National Association of Older Worker Employment Services whose purpose would be information sharing, knowledge building, model program development and public policy recommendations. In this regard, NCOA is now engaged in collecting information on the clients characteristics and the kind of job services being offered before any specific activities are outlined or any long range goals are set.

Volunteer Programs

One of the major accomplishments of the Older Americans Act of 1965 was the establishment of a federal initiative to address the psychological and social needs of older persons as well as providing a legislative framework for additional income-supplementing programs. In 1971, under authority of this Act, ACTION, the federal volunteer agency was established. This agency, through its Older Americans Volunteer Programs (OAVP) division administers three major programs, the Foster Grandparent Program (FGP), Senior Companion Program (SCP), and Retired Senior Volunteer Program (RSVP), (see Table 5-4), all designed to provide meaningful roles for retirees, to relieve the effects of poverty, to improve human services, and to enable retirees to receive the rewards that come from volunteer service. (Bowles, 1976)

There are no formal education or skill requirements for entrants. FGP and SCP require 40 hours of orientation covering the program, and the special needs of clients. Both programs provide monthly in-service training. RSVP training is on-the-job and limited to specific tasks and functions.

Although officially designated as a "volunteer" rather than an "employment" program and sharing a similar purpose, there is one fundamental difference: FGP and SCP are designed for persons at

Table 5-4. Older Americans Volunteer Programs: Data Summary 1979.

	FGP	SCP	RSVP
Year Established	1965	1973	1969
Scope of Operations	50 states, District of Columbia, Puerto Rico, Virgin Islands	26 states, Puerto Rico	50 states, District of Columbia, Puerto Rico, Virgin Islands
Local Projects	198	54	682
Volunteers	16,640	3,350	250,000
Federal funding (millions)	$34.9	$7.0	$20.1
Federal/local cost-sharing ratio	90/10	90/10	Year 1: 90/10; Year 2: 80/20; Year 3: 60/40

Source: Stan Volens, Senior Program Specialist, Older Americans Volunteer Programs, ACTION, 1979.

or below the poverty level and provide participants with a small hourly nontaxable stipend. Volunteers work four hours daily and receive such fringe benefits as vacation, sick leave, and insurance coverage as well as transportation and meals. Such provisions have led to considerable debate on the legitimacy of designating these two programs as volunteer. (Bowles, 1976) In effect FGP and SCP are hybrids falling somewhere between paid employment and volunteerism.

Unlike FGP and SCP, RSVP is an orthodox volunteer program. Participants receive no stipend, have no stipulation regarding the number of hours, have considerable flexibility regarding assignments, and receive neither sick leave nor vacation. Modeled after SERVE, a demonstration project undertaken by the Community Service Society of New York, RSVP is designed specifically to reach the nontraditional volunteer—those adults who would not ordinarily participate in volunteer programs. Nationally about 27 percent of RSVP volunteers have had no volunteer experience. It also attempts to engage nontraditional volunteer stations, such as parks and zoos, police and court programs, senior centers, and government agencies. (Bowles, 1976) The program is seen by many professionals as a model for older volunteers who increasingly fill the gaps created by the movement of the traditional volunteers, young and middle-aged women, into the work force.

CONCLUSIONS

A review of the current employment situation of older persons reveals a continuing decline in participation rates and, among workers a dominance of part-time positions which are below the skill level of previous positions. Despite this pattern, attitudinal surveys have demonstrated that older persons prefer to be active in retirement through either income generating or nonremunerative positions which provide services to others and opportunities to remain useful.

Structural and attitudinal barriers which serve to limit the options of retirees include age discrimination, the generally lower educational attainment of older workers, and the reluctance of employers to invest in training older persons. Federally funded programs which have sought to improve the employment situation for retirees, the

U.S. Employment Service and programs funded under MDTA and CETA, have had mixed success. Despite their differing approaches, the USES and MDTA and CETA programs have consistently underserved older workers and retirees.

Like their employment program counterparts federally sponsored volunteer programs have had mixed success. The Foster Grandparent and Senior Companion programs are designed to provide meaningful roles along with income and related benefits to low income elderly volunteers. RSVP, a nonstipended volunteer program, provides a remarkably wide range of services in nontraditional volunteer stations. The shortcoming of these programs lies in neither their design, execution, nor acceptance by participants and host communities; rather it lies in the low level of funding in the face of enormous needs; a corps of over 270,000 volunteers appears impressive until one realizes that an additional 7 million retirees are interested in volunteer service.

The concern for job opportunities for retirement age workers, however, remains the focus of this chapter. We began with a review of the employment systems which have been developed to serve all age groups. We have examined the legislation, and described some of the general programmatic efforts to serve all job seekers.

The Employment Service provided a labor exchange for the person who simply wishes to do another kind of work. The categorical programs, in contrast, serve "special segments" of the labor force: the poor, veterans, and the racial and ethnic disadvantaged. We have reviewed, as well, the background and pattern of CETA legislation which sought to correct inadequate and sometimes discriminatory manpower delivery systems, while seeking to address regional and political differences as well.

The unbroken thread running through the background is the resistance of manpower efforts to serve a group with the one characteristic that affects us all—age. There have been some bright movements such as the MDTA Older Worker demonstration, Mainstream, and the Senior Community Service Employment Program. Except for the SCSEP, these are fragmented approaches that have had little lasting effect on legislation and establishment of priorities for a workable employment policy.

Past experience points up the necessity for an equitable age distribution of all employment resources. There is little doubt that, in a democracy, the acute job-disadvantaged deserve a high proportion of available resources, but when only the disadvantaged are served, a serious threat is posed to the welfare of all other applicant groups. This has been the fate of older worker programs and suggests that age equity be restored by a federal requirement that CETA prime sponsor plans reflect the age composition of their jurisdictions.

While no one system can "do it all," there is a matter of counterproductivity when two tax-supported employment agencies (USES and CETA) are frequently sharing the same jurisdiction, competing for the same clients, and duplicating many services. With a review of the Wagner-Peyser Act, now a matter of Congressional decision, it might be appropriate to consider a reallocation of functions with responsibility for overview, national policy, and maintenance of operating standards being returned to the government by repealing Wagner-Peyser and federalizing these functions of the employment service.

In his "Mission of Manpower Policy" the late E. Wight Bakke supports such a concept when he states:

". . . it is essential that a single agency have responsibility and authoritative opportunity to plan for and to propose modifications in the action programs involved, and to monitor the performance of agents and agencies charged with carrying out those programs."

We have now had sufficient experience and made enough mistakes to have learned a great deal. It would be sad, indeed, if as a nation we traded that knowledge for short-range employment programs which do not consistently aim for age equity and which fail to take advantage of the experience of mature persons who wish to continue to work.

SOURCES

Arvey, R., and Mussio, S. Test discrimination, job performance and age," *Industrial Gerontology*, N. 16, Winter, 1973.

Bakke, E. Wight. *The Mission of Manpower Policy,* Kalamazoo, Michigan: Upjohn Institute, April 1969.

Bauer, Dorothy. Economic development and the older worker: A technical assistance guide for economic development districts, prepared under Grant # 99-6-0919, Office of Technical Assistance, Economic Development Administration, U.S. Department of Commerce, Washington, D.C.: NCOA, 1978.

Bowles, Elinore. Older persons as providers of services: Three federal programs, *Social Policy,* November/December, 1976, pp. 81-88.

Brown, Robert J. A department of labor look at the older worker, *Industrial Gerontology,* 4 (2):73-76. Spring, 1977.

Butler, Robert. *Why Survive?: Being Old in America,* New York: Harper & Row, 1973.

Harris, Charles S., ed. *Fact Book on Aging: A Profile of America's Older Population,* Washington, D.C.: NCOA, 1978.

Harris, Charles, Goldberg, David, Jones, Valinda, Peavy, Nancy, and Whitman, Sue. Changing the mandatory retirement age: Its effects on employing older workers and selected members of the labor force, unpublished paper, NCOA, July 1978.

Heidbreder, Elizabeth M. Pensions and the single woman, *Industrial Gerontology,* Fall, 1972, pp. 52-62.

Holly, W. H., Field, H. S., and Holly, B. B. Age and reactions to jobs: An empirical study of paraprofessional workers, *Aging and Work,* 1 (1), Winter, 1978.

Johnson, Miriam and Sugarman, Marged. *Job Development and Placement: CETA Program Models,* U.S. Department of Labor, 1978 (revised).

Kirschner Associates, *National Evaluation of Operation Mainstream,* Albuquerque, New Mexico: The Senior Aides Program, May 1971.

Kunze, Karl. Age and occupations at Lockheed-California: Versatility of older workers, *Industrial Gerontology,* 1 (2), Spring, 1974, pp. 59-64.

Leiter, Sarah F. *Training and Employment of the Older Worker,* U.S. Department of Labor, February 1968.

Meier, Elizabeth L. *Aging in America, # 7: Implications for Employment,* Washington, D.C.: NCOA, 1976.

Meier, Elizabeth L. and Kerr, Elizabeth. Capabilities of middle-aged and older workers: A survey of the literature, *Industrial Gerontology,* 3, 1976.

Schwab, Donald P. and Heneman, Herbert G. Effects of age and experience on productivity, *Industrial Gerontology,* 4 (2):113-119, Spring, 1977.

Sheppard, Harold L. and Rix, Sara E. *The Graying of Working America: The Coming Crisis of Retirement-Age Policy,* New York: The Free Press, 1977.

Snedeker, Bonnie B. and Snedeker, David M. *CETA: Decentralization on Trial,* Olympus, Salt Lake City, Utah, 1978.

Thompson, P. H. and Dalton, G. W. Are R & D organizations obsolete? *Harvard Business Review,* 54: 105-116, 1976.

Wirtz, Willard. *MDTA—A Summary of the Manpower Development and Training Act of 1962, as amended,* U.S. Department of Labor, December 1965.

6

AGE DISCRIMINATION AND MANDATORY RETIREMENT

Edward Howard, Nancy Peavy, and Lauren Selden

On April 6, 1978, President Jimmy Carter, surrounded by Congressional leaders, Cabinet secretaries, and the heads of a dozen voluntary groups representing older Americans, signed into law amendments to the Age Discrimination in Employment Act (ADEA) of 1967 (Public Law 95–256). Under the provisions of the amended ADEA, most federal employees were freed from the requirement that they retire at age seventy, the first time the federal law explicitly banned involuntary termination based on an individual's age. The restraint placed on mandatory retirement throughout the majority of the labor force was hailed as the first step in the inevitable abolition of a practice that had come to symbolize age discrimination. Additionally, under the amended ADEA, most nonfederal governmental units and private employers were prohibited from imposing compulsory retirement on their workers any earlier than age seventy.

In 1978 legislation plainly altered the law, but the impact of the changes upon national policy is less clear. For decades the law has reflected a long-term employment outlook. A primary component of that outlook has been the exclusion of large numbers of older people from work opportunities for which they were objectively qualified.

This chapter explores the origins of a ''nonwork'' posture and the evolution and development of modifications in that posture. It also examines the role of the courts and the Federal Government in enforcing the law. Finally, the chapter suggests what the future is likely to hold for older people and their right and opportunity to work.

THE EVOLUTION OF NONWORK

For most of the nation's history, advancing age rarely qualified a person's opportunity to earn a livelihood. In 1890 seven out of every ten men over the age of 65 held a job. Few had any other choice. Private pensions were virtually unknown. Even those who were receiving Civil War military benefits typically needed to work. By 1979, despite the revolution in the labor force status of women, only 14 percent of the entire population of 24 million people 65 and over held a job. For the most part, nonworkers were "retirees." At least 4.5 million of them would trade retirement for employment (Louis Harris, 1975), but were unable to find satisfactory job opportunities.

The transition of the older American from an individual who had to work in order to survive to an individual often excluded from work reflects two distinct, yet implicit and connected, themes in modern industrial society.

Although preindustrial America suffered from an apparent shortage of labor, the modern era has witnessed the periodic inability of the economic system to produce work for everyone who wanted and needed a job. The period from 1873 through the end of the 1930's was marked by a cycle of recessions and depressions, and thus by frequent rates of high unemployment. Between 1893 and 1898 unemployment never dropped below 11.7 percent. In 1897 it reached a high of 14.5 percent. During the first decade of the 20th century, unemployment exceeded 5.1 percent in four separate years. Except for the war years (1917–18), joblessness averaged over 6 percent throughout the next decade. The figures are probably understated because society did not perceive itself as obligated to provide work for nonwhites, aliens, and women, these classes may have been ignored by analysts of the labor force.

The reality of nonwork for substantial numbers of people found expression in law and societal values, an expression that was both exclusionary and reformist. Nearly 25 million immigrants from southern and eastern Europe entered the country between the end of the Civil War and the early 1920s. In popular imagination, if not in fact, immigrants were considered a primary cause of depressed wages and high unemployment among native white males. This perception, in turn, gave rise to political movements by working men in the western states and trade unionists in the eastern states to limit immigration. By the early 1900s the immigration of Asians was largely shut down by federal statute and executive agreements. The nascent urban political machines, often based on immigrant support, resisted curbs on European immigration. By the second decade of the century, the spread of World War I curbed the movement of people. But when the end of that war triggered another massive wave of immigration, Congress quickly imposed quotas on admission into America.

The curb on immigration was only one means of controlling the size of the population seeking work. Other classes were also excluded from the labor force. Child labor laws, enacted in most states during the Progressive Era, restricted dramatically the type of employment in which children could engage. Opportunities for nonwhites and women were confined by both statute and tradition. In the case of nonwhites, segregation included explicit limitations on access to numerous occupations as well as to education. Women, particularly single women, were accepted as teachers, factory workers and, after the introduction of the office typewriter, secretaries. But in many states the law limited the jobs women could hold, the hours they could work, the hazards to which they might be exposed, and their right to obtain advanced education.

In each instance, reform notions of protecting society and the individual underlie the development of the law. For example, reformers perceived that work exploited children, condemned them to permanent poverty, and led to a variety of social evils (alcoholism, prostitution, and a weakening of the family). Unions often supported child labor laws as a method of eliminating competition for scarce employment. The same set of values prompted "protective" legislation for women. Even the segregation of blacks was seen by some as beneficial, a shield against a hostile white community.

Nevertheless, the statutory law and social values effectively merged into a national attitude toward employment, an attitude defined by the recognition that some classes *required* work, but others did not. Because some classes did not require work, the economic system was under no obligation to create work for them. This was an attitude rather than an explicit public policy. Thus, its premises and operation encountered less than substantial resistance for most of the century.

The significance of such an attitude for this chapter is that older people too came to be counted out. As in the case of women and children, exclusion flowed from benevolent impulse. Indeed, exclusion of older people is inseparable from a reform impulse: the establishment of a national system of old age pensions.

In the early years of the 20th century, progressive economists, academicians and social workers attempted to put pensions on the national agenda. No significant headway was made until the Great Depression compelled policymakers to deal with massive unemployment and old age indigency. Franklin D. Roosevelt assigned to a Cabinet-level task force the responsibility for designing a federal system to provide income to the jobless and the elderly. With at least one-quarter of the labor force out of work, it is hardly surprising that the two, unemployment and the older person, were linked. The end product of FDR's Committee on Economic Security, the Social Security Act of 1935, embodies both the linkage and the national attitude.

By providing pensions to people 65 and older, the Social Security Act made retirement (labor force withdrawal) feasible. After examining the public record and the inner workings of the Roosevelt Administration, New Deal historians conclude that the Act, for all its humanitarian roots, cannot be understood apart from the economic problems exposed by the Depression. An implicit goal of the Social Security Act was to discourage older people from work.*

The Social Security Act did not legislate retirement; it simply made it practical. Inadvertently, voluntary retirement and, subsequently, exclusion emerged as the dominant employment themes among older people. Within two decades of the Social Security Act, both themes were codified in law and institutional practice.

The process was slow. The Act initially covered very few workers. Nearly universal coverage did not come until after the Korean War. Moreover, overseas events provided a natural break upon the drift of aging workers into retirement. Preparation for World War II, the war itself and the Korean conflict, which pressed millions of young

---

*Older citizens were ready to accept an explicit trade-off, no work in exchange for economic security. A contemporaneous and far more generous scheme than Social Security, the Townsend Plan, favored overwhelmingly by older people, would have conditioned receipt of a pension upon renunciation of employment. In general see Schlesinger, 29–41, 1960; Leuchtenburg, 103–106, 131–133, 1963; Pratt, *The Gray Lobby* at 11–35, 1976.

men into military service, demanded the labor force participation of women and older men. By the end of the Cold War era, the decline in work among the older population had become pronounced. Between 1948 and 1968, work among people 65 and older dropped from 27 percent to 17 percent. In 1979 only 14 percent worked.

Specific provisions of the Social Security Act encouraged retirement. The "earnings limitation test" placed a ceiling on the amount of wages a Social Security beneficiary may earn without incurring a reduction in benefit. The ceiling has always been low; until a recent amendment to the Act it was $3000. Because Social Security income is not taxed, a prospective older worker must calculate whether it pays to accept modest wages. In addition, in 1961 the Act was "liberalized" to permit men to collect retirement income (albeit reduced) at 62, the same age at which women become eligible. Since 1974, 72 percent of all initial retirement benefits to men have in fact been drawn before age sixty-five.

Although the changes proceeded slowly, retirement became the rule. While the new freedom to choose to stop work was a long overdue development, the fact remains that withdrawal from work was dictated by business practice, pension plans and public law. Prior to the Social Security Act, mandatory retirement was rare. After the Act, public employees forced retirement statutes covered virtually all government workers. Private pension plans, which experienced remarkable growth after World War II, usually mandated involuntary retirement. When the Social Security Act permitted men to retire at age 62 and draw benefits, many private plans lowered the age of forced retirement accordingly.

Collective bargaining agreements permitted, even encouraged, aging workers to retire. In part, unions responded to the demand of older industrial workers for the freedom to leave tedious and often unpleasant jobs. Unions, however, were also responsive to the desire of younger people anxious to see older workers depart in order to accelerate an upward movement in authority and wages. In some industries, management agreed to "thirty and out" contracts (full retirement benefits after thirty years of employment), for the plans generated a significant savings in current operating costs. At General Motors, for example, the average age at which a United Automobile Worker retired dropped to 53; only 2 percent of the union work force stayed on to the mandatory retirement age of 68. In other industries, at both the managerial and blue collar level, voluntary retirement in the fifties became common. (See Walker and Lazer, 1978.)

Retirement practices served a business or managerial strategy.* At one level, involuntary retirement permitted easier control over the size of a workforce. More importantly, retirement rules became a mechanism for implementing corporate changes that leaned toward the talents and plans of upwardly mobile younger executives. Instead of firing older managers and supervisors, firms offered to "load up" a retirement plan; in exchange for a voluntary resignation, the departing employee received additional benefits. (Walker and Lazer, 1978.)

Because most retirement data are based on Social Security claims, precise figures about the scope of mandatory retirement rules are impossible to obtain. Specialists in labor force trends are confident that well over half the work force has for decades been employed in institutions that compel retirement at a specific age. By no means was 65 *the* retirement age. The Labor Department estimated in 1977 that perhaps as many as 11 million people faced involuntary retirement at younger ages.

The national stance toward older people has been effectuated in two other ways. First, until 1968 when the ADEA became effective, the termination of an employee because of age did not violate any federal law. A few states prohibited age discrimination, but in every state mandatory retirement was lawful.

Second, retirement was transformed into a big business and a way of life. American business marketed retirement. The larger culture communicated positive images of a life of leisure.** For many, retire-

---

*Other rationales asserted in defense of involuntary retirement—the unfitness of aging workers, the desirability of sparing the feelings of older people who would otherwise be singled out for discharge based upon cause—surfaced after the practice became widespread. On the development of such rationales, see: Walker and Lazer, 1978; Butler, 1975; and Kaplan, 1971.

**There is a large and growing literature on retirement and retirees, including an abundance of books advising people on adjustment to leisure and where to live. But there is no authoritative institutional analysis of retirement as an industry. Since retirees constitute a multibillion dollar market, involving such powerful private interests as insurance, real estate and travel, an institutional analysis would make a major contribution to public policy analysis. The U.S. Commerce Department has awarded a grant to the National Council on the Aging to begin such an analysis.

ment was the fulfillment of a dream, but not for everyone. Some people did not want to stop working either because they loved their work or needed the income, or both. Others discovered *after they were retired* that their economic resources were inadequate. Astonishing numbers, according to one in-depth study of the older population, found that they missed work and the network of associations organized around employment (Louis Harris, 1975). For the most part, the law and private practice combined to circumscribe options.

RESTRAINING DISCRIMINATION: THE AGE DISCRIMINATION IN EMPLOYMENT ACT OF 1967.

The United States Congress first considered the need to prohibit age discrimination in employment while debating the legislation that became Title VII of the Civil Rights Act of 1964.

The genesis of Title VII had nothing to do with older people. That landmark legislation traces its roots to the movement for equality by blacks in the years after the historic Supreme Court decision in *Brown v. Board of Education,* 347 U.S. 483 (1954). Title VII, the basic federal fair employment practices statute, could not create jobs, but it did establish a legal means to challenge racially and sexually based employment exclusion. Although there is no evidence that older Americans or their voluntary organizations sought to include age in the list of classes protected by the Civil Rights Act, an amendment was offered on the floor of both Houses.* The legislative history makes clear that the sponsors of the amendment intended that no upper or lower age ceiling qualify the prohibition against discrimination.

Congress rejected the amendment, ostensibly on the grounds that little was known about the magnitude or causes of age discrimination. Section 715 of the Act, however, directed the Secretary of Labor to study the employment status of "older people" and report both his findings and recommendations for remedial legislation back to Congress.

*Unlike the authors of the amendment that added sex to the roster of protected classes in the hopes that the inclusion would dilute enforcement, the sponsors of the age amendment responded to perceptions that age discrimination was a serious problem.

The Secretary's study led ultimately to the enactment of the Age Discrimination in Employment Act of 1967. The study and the final legislation, however, were limited products.

Apparently on its own authority, the Department of Labor ignored section 715's mandate to study "older people." Only those between 45 and 65 were actually examined. Those over age 65 were left out, presumably because they were "retirees" living on Social Security or other pensions.

The Labor Department did discover, however, the astonishing magnitude of nonwork among those they chose to study (age 45-65). In 1966, the last boom year before the prolonged economic decline associated with the war in Indo-China, unemployment among those 45 to 65 never fell below 750,000. The average duration of joblessness lasted six weeks longer than among younger people. Unemployment compensation payments to the class exceeded $750 million annually. One out of every three families in poverty was headed by an unemployed older person. Then-Secretary of Labor Willard Wirtz told Congress that the "older worker" formed the most significant segment of the national unemployment problem.*

The witnesses who appeared before the Congressional Committees reviewing the various proposals to ban age discrimination in employment offered two theories to explain the employment plight of the older worker. One theory emphasized the industrial community's need for a work force possessing better education than aging individuals could offer. The second theory focused on "attitude." Secretary Wirtz argued that employers were insensitive to the capabilities of older workers. Discrimination, in his view, reflected "managerial oversight." The Chamber of Commerce placed the blame squarely on the older person for failing to learn the kind of "marketing skills" necessary to sell oneself.

Only one witness, an official of the National Council on the Aging (NCOA), saw the connection between the national employment posture with respect to those 65 and over and the unemployment problem of people age 45-65. The rise in unemployment among those between 45 and 65 tracked precisely the sharp decline in labor

*This construction of the legislative history is drawn from U.S. Senate Committee on Public Welfare, 1967, and U.S. House of Representatives Committee on Education and Labor, 1967.

force participation by persons 65 and over (then down to one in four) and the drop in the age at which retirement was forced or coerced upon workers. As "normal retirement age" fell below 65, the age at which new workers were hired declined, as did the age at which older people were pushed out.*

A Labor Department study, incorporated into the hearing record but uncommented upon by the witnesses, confirmed the NCOA hypothesis. That analysis showed a direct relationship between prevailing retirement practices and the rise in joblessness among people between 45 and 65. The Department ventured the opinion that many people presumed to have retired voluntarily had actually been forced into leaving their jobs. (U.S. Department of Labor, 1966.)

The ADEA passed the Congress in December 1967 by an overwhelming bi-partisan majority, and became effective in June of 1968.

- As enacted, the ADEA protects individuals 40 years of age and over, until they reach their 65th birthday. In 1979 the ceiling was raised to 70.
- The law prohibits discrimination because of age in matters of hiring, job retention, compensation, and other terms, conditions, and privileges of employment.
- Employers of 25 or more persons are subject to the law, as are public and private employment agencies serving those employers. Labor organizations with 25 or more members are covered by the Act; so are labor organizations which refer persons for employment to covered employers, or to representatives of covered employers. The Act originally applied to employers of 25 or more persons and was later amended.
- The term "employer" at the time of passage did not include federal, state or local governments. The Act was amended in 1974 to include these workers.
- Employers, employment agencies and labor organizations under the Act's jurisdiction are not permitted to use printed or

*The process made apparent economic sense. Younger people commanded lower wages than older people. Moreover, a person hired at age 30 could be expected to work for 25 or 30 years; a 45-year-old not only commanded higher wages and benefits, but might face retirement after only 15 years on the job.

published notices or advertisements relating to employment which indicate any preference, limitation, or specification or discrimination based on age.

- There are certain exceptions from the Act's prohibitions. These involve situations where age is a *bona fide* occupational qualification (BFOQ) (section 4(f)(1)), reasonably necessary to the normal operation of the particular business; where a differentiation is based on reasonable factors other than age (section 4(f)(1)); where a differentiation is caused by observing the terms of a *bona fide* seniority system or employee benefit plan (section 4(f)(2)), which is not a subterfuge to avoid the purposes of the Act. The Act does state that no employee benefit plan may excuse the failure to hire an individual within the scope of the law. As so often included in labor standards, there is an exception provided where discharge of an individual is for good cause. This exception has been significantly narrowed (see discussion below).

- Each covered employer, employment agency, or labor organization was required to post in a conspicuous place on its premises the official notice by the Secretary of Labor which outlines the rights of individuals covered by the Act and provides information on how to locate and contact the nearest office of the enforcement agency, which was the Wage and Hour Division within the Employment Standards Administration of the Department. (In 1979, this jurisdiction was transferred to the Equal Employment Opportunity Commission.)

Congress chose not to recognize the nexus between retirement and nonwork. The two were to be kept discrete. In enacting Medicare, Medicaid, and the early retirement provision in the Social Security Act, Congress, had, in the words of Senator Ralph Yarborough, floor manager of the bill that became the ADEA, "concentrated on the problems of the retired individual." The ADEA, Yarborough claimed, would provide relief for "the older worker who is not ready for retirement" by outlawing the age distinctions." As Senator Jacob Javits put it, the ADEA was the vehicle "to break down wholly irrational barriers to employment."

None of the various fair employment practices proposals introduced in 1967 explicitly prohibited forced retirement before age 65 in all cases. Only one group testified in express support of a provision almost that broad. The AFL/CIO suggested that the bills be amended to ban involuntary retirement before 65 where workers had no legal say in the design of pension plans or employment rules. That recommendation went unheeded.

Subsequently the language of section 4(f)(2) of the Act engendered protracted litigation as to whether the law in fact had banned compulsory retirement before age 65, the ceiling on protection provided in the statute. As finally enacted by Congress, that section provided that it was not unlawful for an employer:

> to observe the terms of a bona fide seniority system or any bona fide employee benefit plan such as retirement, pension, or insurance plan, which is not a subterfuge to evade the purposes of this Act, except that no such employee benefit plan shall excuse the failure to hire any individual. . .

A careful reading of the legislative history, including the hearing record, indicates that the language reflected the desire of the business community to avoid any obligation to incur the expense of providing newly hired older workers with a full range of costly employee fringe benefits. During floor debate, rather than state that employers were exempted from an obligation to offer older workers benefits on a nondiscriminatory basis, legislators in both House and Senate spoke of the provision *as a means to encourage the hiring of older workers.* Not a single legislator claimed that forced retirement before 65 was being prohibited, although there was no serious denial. When the United States Supreme Court in *United Air Lines v. McMann,* 434 U.S. 192 (1977) validated pre-65 mandatory retirement under the Act, the Court's reading of the Act was fully consistent with Congressional design.*

*A collaborative writing project requires considerable willingness to tolerate disagreements over emphasis. Unlike justices of the Supreme Court, however, concurring opinions explicating such disagreements are denied us. However, we wish to add this note, although our unanimity on the point is less than enthusiastic. In *United Air Lines,* the Court could, because of the ambiguity in the language of the statute, the incompatability of forced retirement before 65 with the antidiscrimination provisions of the law, and the confusing nature of the speeches made on the floor prior to passage, reasonably have decided just the other way.

Passage of the legislation resulted in praise for a bill that left citizens over 65 without any legal protection. Although it was publicly recognized that the number of those 65 and over who wanted work but were without jobs constituted 2 million persons—more than twice the size of the population between 45 and 65 without work—the legislation addressed only the needs of those 40 to 65 years of age. Representative Dent, a leading ADEA advocate, summed it up accurately: The principle of retirement was "universally accepted."

In its final form the ADEA banned discriminatory practices predicated upon age—refusals to hire, terminations, disparate treatment in leave or vacation policies and on-the-job rights, bias in employment advertisements—and protected individuals between 40 and 65. But the ADEA proposed an enforcement mechanism that hindered many individuals in seeking relief from these discriminatory practices.

Early drafts of the Act vested enforcement in the Federal Government, charging the Secretary of Labor with responsibility to investigate allegations of discrimination and empowering the Secretary, on a finding of discrimination, to issue a "cease-and-desist" order. A violator could seek review of that on order in a Federal Court of Appeals; a complainant dissatisfied with an adverse finding could similarly compel judicial scrutiny. This approach, used successfully to enforce the rights created by the National Labor Relations Act, would have put the enormous power and resources of the government behind the statute.

As it had done when the same technique was initially proposed as the enforcement scheme for Title VII of the Civil Rights Act of 1964, the business community objected and won. As enacted the ADEA placed the primary enforcement burden on the individual alleging discrimination. The Act required any person charging an ADEA violation to file a complaint with the Secretary, and mandated that the Labor Department attempt conciliation. The Secretary was empowered to sue on behalf of a complainant, but Congress sharply limited Department appropriations for this purpose. During the first decade of enforcing the Act, the Labor Department never filed more than 50 suits in any year. While many of those suits were significant, the fact remains that most individuals attempting to vindicate their right to be free from age discrimination were left to their own resources.* For thousands of potential plaintiffs, many of whom were unemployed, the costs of paying lawyers and taking on large corporations were surely prohibitive.

Moreover, ambiguous wording of the statute guaranteed problems for the first generation of ADEA litigants. The task of deciphering the meaning of the procedural and substantive provisions of the Act produced a decade of bewildering and confusing Federal court decisions. Also, the Labor Department interpreted the Act to exclude apprenticeship and training programs from the reach of the prohibitions. Because such programs are critical avenues to employment, the effectiveness of the Act in dealing with unemployment among older persons—the very problem to which the law was addressed—was further constrained.

The 1967 Act marked the beginning of a new era in attacking job discrimination on the basis of age. Condemnation of "arbitrary age limits regardless of potential for job performance" became explicit national policy. In the classified advertising sections of newspapers, employers no longer could deter older applicants by stating their need for a "bright young assistant." More tangibly, over the first ten years of the Act's existence, some 14,000 victims of discrimination were found to be owed damages totaling more than $50 million.

If the original statute was a clear step forward, it was just as clearly not the end of the race to ban age discrimination. The 1978 ADEA amendments, discussed below, dealt with several of the larger defects, both substantive and procedural. However, protection under the Act is still denied to persons above certain ages, claimants must still jump through complicated procedural hoops, and exceptions to the Act's prohibitions have the potential for becoming major loopholes.

Enforcing the ADEA: The Government and the Courts

Prior to July 1979, in order to assert a right created by the ADEA, an individual was required to complain to the Department of

---

*The Department confined its litigation to suits involving plaintiffs attacking practices in large national corporations, and cases fleshing out the meaning of important substantive and procedural sections. In light of its limited resources, the Department's focus was wise.

Labor.* The Department's published records provide no clear index to the number of complaints received during the initial years of the Act's existence, but recent figures suggest that an explosion in the volume of charges did occur in the middle 1970s. By then over 5000 individuals annually alleged violations of the law. In nearly 30% of the charges, the Department found one or more violations to have taken place.**

The Department, through use of its conciliation powers, has helped thousands of discrimination victims recover lost wages and benefits. In 1978, the most current year for which data are available, nearly $4.8 million was restored to 1,363 individuals. That amount represented only one-third of the total amount of money the Department determined was owed to individuals. Three thousand people, owed another $10 million, were awaiting final resolution of their complaints or the initiation of legal proceedings.

Between 1969 and 1979, the decade during which the Labor Department was responsible for the ADEA, over $15 million was actually restored to injured parties. Despite this demonstrated effectiveness in assisting individuals, the major burden for enforcement has fallen upon the federal courts. In part that reflects the substantial responsibility placed upon individuals to vindicate their own rights. Accordingly, the development of the case law must be discussed briefly.

Procedural aspects of the ADEA generated case law conflict sufficiently great to lead the Labor Department to estimate that one-fourth of all complaints were dismissed before the merits of the discrimination claims were reached, for failure to conform to procedural requirements as *defined differently by different courts.* For example, most but not all courts held that the ADEA's "notice of intent to sue" provision demanded that to preserve the right to go to

*Section 7 (d) of the 1967 Act required an individual to file a notice of intent to sue with the Secretary of Labor in order to begin proceedings. P. L. 95–256 (1978) amended that provision to permit a simple filing of a charge. As of July 1, 1979, responsibility for enforcing the Act was transferred to the Equal Employment Opportunity Commission.
**The Secretary filed annual reports on the activities of the previous year under the Act (*Age Discrimination in Employment Act of 1967, A Report Covering Activities. . .).* That series is an invaluable resource for tracking government enforcement efforts. The data above are drawn from the 1978 report.

court, the notice had to meet strict legal standards even if filed by a nonlawyer.*

The ADEA requires that notice be given to the employer within 180 days of an allegedly discriminatory act (300 days if the violation occurs in a state with comparable prohibitions against discrimination). Is this notice requirement strictly jurisdictional, that is, a requirement that must be met before a court can consider the case? Or is it more on the order of a statute of limitations? If the latter, the federal courts are empowered to excuse an untimely filing when equity demands it. Otherwise, one day after the statutory period expires, the right to sue is forfeited forever. The courts have split on this issue.**

The ADEA recognizes that numerous state laws, enforced by local agencies, also prohibit discrimination.*** The different notice requirements take cognizance of the state procedures. But does the Act require, as a condition precedent, that an individual actually utilize the state agencies in order to preserve federal rights? Six Courts of Appeal split down the middle; in one circuit alone, eight trial courts developed eight different rationales to explain their rulings. Finally, in *Oscar Mayer v. Evans* (1979) the Supreme Court ruled that invocation of state remedies were required. One justice explained that his concurrence was based not on the logic of the majority opinion but, rather, on the need to end the case law conflict.

Nor were procedural issues the only ones to split the judiciary. No issue produced, and continues to produce, more disarray than defining the scope of relief available to successful plaintiffs. Section 7(b) and (c) of the Act clearly state that a prevailing plaintiff is entitled to injunctive relief, an offer of employment, reinstatement or promotion, and recovery of lost wages and benefits. If the violation of the Act is willful, liquidated (double) damages may be awarded.

---

*See e.g., *Eklund v. Lubrizol Corp.*, 529 F. 2d 247 (6th Cir. 1978); *Reich v. Dow Badische*, 16 EPD 8224 (2d Cir. 1978); *contra Sutherland v. SFK Industries, Inc.*, 419 F. Supp. 610 (E. D. Pa. 1976).

**Compare *Dartt v. Shell Oil*, 539 F. 2d 1256 (10th Cir. 1976), *aff'd by an equally divided Court* 98 S. Ct. 600 (1977) with *Hiscott v. General Electric*, 521 F. 2d 632 (6th Cir. 1975). Congress felt compelled to comment on this issue during the enactment of the 1978 ADEA amendments, expressing the view that the filing requirements are not jurisdictional, and therefore were subject to equitable modification by the courts.

***The Secretary's annual report, noted *supra*, lists those laws and agencies.

However, does the law permit recovery for compensatory damages (emotional distress, pain, and suffering)? The statute does not explicitly state that such damages may be awarded, but it does permit (section 7(c)) the award of such "equitable relief as will effectuate the purposes" of the Act. Arguing that such monetary recovery must be available, the trial court in *Rogers v. Exxon Research** declared that ". . . the most pernicious effect of age discrimination is not to the pocketbook, but to the victims' self respect." Some courts have concurred, but an even larger number have held that the ADEA precludes compensatory damages.** The ultimate resolution of the matter is of no little import; the prospect of having to pay out sums far larger than back wages is likely to deter violations of the law.

Standards for scrutinizing defenses to claims of discrimination also required judicial interpretation.*** Like the Civil Rights Act with respect to sex, religion, and national origin, the ADEA permits employers to use age classifications when age is a "bona fide occupational qualification" (BFOQ). (Section 4(f)(1).) The underlying theory of the BFOQ is that there are occasions in which an otherwise impermissible classification correlates directly with the ability to perform certain work. Ceilings on age of entry and mandatory retirement at youthful ages are common in law enforcement, security work, fire fighting, and occupations that implicate public safety concerns. In all instances, the use of age for hiring and retirement purposes are defended as BFOQ's.

The Department of Labor challenged those employment practices. In essence, the Department sought to establish for age cases the same

---

*404 F. Supp. 324 (D. N. J. 1975). This holding was reversed, 550 F. 2d 834 (3rd Cir. 1977).
**A detailed discussion of the case law may be found in Selden and Sylvia, 1977. In 1978 Congress attempted to settle the dispute through construction of a legislative history attached to the ADEA amendments, P. L. 95-256. The Conference Committee Report asserted that "The ADEA as amended by this Act does not provide for remedies of a punitive nature." (Conference Report at 14). This continued to leave open the question of whether nontangible, yet nonpunitive damages, e.g., pain and suffering, are available.
***Besides the BFOQ defense discussed, the Act creates two additional defenses: cause and reasonable factors other than age. The federal regulations spelling out the meaning of reasonable factors other than age offered excellent protection for older people. Very little case law has evolved around this defense, but see *Coates v. National Cash Register Co.*, 433 F. Supp. 655 (W.D.Va. 1977). In *Coates* the defendant argued that the discharged employees were not the victims of age discrimination but had been terminated because they lacked the training possessed by younger people. The court found that the firm had systematically provided educational opportunities for younger workers but denied the same training and education to older workers.

rule that governed sex-BFOQ litigation under Title VII. That standard was enunciated in *Weeks v. Southern Bell Telephone and Telegraph,* 408 F. 2d 228, 235 (5th Cir. 1969):

> . . . the principle of non-discrimination requires that we hold that in order to rely upon the bona fide occupational qualification exception an employer has the burden of proving that he had reasonable cause to believe, that is, a factual basis for believing that all or substantially all women would be unable to perform safely and efficiently the duties of the job involved.

At first, the Department was not successful. In *Hodgson v. Greyhound Lines, Inc.,* 499 F. 2d 859 (7th Cir. 1974), the Court upheld the validity of a refusal to hire bus drivers over age 35, asserting that even a miniscule increase in the safety risk, documented only through generalized evidence of risk, could justify invoking a BFOQ. The Court held that *suppositions* connecting age, fitness, and safety were legally sufficient. Three years later in *Houghton v. McDonnell Douglas,* 553 F. 2d 561 (8th Cir. 1977), the Court rejected the *Greyhound* approach, ruling that a defendant had to show that advancing age precluded reliable individualized determinations of fitness and competence. The Supreme Court declined to review *Houghton:* at this writing it is unclear how widely the holding will be applied.

PRESSURES FOR STRONGER AGE LAW

At the same time the courts were grappling with discrete provisions of the ADEA, other litigation as well as nonlegal developments were combining to put pressure on Congress to enhance the quality and scope of protection afforded to older people. In 1974, Lt. Col. Robert Murgia, a retired Massachusetts police officer, contested his involuntary termination. Because nonfederal public employees were not covered by the ADEA at the time of his retirement, Murgia contended that mandatory retirement at age 50 violated the Equal Protection Clause of the Fourteenth Amendment to the Constitution. Murgia's arguments reflected what came to be the conventional constitutional attack on public employee forced retirement: that inflexible rules treat two identical classes of workers (those under and over the retirement age) differently on the basis of a wholly arbitrary and irrationally selected characteristic, thus intruding on an important right (continued governmental employment).*

The three-judge court hearing the case agreed with Murgia. The Commonwealth could introduce no evidence demonstrating either that at age 50 police became unfit or that medical testing was inadequate to measure significant decline or impairment. The court ruled that the Massachusetts statute was unconstitutional as applied to Murgia—the first time any Federal court had declared mandatory retirement illegal.**

As expected, the United States Supreme Court agreed to review *Murgia,* for the holding put *every* public employee mandatory retirement statute in jeopardy. Supreme Court review meant that for the first time national attention would be focused upon mandatory retirement and age discrimination. The Court ruled two years later (427 U.S. 307 (1976)). With only Justice Marshall in dissent, the Court held that mandatory retirement statutes need not be drawn precisely or even reflect legislative wisdom. The federal courts were ordered to defer to virtually any legislative judgments about the relationship between aging and ability to perform.***

Stimulated in part by the publicity surrounding *Murgia,* others, particularly teachers and civil servants whose work responsibilities raised none of the safety concerns surrounding law enforcement, pressed other courts to overturn forced retirement statutes.****

Still others disputed the view that the ADEA permitted com-

---

* Some subsequent plaintiffs alleged that forced retirement violated the due process prohibition against "irrebuttable presumptions," i.e. assumptions about characteristics attributed to an entire class without any opportunity for an individual class member to show his/her lack of that characteristic. For extended discussions of the constitutional doctrines, see the various law review articles cited at the end of the chapter.

** *Murgia v. Massachusetts Board of Retirement,* 376 F. Supp. 1140 (D. Mass. 1974). Prior to *Murgia* the courts generally held that mandatory retirement laws did not raise an issue of constitutional right. *McIlvaine v. Pennsylvania,* 415 U.S. 986 (1974), *dismissing* 309 A. 2d 810 (1973); *Weisbrod v. Lynn,* 420 U.S. 940 (1975), *aff'd* 383 F. Supp. 937 (D.D.C. 1974).

***The Murgia case is discussed in considerable detail in two articles by Selden, June, 1979; Spring, 1979.

****See for example *Gault v. Garrison,* 569 F. 2d 993 (7th Cir. 1977); *Klain v. Pennsylvania State University,* 434 F. Supp. 571 (M.D.Pa. 1977), *aff'd without opinion* 18 EPD 8681 (3rd Cir. 1978); *Johnson v. Lefkowitz,* 566 F. 2d 866 (2d Cir. 1977); and *Palmer v. Ticcione,* 433 F. Supp. 653 (E.D.N.Y. 1977), *aff'd* 16 EPD 8314 (2d Cir. 1978).

pulsory retirement earlier than age 65. This controversy played a major role in generating the public law changes of 1978.

When it first wrote regulations implementing the ADEA, the Labor Department took the position that Section 4(f)(2) permitted compulsory retirement at any age. But the Department reversed itself and initiated litigation asserting the right of employees to escape mandatory retirement until 65. Courts uniformly ruled that forced retirement at any age was sanctioned by the ADEA.* In 1976, the Court of Appeals for the Fourth Circuit held that United Air Lines had violated the Act in retiring Harris McMann, an executive, at age 60. The Court could not imagine that Congress had intended to permit a firm to retire a person one day but make it a violation of the law to refuse to hire that person for a job the very next day. *McMann v. United Air Lines*, 542 F. 2d 217 (4th Cir. 1976). The case was accepted for review by the Supreme Court, which prompted a group of Congressmen to undertake an effort to amend the Act to ban forced retirement completely before the Court could rule.

That there was by early 1977 a substantial congressional sentiment to amend the law traces its roots to these and other sources. Some legislators, notably Representatives Claude Pepper, Augustus Hawkins, and Paul Findlay, were long-time advocates of abolition. Without their commitment, nothing would have happened. But the economy, public opinion, and a unique public focus on older people played critical roles.

The publication in 1975 by the National Council on the Aging of a study done for it by pollster Louis Harris was vital. *The Myth and Reality of Aging in America* revealed that retirement was not the idyllic world so many people had envisioned. In addition to finding that millions of retirees wanted to work, Harris documented that forced retirement was overwhelmingly opposed by American citizens. Indeed, 86 percent of the public thought mandatory retirement wrong; even trade unionists, presumed to be strong supporters of involuntary retirement, opposed the practice.

Throughout the 1960s and 1970s an enormous body of literature was developed by NCOA and others that conclusively demonstrated the extraordinary capability of older people to work. NCOA

---

* See *Brennan v. Taft Broadcasting*, 500 F. 2d 212 (5th Cir. 1974).

pioneered sophisticated age-neutral testing procedures by which employers could accurately determine the competence and fitness of aging workers.*

A committee of the American Medical Association publicly declared that mandatory retirement was destructive of both the physical and emotional well-being of many who were forced out of work. (*AMA*, 1966). Perhaps even more critical, policy makers were being made aware that changing population and labor force trends posed serious problems for private and public treasuries. The population was unquestionably "graying." In absolute numbers and as a percentage of the whole, senior citizens had come to constitute a huge and growing minority. With younger people electing to have fewer children and more of the elderly actually living longer, demographers forecast that by the end of the 20th century America would be an older society. Given the persistence of existing rates of retirement and nonwork, a shrinking population of workers would have to support vast numbers of older citizens. Some labor force analysts projected that by the early years of the 21st century, there would only be two active workers to support each retiree, for of the anticipated 50 million persons 65 and over, only 5 million would be employed.**

The escalating costs of dependency were not simply for the future. One of the major items on the agenda of the 95th Congress, as it convened in early 1977, was a proposal to increase dramatically the Social Security tax paid by active workers to sustain some 19 million retirees and 11 million other Social Security beneficiaries. Not only, it should be added, was the Social Security system facing unique problems. Unfunded private pension liabilities, exacerbated by the pressure of early retirement, were reported to exceed $200 billion. The total of all unfunded pension liabilities, public and private, equalled the national debt of $600 billion (U.S. Senate Committee on Aging, 1975; Califano, 1978).

In addition, it was clear that older people continued to be victimized by joblessness. Between 1966 and 1977 the size of the unemployed population between 45 and 65 had increased, as had the size

* Readers interested in reviewing that literature would do well to read NCOA's quarterly publication *Aging and Work* (formerly *Industrial Gerontology*).
**See esp. Sheppard and Rix, 1977.

of the class of retirees who were willing and able to work but unable to secure good jobs.

Finally, all of these developments caught the attention of the media. In 1976 and 1977 the press discovered old people. *Time* and *Newsweek* devoted major cover stories to "the graying of America." CBS aired a one-hour documentary on retirement. Gray Panther founder Maggie Kuhn became an occasional guest on the Johnny Carson program. Indeed, Representative Pepper deftly used the sudden media interest in the elderly. In May 1977, a group of prominent older citizens who were media celebrities in their own right—actors Will Greer and Ruth Gordon, political figures Averell Harriman and Tommy Corcoran, and Kentucky Fried Chicken founder Colonel Harlan Sanders—appeared before the House Committee on Aging, chaired by Pepper to condemn mandatory retirement and discrimination. (U.S. House of Representatives Select Committee on Aging, 1977.)

THE 1978 AMENDMENTS TO THE AGE DISCRIMINATION IN EMPLOYMENT ACT

The growing public pressures for a stronger age law and abolition of compulsory retirement, the concern over labor force trends and the increasing tax burden on workers led to the enactment of the 1978 amendments to the ADEA. Those amendments constituted a major though less than total victory for senior citizens and their advocates.

The 1978 legislation eliminated most federal government forced retirement.* Abolition of civil service mandatory retirement reflected something more than age discrimination concerns. As part of his campaign for the presidency, Jimmy Carter promised to reorganize and reform the federal bureaucracy. In 1977 the administration attacked the rules that were perceived to give civil servants unbreachable job security. The administration's proposals were aimed at eliminating inflexible rules that subordinated judgments about individual merit to tenure. Thus the administration was logically compelled to support abolition of compulsory retirement: the practice blatantly contradicted the emphasis upon merit since it resulted

---

* Forced retirement in law enforcement and intelligence work, diplomatic service, and several other areas was left in place.

in the termination of competent employees. As Civil Service Commission Chair Alan K. Campbell told a House Committee, "Repeal of the mandatory age 70 retirement provision would certainly be more in keeping with the principles of true merit. . . ."

The fact that the government work force is young—between 1977 and 1981 only 30,000 federal workers would be affected by abolition—helped to make this provision noncontroversial. (U.S. House of Representatives Committee on Post Office and Civil Service, 5-9, 1977). The size of the *affected work force* was so small that abolition was viewed as an attractive experiment to test its impact on personnel practices and labor force trends.

Beyond the federal work force provision, the legislation raised the ceiling on Act protection to 70 and explicitly banned mandatory retirement earlier than that age except where age is a BFOQ.* The bill evoked virtually no opposition in the House, but not because none existed. The proposal had at least two powerful enemies: the leadership of the AFL-CIO and the business community. But those two groups were themselves engaged as adversaries in ferocious battles over labor law reform and the minimum wage. Neither anticipated Congressional action in 1977; both declined invitations to testify. With no visible resistance to the measure, and the press following the legislation closely, House members had every reason to vote for a measure being characterized as an employment bill of rights for older Americans. Passage through the Senate was not nearly so smooth. In public, and more passionately in private, lobbyists from several universities, unions, and the business community (the Chamber of Commerce and Business Roundtable) fought to preserve their discretionary power.

The opposition was cast as a defense of the prevailing employment posture. The major impact of the law would be to permit people who were going to be forced to leave work in their 50s or early 60s to work until age 70. That, opponents argued, would significantly reduce job opportunities for young people entering the labor force as well as block promotions for those already employed. The Chamber

---

* The final bill provided for the right to a jury trial, but between the time the House and Senate each passed the bill in 1977, and the time the compromise version was enacted in April 1978, the Supreme Court ruled that the 1967 Act guaranteed that right. *Lorilard v. Pons,* 434 U.S. 575 (1978). Another provision of the new law changed the notice requirement to a simple charge. (See Selden, *EEOC Manual,* 1979.)

of Commerce and some unions contended that the amendments would have a devastating impact on affirmative action programs for women and racial minorities, a charge echoed by the National Association for the Advancement of Colored People and the National Urban League.

As a consequence of this opposition, Senators wanted assurances from the Labor Department and aging advocacy groups that the law reform did not threaten existing labor force practices. They received those assurances. Officials of the Labor Department and the National Retired Teachers Association/American Association of Retired Persons predicted that no more than 200,000 people a year would exercise their right to work beyond age 65, hardly sufficient to affect affirmative action, promotions or new opportunities.*

By the time the bill reached the Senate floor, it was no longer spoken of as a vehicle to ease the tax burden on younger people, relieve the pressure on pension systems, or stem unemployment; the measure had become a bill of rights for that small minority of older people who wanted to work a little longer. Leading off the Senate debate, Harrison Williams took note of the arguments that the amendments would have "a severe impact" on employment trends. That gave him pause, but, he told the Senators, the experts assured him that almost no one was going to take advantage of the law. On the House side, Representative Paul Findlay, a long-time abolitionist, described the Act as preserving "an important right for the few who need or want to keep working. . . ."

As finally enacted, the bill contained some exceptions affecting highly compensated executives, college professors, and collective bargaining agreements.** More importantly, at the insistence of the Senate, the Congress carefully constructed a legislative history designed to shape new regulations governing the benefit rights of

---

* See the testimony of Carin Ann Clauss, Lauren Selden, and the representatives of the Chamber of Commerce and the AFL-CIO (U.S. Senate Human Resources Committee, 1977). The basis for the forecast is explained in the Clauss and Selden testimony. The figure was extrapolated from old studies of labor force trends that included information on institutions with flexible retirement rules. There is a weakness in those studies—they cover time periods when pre-65 forced retirement was lawful.

**The Act sanctions forced retirement at 65 for executives receiving $27,000 annually in retirement pay, permits until 1982 some professors to be forced to retire at 65, and phased in the age 70 rule where agreements were negotiated through collective bargaining. Selden, (*EEOC Manual,* 1979) discusses the exceptions in detail.

those who elected to work past age 65. The rules dictated by Congress permit employers to limit the amount spent on the benefits of the over-65 employee to that spent on behalf of those under 65, even though that may entail lesser benefits for the older worker. The floor managers of the Act in both Houses stated that the amended law did not require accrual of pension benefits by those working beyond "normal retirement age." Subsequent Labor Department regulations faithfully followed the legislative history. In most instances, pension benefits may be frozen at age 65.* Some critics of the benefit regulations argue that the Act has been interpreted to sanction the type of disparate treatment the law should prohibit. Only time will tell if the rules actually discourage longer careers.

In the final analysis, however, the 1978 legislation unquestionably enhanced the employment rights of older people and continued Congress on the path first embarked upon a decade earlier.

THE FUTURE

In the opening Section of the 1967 Act, Congress declared that:

1. In the face of rising productivity and affluence, older workers find themselves disadvantaged in their efforts to retain employment, and especially to regain employment when displaced from jobs;
2. The setting of arbitrary age limits regardless of potential for job performance has become a common practice, and certain otherwise desirable practices may work to the disadvantage of older persons;
3. The incidence of unemployment, especially long-term unemployment with resultant deterioration of skills, morale, and employer acceptability is, relative to younger ages, high among older workers; their numbers are great and growing, and their employment problems grave . . . . . (29 U.S.C. § 621).

---

*That legislative history may not have provided infallible guidance. Several legislators claimed that their formulation of the impact of the Act on benefits was supported by the Department of Labor's analysis of the issues. The only Department communication placed in the record, and the communication to which those legislators specifically referred, addressed only defined benefit plans. Selden, 1979, discusses the regulations. The Equal Employment Opportunity Commission, which now enforces the ADEA, is reviewing the rules.

During the decade between the original enactment and the 1978 amendments, unemployment among those protected by the ADEA increased, as did the number of retirees wanting work.

That is only part of the story. The big boost in Social Security benefits that occurred in the early 1970s reduced dramatically the number of persons over 65 with incomes below the official poverty line. But the economic crisis of the 1970s hit the elderly hard indeed. In 1979 Mollie Orshansky, the Social Security Administration's foremost poverty expert, reported that 36 percent of the older citizenry lives in poverty—two-and-one-half times the official rate. (Binstock, 5, 1979).

Unleavened optimism hardly seems warranted, but there are some grounds for hope.

The seeds for "uncapping" the ADEA, that is, protecting even persons over 70 from age discrimination, were sown in the enactment of the 1978 amendments. Unable to eliminate age 70 as the upper limit for protection under the Act, the "abolitionists" insisted on a requirement designed to lead to that result. Section 5(a)(1) of ADEA requires the Secretary of Labor to study the impact of increasing the maximum age of protection from 65 to 70, and report on "the feasibility of eliminating such limitation. . . ." The report must be submitted to Congress and the President by January 1, 1982 (an interim report was due a year earlier). If the report finds that raising or removing the upper age limit would be "feasible" it will trigger efforts in Congress to legislate changes to ADEA in that direction. Close scrutiny is also likely for the various exceptions to the Act's prohibitions—specific ones like that for certain highly paid executives, and more general ones such as the use of age as a bona fide occupational qualification.

The Congress is not the only forum in which mandatory retirement is open to attack. Increasingly, state legislatures are rejecting the notion that arbitrary age terminations serve any purpose other than administrative convenience. California has abolished involuntary retirement altogether; Florida, Maine, Connecticut, Massachusetts and several localities have repealed their public employee forced retirement laws.* With older Americans increasingly organized,

* On Maine see Riley, 1978. On California see Schickman, 1979.

pressure will surely be exerted in other states. The example set by the
states may well make it easier for Congress to take the final step and
remove the ADEA ceiling on the age of protection entirely.* Indeed, if several large states ban compulsory retirement there will be
no incentive for firms in interstate commerce to resist a national prohibition.

As the issue continues to come before legislative bodies, business
opposition to abolition is likely to be muted. In the 1960s and 1970s,
managers articulated defenses of retirement rules that had questionable substance—for example, the role of forced retirement in facilitating both employee planning for retirement and employer calculations of pension funding obligations. During the 1977–1978 battle
in Congress, business argued that abolition would undermine affirmative action, slow down promotional opportunities and diminish
new job openings. Shortly after the amendments passed, the pres-
tigious Conference Board released a study showing that retirement
practices have little or nothing to do with these processes. (Meyer,
1978.)

The greatest single source of managerial support for inflexible retirement rules has been human inertia, and bureaucratic convenience. Most present-day personnel directors, supervisors, and executives have known no system but mandatory retirement. Yet as
management consultant James Walker has demonstrated, and several large corporations have discovered, administering a personnel
system predicated upon flexible retirement presents no insurmountable business problem. (Walker and Lazer, 1978)**

Even if mandatory retirement does not disappear soon, greater
compliance with the Act is likely. Perhaps more accurately, it is
reasonable to anticipate better ADEA enforcement. In part, more
widespread awareness of the Act on the part of aging workers should
generate more complaints. A changing political climate, coupled
with the recent shift in federal enforcement responsibility, may help
bring about a reduction in instances of discriminatory practices.

---

*The ADEA is not the only federal age discrimination statute likely to affect employment in
the 1980s. The Age Discrimination Act of 1975, 42 U.S.C. § 6001, went into effect in
mid-1979. The ADA bans age discrimination in programs and services receiving Federal
money. Once fully implemented, the ADA could have substantial impact on the operations of
the U.S. Employment Service and state employment agencies, as well as those of prime sponsors under the Comprehensive Employment and Training Act, 29 U.S.C 801.
**Also see Mercer, 1977.

The commitment of Labor Department professionals to the civil rights principles of the ADEA over the years has been singular. The goal of combatting age discrimination, however, was forced to compete for resources within the Department with far broader employment policy objectives. Until 1978, ADEA enforcement expenditures were limited by statute to a maximum of $5 million. Actual expenditures never exceeded 60 percent of that amount.

The ADEA is now the responsibility of the Equal Employment Opportunity Commission (EEOC), an independent agency with strong ties to the civil rights movement and considerable support in Congress. Aging community leaders at first expressed reservations about the transfer, fearing that age complaints might receive something less than high priority in light of the volume of race and sex discrimination charges filed with the Commission. That possibility still remains. But the shift could lead older citizens' organizations into an alliance with the women's movement and the civil rights coalitions. An alliance of all discrimination victims might help effect the changes necessary to upgrade the EEOC's ability to root out illegal practices. Indeed, for several years, legislative proposals to amend Title VII to include age among the protected classes have been discussed. The transfer of ADEA enforcement to the EEOC may give new impetus to those proposals.

Yet another dividend could flow from the shift to the EEOC. *Oscar Mayer v. Evans, supra,* requires that state agencies, where they exist, be given first crack at ADEA complaints. The Commission is now channeling federal funds to the agencies to improve their operations, as they have done in the past for Title VII state agencies. The greater involvement of state officials in age problems *may* build yet another institutional force for more law reform on the local level.

Changing business attitudes, increased awareness of the law by employers and employees, and a greater enforcement effort may well reduce age-based discrimination in hiring, firing, and on-the-job conditions. The ADEA no doubt plays a role in keeping aging workers in the labor force, but it is by no means clear that a prohibition against discrimination can in the long run deal with the more fundamental problem of opportunity.

Some students of public policy predict that the demographics of American society will lead to expanding work choices for older people. As the population "ages," and relatively fewer young people enter the labor market, the work of people in their 60s and 70s will be necessary, it is presumed, to sustain economic growth and productivity. Moreover, the costs of dependency should create additional incentives to keep people working longer. (Sheppard and Rix, 1977.) Already there is considerable discussion of job sharing, second careers, and alternatives to the existing cycle of work and leisure. Nevertheless, long-term change demands a reversal of the national employment policy.

The fact remains that at present about 5 million citizens over age 40 are out of work and want employment. Over 4 million of them are not classified as unemployed because they are "retirees." The Humphrey-Hawkins Full Employment and Balanced Growth Act of 1978, which theoretically committed government resources to full employment, remains to be implemented. Representative Hawkins recently charged that the administration has ignored the law and thus delayed any hope that full employment can be achieved for several years. (Hawkins, 1979)

The great economic boom of the post-World War II era has apparently ended. Hard times produce victims and exclusion. A prolonged slump is bound to delay the time when our society dedicates itself to producing work for all who need and want work. But that in the final analysis is the one necessary change in public posture which can end discrimination against aging Americans.

REFERENCES

American Medical Association. *Retirement, A Medical Philosophy and Approach,* Chicago: AMA, 1966.

Binstock, Robert H. A policy agenda on aging for the eighties, *Aging: Agenda for the Eighties,* Washington, D.C.: A National Journal Issues Book, 1979.

Butler, Robert N. *Why Survive? Being Old in America,* New York: Harper & Row, 1975.

Califano, Joseph A., Jr. Aging of America, questions for the four-generation society, Washington, D.C.: **438** *The Annals* 96.

Harris, Louis and Associates. *The Myth and Reality of Aging in America,* Washington, D.C.: National Council on the Aging, 1975.

Hawkins, Augustus. What ever happened to the Humphrey-Hawkins act?, *Equal Opportunity Forum,* February 1979.

Howard, Edward. Public policy report, *Perspective,* **VIII** (3):23, May/June 1979.

_____. Public policy report, *Perspective,* **VIII** (4):26, July/August 1979.

_____. Public policy report, *Perspective,* **VIII** (5):27, November/December 1979.

_____. On Capitol Hill—ADEA: Passing the torch, *Aging and Work,* **2**(3):210 Summer 1979.

_____. Mandatory retirement: Traumatic evidence of age discrimination, *Trial,* **13** (11):46–51, November 1977.

Law Review Articles:

The Age Discrimination in Employment Act of 1967, 90 Harv. L.R. 380, 1976.

August, Richard Lee. *Age Discrimination in Employment: Correcting a Constitutionally Infirm Legislative Judgement,* 47 So. Cal. L.R. 1311, 1974.

Bothelho, Bruce M., Cain, Leonard D. and Friedman, Stephen. *Mandatory Retirement: The Law, The Courts, and The Broader Social Context,* 11 Willamette L.J. 398, 1975.

Fox, Elaine S. *Mandatory Retirement—A Vehicle for Age Discrimination,* 51 Chi-Kent L.R. 116, 1974.

Kaplan, Terry S. *Too Old To Work: The Constitutionality of Mandatory Retirement Plans,* 44 So. Cal. L.R. 150, 1971.

Leuchtenburg, William E. *Franklin D. Roosevelt and the New Deal.* New York: Harper & Row, 1963.

Meier, Elizabeth. Implications for employment, *Aging in America,* Number 7, Washington, D.C.: National Council on the Aging, 1976.

Mercer, William M. *Employer Attitudes Toward Mandatory Retirement,* New York: William M. Mercer, Inc., 1977.

Meyer, Mitchell. *The Ban on Mandatory Retirement at 65: Managerial Responses,* New York: The Conference Board, 1978.

Peavy, Nancy. Approaching retirement age: Attitudes toward older workers and retirement policies in three companies, *Industrial Gerontology,* Winter 1975.

_____. NIIG conference on middle-aged and older workers: Costs and benefits to management, *Industrial Gerontology,* Winter 1973.

_____. The impact of middle-aged and older persons in the population and in the labor force, *Middle-Aged and Older Workers in Industry, Facts and Trends,* No. 2 (a five-part series), May 1973.

_____. Summary of provisions under state laws on age discrimination in employment, *Industrial Gerontology,* Summer 1973.

_____. The industrial health counseling service: An interview with three employer participants, *Industrial Gerontology,* Fall 1973.

_____. A comparative view of services to age groups as reported in the employment security automated reporting system, *Middle-Aged and Older Workers in Industry, Facts and Trends,* National Council on the Aging, Washington, D.C., No. 3, March 1974.

_____. ADEA: Recent decisions, settlements and pending cases, *Industrial Gerontology,* 198–202, Summer 1976; 252–258, Fall 1976; 46–52, Winter 1977; 126–129, Spring 1977; 198–204, Summer 1977; 264–271, Fall 1977.

_____. ADEA: A look at the courts, *Aging and Work* (formerly *Industrial Gerontology*) **1**(1):42–48, Winter 1978; **1**(2):122–127, Spring 1978; **1**(3):190, Summer 1978; **1**(4):260–263, Fall 1978: **2**(1):70–74, Winter 1979; **2**(2)114–117, Spring 1979; **2**(3):190–194, Summer 1979; *2*(4):260–265, Fall 1979.

Pratt, Henry J. *The Gray Lobby,* Chicago: University of Chicago Press, 1976.

Riley, Patricia A. Abolishing mandatory retirement in Maine, *Aging and Work* (formerly *Industrial Gerontology*), 1(1):15–24, Winter 1978.

Schickman, Mark I. California's new age discrimination law: An end to mandatory retirement, *Aging and Work* (formerly *Industrial Gerontology*) 2(1):53–58, Winter 1979.

Schlesinger, Arthur M., Jr. *The Age of Roosevelt: The Politics of Upheaval,* Chicago: Houghton-Mifflin, 1960.

Selden, Lauren. Less than superior performance: Mandatory retirement upheld, *Aging and Work* (formerly *Industrial Gerontology,* 2(2):118–124, Spring, 1979.

_____. The 1978 amendments to the age discrimination in employment act, *Equal Employment Opportunity Compliance Manual,* 1979.

_____. The over-65 worker and employee benefits under the ADEA amendments, *Equal Employment Opportunity Compliance Manual,* 1979.

_____. The supreme court and mandatory retirement, *Equal Opportunity Forum,* June 1979.

_____. and Corrine, Sylvia. Proposed amendments to the age discrimination in employment act, reprinted in *Senate Committee on Human Resources, Age Discrimination in Employment Amendments of 1977,* 95th Congress, 1st Session, 1977.

Sheppard, Harold and Rix, Sara E. *The Graying of America: The Coming Crisis in Retirement-Age Policy,* New York: Free Press, 1977.

United States Department of Labor. *Labor Force and Employment in 1965,* SLF Report No. 69, 1966.

United States Congress: House of Representatives Committee on Education and Labor Hearings, *Age Discrimination in Employment,* 90th Congress, 1st Session, 1967.

_____. House of Representatives Committee on Post Office and Civil Service, Hearings, *Elimination of Mandatory Retirement at Age 70,* 95th Congress, 1st Session, 1977.

_____. House of Representatives Select Committee on Aging, Hearings, *Active Americans Over 65 Speak Out on Retirement Age Policies,* 95th Congress, 1st Session, 1977.

_____. Senate Special Committee on Aging, Hearings, *Future Directions in Social Security,* Part II, 94th Congress, 1st Session, 1975.

_____. Senate Committee on Human Resources, Hearings, *Age Discrimination in Employment, Amendments of 1977,* 95th Congress, 1st Session, 1977.

_____. Senate Committee on Public Welfare, Hearings, *Age Discrimination in Employment,* 90th Congress, 1st Session, 1967.

Walker, James and Lazer, Harriet L. *End of Mandatory Retirement: Implications for Management,* New York: John Wiley and Sons, 1978.

_____. and Lupton, Daniel E. Performance appraisal programs and age discrimination law, *Aging and Work,* (formerly *Industrial Gerontology),* 1(2):73–83, Spring 1978.

The Age Discrimination in Employment Act of 1967, as amended*

(29 U.S.C. 621, et seq.)

AN ACT

To prohibit age discrimination in employment

Be it enacted by the Senate and House of Representatives of the United States of America in Congress assembled, that this Act may be cited as the "Age Discrimination in Employment Act of 1967".

STATEMENT OF FINDINGS AND PURPOSE

Sec. 2. (a) The Congress hereby finds and declares that—

(1) in the face of rising productivity and affluence, older workers find them-

---

* The original text of the Age Discrimination in Employment Act of 1967 is set in the "Century" typeface. Added or amended language as enacted by subsequent amendments is represented by other typefaces as indicated below.

Amendments	Typeface Used	Public Law	Date Enacted	Statute Citation
Original	Century	90–202	12/15/67	81 Stat. 602
1974	**Century Boldface**	**93–259**	**4/8/74**	**88 Stat. 55**
1978	*Century Italics*	*95–256*	*4/6/78*	*92 Stat. 189*

U.S. DEPARTMENT OF LABOR
Employment Standards Administration
Wage and Hour Division

WH Publication 1387 (Revised July 1978)

For sale by the Superintendent of Documents, U.S. Government Printing Office
Washington, D.C. 20402

Stock Number 029-005-00026-5

selves disadvantaged in their efforts to retain employment, and especially to regain employment when displaced from jobs;

(2) the setting of arbitrary age limits regardless of potential for job performance has become a common practice, and certain otherwise desirable practices may work to the disadvantage of older persons;

(3) the incidence of unemployment, especially long-term unemployment with resultant deterioration of skill, morale, and employer acceptability is, relative to the younger ages, high among older workers; their numbers are great and growing; and their employment problems grave;

(4) the existence in industries affecting commerce, of arbitrary discrimination in employment because of age, burdens commerce and the free flow of goods in commerce.

(b) It is therefore the purpose of this Act to promote employment of older persons based on their ability rather than age; to prohibit arbitrary age discrimination in employment; to help employers and workers find ways of meeting problems arising from the impact of age on employment.

EDUCATION AND RESEARCH PROGRAM

Sec. 3. (a) The Secretary of Labor shall undertake studies and provide information to labor unions, management, and the general public concerning the needs and abilities of older workers, and their potentials for continued employment and contribution to the economy. In order to achieve the purposes of this Act, the Secretary of Labor shall carry on a continuing program of education and information, under which he may, among other measures—

(1) undertake research, and promote research, with a view to reducing barriers to the employment of older persons, and the promotion of measures for utilizing their skills;

(2) publish and otherwise make available to employers, professional societies, the various media of communication, and other interested persons the findings of studies and other materials for the promotion of employment;

(3) foster through the public employment service system and through cooperative effort the development of facilities of public and private agencies for expanding the opportunities and potentials of older persons;

(4) sponsor and assist State and community informational and educational programs.

(b) Not later than six months after the effective date of this Act, the Secretary shall recommend to the Congress any measures he may deem desirable to change the lower or upper age limits set forth in section 12.

PROHIBITION OF AGE DISCRIMINATION

Sec. 4. (a) It shall be unlawful for an employer—

(1) to fail or refuse to hire or to discharge any individual or otherwise discrimi-

nate against any individual with respect to his compensation, terms, conditions, or privileges of employment, because of such individual's age;

(2) to limit, segregate, or classify his employees in any way which would deprive or tend to deprive any individual of employment opportunities or otherwise adversely affect his status as an employee, because of such individual's age; or

(3) to reduce the wage rate of any employee in order to comply with this Act.

(b) It shall be unlawful for an employment agency to fail or refuse to refer for employment, or otherwise to discriminate against, any individual because of such individual's age, or to classify or refer for employment any individual on the basis of such individual's age.

(c) It shall be unlawful for a labor organization—

(1) to exclude or to expel from its membership, or otherwise to discriminate against, any individual because of his age;

(2) to limit, segregate, or classify its membership, or to classify or fail or refuse to refer for employment any individual, in any way which would deprive or tend to deprive any individual of employment opportunities, or would limit such employment opportunities or otherwise adversely affect his status as an employee or as an applicant for employment, because of such individual's age;

(3) to cause or attempt to cause an employer to discriminate against an individual in violation of this section.

(d) It shall be unlawful for an employer to discriminate against any of his employees or applicants for employment, for an employment agency to discriminate against any individual, or for a labor organization to discriminate against any member thereof or applicant for membership, because such individual, member or applicant for membership has opposed any practice made unlawful by this section, or because such individual, member or applicant for membership has made a charge, testified, assisted, or participated in any manner in an investigation, proceeding, or litigation under this Act.

(e) It shall be unlawful for an employer, labor organization, or employment agency to print or publish, or cause to be printed or published, any notice or advertisement relating to employment by such an employer or membership in or any classification or referral for employment by such a labor organization, or relating to any classification or referral for employment by such an employment agency, indicating any preference, limitation, specification, or discrimination, based on age.

(f) It shall not be unlawful for an employer, employment agency, or labor organization—

(1) to take any action otherwise prohibited under subsections (a), (b), (c), or (e) of this section where age is a bona fide occupational qualification reasonably necessary to the normal operation of the particular business, or where the differentiation is based on reasonable factors other than age;

(2) to observe the terms of a bona fide seniority system or any bona fide employee benefit plan such as a retirement, pension, or insurance plan, which is not a subterfuge to evade the purposes of this Act, except that no such employee benefit plan shall excuse the failure to hire any individual, *and no such seniority system or employee benefit plan shall require or permit the involuntary retirement*

of any individual specified by section 12(a) of this Act because of the age of such individual;[1] or

(3) to discharge or otherwise discipline an individual for good cause.

STUDY BY SECRETARY OF LABOR

Sec. 5. (a)(1) The Secretary of Labor is directed to undertake an appropriate study of institutional and other arrangements giving rise to involuntary retirement, and report his findings and any appropriate legislative recommendations to the President and to the Congress. *Such study shall include—*

(A) an examination of the effect of the amendment made by section 3(a) of the Age Discrimination in Employment Act Amendments of 1978 in raising the upper age limitation established by section 12(a) of this Act to 70 years of age;

(B) a determination of the feasibility of eliminating such limitation;

(C) a determination of the feasibility of raising such limitation above 70 years of age; and

(D) an examination of the effect of the exemption contained in section 12(c), relating to certain executive employees, and the exemption contained in section 12(d), relating to tenured teaching personnel.

(2) The Secretary may undertake the study required by paragraph (1) of this subsection directly or by contract or other arrangement.

(b) The report required by subsection (a) of this section shall be transmitted to the President and to the Congress as an interim report not later than January 1, 1981, and in final form not later than January 1, 1982.

ADMINISTRATION

Sec. 6. The Secretary shall have the power—

(a) to make delegations, to appoint such agents and employees, and to pay for technical assistance on a fee for service basis, as he deems necessary to assist him in the performance of his functions under this Act;

(b) to cooperate with regional, State, local, and other agencies, and to cooperate with and furnish technical assistance to employers, labor organizations, and employment agencies to aid in effectuating the purposes of this Act.

---

[1] As amended by section 2(a) of the Age Discrimination in Employment Act Amendments of 1978. The effective date of this amendment is set forth in section 2(b) of the 1978 amendments: *"The amendment made by subsection (a) of this section shall take effect on the date of enactment of this Act, except that, in the case of employees covered by a collective bargaining agreement which is in effect on September 1, 1977, which was entered into by a labor organization (as defined by section 6(d)(4) of the Fair Labor Standards Act of 1938), and which would otherwise be prohibited by the amendment made by section 3(a) of this Act, the amendment made by subsection (a) of this section shall take effect upon the termination of such agreement or on January 1, 1980, whichever occurs first."* The revision of section 12 of the ADEA is the "amendment made by section 3(a) of this Act" referred to in the previous sentence.

RECORDKEEPING, INVESTIGATION, AND ENFORCEMENT

Sec. 7. (a) The Secretary shall have the power to make investigations and require the keeping of records necessary or appropriate for the administration of this Act in accordance with the powers and procedures provided in sections 9 and 11 of the Fair Labor Standards Act of 1938, as amended (29 U.S.C. 209 and 211).

(b) The provisions of this Act shall be enforced in accordance with the powers, remedies, and procedures provided in sections 11(b), 16 (except for subsection (a) thereof), and 17 of the Fair Labor Standards Act of 1938, as amended (29 U.S.C. 211(b), 216, 217), and subsection (c) of this section. Any act prohibited under section 4 of this Act shall be deemed to be a prohibited act under section 15 of the Fair Labor Standards Act of 1938, as amended (29 U.S.C. 215). Amounts owing to a person as a result of a violation of this Act shall be deemed to be unpaid minimum wages or unpaid overtime compensation for purposes of sections 16 and 17 of the Fair Labor Standards Act of 1938, as amended (29 U.S.C. 216, 217): *Provided,* That liquidated damages shall be payable only in cases of willful violations of this Act. In any action brought to enforce this Act the court shall have jurisdiction to grant such legal or equitable relief as may be appropriate to effectuate the purposes of this Act, including without limitation judgments compelling employment, reinstatement or promotion, or enforcing the liability for amounts deemed to be unpaid minimum wages or unpaid overtime compensation under this section. Before instituting any action under this section, the Secretary shall attempt to eliminate the discriminatory practice or practices alleged, and to effect voluntary compliance with requirements of this Act through informal methods of conciliation, conference, and persuasion.

(c)*(1)* Any person aggrieved may bring a civil action in any court of competent jurisdiction for such legal or equitable relief as will effectuate the purposes of this Act: *Provided,* That the right of any person to bring such action shall terminate upon the commencement of an action by the Secretary to enforce the right of such employee under this Act.

(2) In an action brought under paragraph (1), a person shall be entitled to a trial by jury of any issue of fact in any such action for recovery of amounts owing as a result of a violation of this Act, regardless of whether equitable relief is sought by any party in such action.[2]

(d) No civil action may be commenced by an individual under this section until 60 days after a charge alleging unlawful discrimination has been filed with the Secretary. Such a charge shall be filed—

(1) within 180 days after the alleged unlawful practice occurred; or

(2) in a case to which section 14(b) applies, within 300 days after the alleged unlawful practice occurred, or within 30 days after receipt by the individual of notice of termination of proceedings under State law, whichever is earlier.

Upon receiving such a charge, the Secretary shall promptly notify all persons named

---

[2] Effective with respect to civil actions brought after April 6, 1978.

in such charge as prospective defendants in the action and shall promptly seek to eliminate any alleged unlawful practice by informal methods of conciliation, conference, and persuasion.[3]

*(e)(1)*Sections 6 and 10 of the Portal-to-Portal Act of 1947 shall apply to actions under this Act.

(2) For the period during which the Secretary is attempting to effect voluntary compliance with requirements of this Act through informal methods of conciliation, conference, and persuasion pursuant to subsection (b), the statute of limitations as provided in section 6 of the Portal-to-Portal Act of 1947 shall be tolled, but in no event for a period in excess of one year.[4]

NOTICE TO BE POSTED

Sec. 8. Every employer, employment agency, and labor organization shall post and keep posted in conspicuous places upon its premises a notice to be prepared or approved by the Secretary setting forth information as the Secretary deems appropriate to effectuate the purposes of this Act.

RULES AND REGULATIONS

Sec. 9. In accordance with the provisions of subchapter II of chapter 5 of title 5, United States Code, the Secretary of Labor may issue such rules and regulations as he may consider necessary or appropriate for carrying out this Act, and may establish such reasonable exemptions to and from any or all provisions of this Act as he may find necessary and proper in the public interest.

CRIMINAL PENALTIES

Sec. 10. Whoever shall forcibly resist, oppose, impede, intimidate or interfere with a duly authorized representative of the Secretary while he is engaged in the performance of duties under this Act shall be punished by a fine of not more than $500 or by imprisonment for not more than one year, or both: *Provided, however,* That no person shall be imprisoned under this section except when there has been a prior conviction hereunder.

---

[3] Effective with respect to civil actions brought after April 6, 1978. Prior to the Age Discrimination in Employment Act Amendments of 1978, section 7(d) read as it does now, except that it required a "notice of intent to sue" rather than a "charge alleging unlawful discrimination."

[4] Effective with respect to conciliations commenced by the Secretary of Labor after April 6, 1978.

DEFINITIONS

Sec. 11. For the purposes of this Act—

(a) The term "person" means one or more individuals, partnerships, associations, labor organizations, corporations, business trusts, legal representatives, or any organized groups of persons.

(b) The term "employer" means a person engaged in an industry affecting commerce who has twenty[5] or more employees for each working day in each of twenty or more calendar weeks in the current or preceding calendar year: *Provided,* That prior to June 30, 1968, employers having fewer than fifty employees shall not be considered employers. **The term also means (1) any agent of such a person, and (2) a State or political subdivision of a State and any agency or instrumentality of a State or a political subdivision of a State, and any interstate agency, but such term does not include the United States, or a corporation wholly owned by the Government of the United States.**

(c) The term "employment agency" means any person regularly undertaking with or without compensation to procure employees for an employer and includes an agent of such a person; but shall not include an agency of the United States.[6]

(d) The term "labor organization" means a labor organization engaged in an industry affecting commerce, and any agent of such an organization, and includes any organization of any kind, any agency, or employee representation committee, group, association, or plan so engaged in which employees participate and which exists for the purpose, in whole or in part, of dealing with employers concerning grievances, labor disputes, wages, rates of pay, hours, or other terms or conditions of employment, and any conference, general committee, joint or system board, or joint council so engaged which is subordinate to a national or international labor organization.

(e) A labor organization shall be deemed to be engaged in an industry affecting commerce if (1) it maintains or operates a hiring hall or hiring office which procures employees for an employer or procures for employees opportunities to work for an employer, or (2) the number of its members (or, where it is a labor organization composed of other labor organizations or their representatives, if the aggregate number of the members of such other labor organization) is fifty or more prior to July 1, 1968, or twenty-five or more on or after July 1, 1968, and such labor organization—

(1) is the certified representative of employees under the provisions of the National Labor Relations Act, as amended, or the Railway Labor Act, as amended; or

(2) although not certified, is a national or international labor organization or a

---

[5] Section 28(a)(1) of the Fair Labor Standards Amendment of 1974 substituted "twenty" for "twenty-five," effective May 1, 1974.

[6] Prior to the Fair Labor Standards Amendments of 1974, the Act's definition of an "employment agency" excluded "an agency of a State or political subdivision of a State, except that such term shall include the United States Employment Service and the system of State and local employment services receiving Federal assistance."

local labor organization recognized or acting as the representative of employees of an employer or employers engaged in an industry affecting commerce; or

(3) has chartered a local labor organization or subsidiary body which is representing or actively seeking to represent employees of employers within the meaning of paragraph (1) or (2); or

(4) has been chartered by a labor organization representing or actively seeking to represent employees within the meaning of paragraph (1) or (2) as the local or subordinate body through which such employees may enjoy membership or become affiliated with such labor organization; or

(5) is a conference, general committee, joint or system board, or joint council subordinate to a national or international labor organization, which includes a labor organization engaged in an industry affecting commerce within the meaning of any of the preceding paragraphs of this subsection.

(f) The term "employee" means an individual employed by any employer except that the term "employee" shall not include any person elected to public office in any State or political subdivision of any State by the qualified voters thereof, or any person chosen by such officer to be on such officer's personal staff, or an appointee on the policymaking level or an immediate adviser with respect to the exercise of the constitutional or legal powers of the office. The exemption set forth in the preceding sentence shall not include employees subject to the civil service laws of a State government, governmental agency, or political subdivision.

(g) The term "commerce" means trade, traffic, commerce, transportation, transmission, or communication among the several States; or between a State and any place outside thereof; or within the District of Columbia, or a possession of the United States; or between points in the same State but through a point outside thereof.

(h) The term "industry affecting commerce" means any activity, business, or industry in commerce or in which a labor dispute would hinder or obstruct commerce or the free flow of commerce and includes any activity or industry "affecting commerce" within the meaning of the Labor-Management Reporting and Disclosure Act of 1959.

(i) The term "State" includes a State of the United States, the District of Columbia, Puerto Rico, the Virgin Islands, American Samoa, Guam, Wake Island, the Canal Zone, and Outer Continental Shelf lands defined in the Outer Continental Shelf Lands Act.

AGE LIMITATION

Sec. 12. (a)[7] *The prohibitions in this Act shall be limited to individuals who are at least 40 years of age but less than 70 years of age.*

(b)[8] In the case of any personnel action affecting employees or applicants for

---

[7] Subsection 12(a) takes effect on January 1, 1979. Prior to the Age Discrimination in Employment Act Amendments of 1978, section 12 provided in its entirety: "The prohibitions in this Act shall be limited to individuals who are at least forty years of age but less than sixty-five years of age."

[8] Subsection 12(b), which was added by the 1978 Amendments, takes effect on September 30, 1978.

employment which is subject to the provisions of section 15 of this Act, the prohibitions established in section 15 of this Act shall be limited to individuals who are at
least 40 years of age.

(c)[9](1) Nothing in this Act shall be construed to prohibit compulsory retirement of
any employee who has attained 65 years of age but not 70 years of age, and who, for
the 2-year period immediately before retirement, is employed in a bona fide executive or a high policymaking position, if such employee is entitled to an immediate
nonforfeitable annual retirement benefit from a pension, profit-sharing, savings, or
deferred compensation plan, or any combination of such plans, of the employer of
such employee, which equals, in the aggregate, at least $27,000.

(2) In applying the retirement benefit test of paragraph (1) of this subsection, if
any such retirement benefit is in a form other than a straight life annuity (with no
ancillary benefits), or if employees contribute to any such plan or make rollover contributions, such benefit shall be adjusted in accordance with regulations prescribed
by the Secretary, after consultation with the Secretary of the Treasury, so that the
benefit is the equivalent of a straight life annuity (with no ancillary benefits) under a
plan to which employees do not contribute and under which no rollover contributions are made.

(d)[10] Nothing in this Act shall be construed to prohibit compulsory retirement of
any employee who has attained 65 years of age but not 70 years of age, and who is
serving under a contract of unlimited tenure (or similar arrangement providing for
unlimited tenure) at an institution of higher education (as defined by section 1201(a)
of the Higher Education Act of 1965).

ANNUAL REPORT

Sec. 13. The Secretary shall submit annually in January a report to the Congress
covering his activities for the preceding year and including such information, data,
and recommendations for further legislation in connection with the matters covered
by this Act as he may find advisable. Such report shall contain an evaluation and appraisal by the Secretary of the effect of the minimum and maximum ages established
by this Act, together with his recommendations to the Congress. In making such
evaluation and appraisal, the Secretary shall take into consideration any changes
which may have occurred in the general age level of the population, the effect of the
Act upon workers not covered by its provisions, and such other factors as he may
deem pertinent.

FEDERAL-STATE RELATIONSHIP

Sec. 14. (a) Nothing in this Act shall affect the jurisdiction of any agency of any
state performing like functions with regard to discriminatory employment practices
on account of age except that upon commencement of action under this Act such action shall supersede any State action.

[9] Subsection 12(c), which was added by the 1978 Amendments, takes effect on January 1,
1979.
[10] Subsection 12(d), which was added by the 1978 Amendments, takes effect on January 1,
1979. It is repealed on July 1, 1982.

(b) In the case of an alleged unlawful practice occurring in a State which has a law prohibiting discrimination in employment because of age and establishing or authorizing a State authority to grant or seek relief from such discriminatory practice, no suit may be brought under section 7 of this Act before the expiration of sixty days after proceedings have been commenced under the State law, unless such proceedings have been earlier terminated: *Provided,* That such sixty-day period shall be extended to one hundred and twenty days during the first year after the effective date of such State law. If any requirement for the commencement of such proceedings is imposed by a State authority other than a requirement of the filing of a written and signed statement of the facts upon which the proceeding is based, the proceeding shall be deemed to have been commenced for the purposes of this subsection at the time such statement is sent by registered mail to the appropriate State authority.

NONDISCRIMINATION ON ACCOUNT OF AGE IN FEDERAL GOVERNMENT EMPLOYMENT

Sec. 15 (a) All personnel actions affecting employees or applicants for employment *who are at least 40 years of age* (except *personnel actions* with regard to aliens employed outside the limits of the United States) in military departments as defined in section 102 of title 5, United States Code, in executive agencies as defined in section 105 of title 5, United States Code (including employees and applicants for employment who are paid from nonappropriated funds), in the United States Postal Service and the Postal Rate Commission, in those units in the government of the District of Columbia having positions in the competitive service, and in those units of the legislative and judicial branches of the Federal Government having positions in the competitive service, and in the Library of Congress shall be made free from any discrimination based on age.

(b) Except as otherwise provided in this subsection, the Civil Service Commission is authorized to enforce the provisions of subsection (a) through appropriate remedies, including reinstatement or hiring of employees with or without backpay, as will effectuate the policies of this section. The Civil Service Commission shall issue such rules, regulations, orders, and instructions as it deems necessary and appropriate to carry out its responsibilities under this section. The Civil Service Commission shall—

(1) be responsible for the review and evaluation of the operation of all agency programs designed to carry out the policy of this section, periodically obtaining and publishing (on at least a semiannual basis) progress reports from each department, agency, or unit referred to in subsection (a);

(2) consult with and solicit the recommendations of interested individuals, groups, and organizations relating to nondiscrimination in employment on account of age; and

(3) provide for the acceptance and processing of complaints of discrimination in Federal Employment on account of age.

The head of each such department, agency, or unit shall comply with such rules, regulations, orders, and instructions of the Civil Service Commission which shall include a provision that an employee or applicant for employment shall be notified of any final action taken on any complaint of discrimination filed by him thereunder. Reasonable exemptions to the provisions of this section may be established by the Commission but only when the Commission has established a maximum age requirement on the basis of a determination that age is a bona fide occupational qualification necessary to the performance of the duties of the position. With respect to employment in the Library of Congress, authorities granted in this subsection to the Civil Service Commission shall be exercised by the Librarian of Congress.

(c) Any person aggrieved may bring a civil action in any Federal district court of competent jurisdiction for such legal or equitable relief as will effectuate the purposes of this Act.

(d) When the individual has not filed a complaint concerning age discrimination with the Commission, no civil action may be commenced by an individual under this section until the individual has given the Commission not less than thirty days' notice of an intent to file such action. Such notice shall be filed within one hundred and eighty days after the alleged unlawful practice occurred. Upon receiving a notice of intent to sue, the Commission shall promptly notify all persons named therein as prospective defendants in the action and take any appropriate action to assure the elimination of any unlawful practice.

(e) Nothing contained in this section shall relieve any Government agency or official of the responsibility to assure nondiscrimination on account of age in employment as required under any provision of Federal law.

(f)[11] Any personnel action of any department, agency, or other entity referred to in subsection (a) of this section shall not be subject to or affected by, any provision of this Act, other than the provisions of section 12(b) of this Act and the provisions of this section.

(g)[12] (1) The Civil Service Commission shall undertake a study relating to the effects of the amendments made to this section by the Age Discrimination in Employment Act Amendments of 1978, and the effects of section 12(b) of this Act, as added by the Age Discrimination in Employment Act Amendments of 1978.

(2) The Civil Service Commission shall transmit a report to the President and to the Congress containing the findings of the Commission resulting from the study of the Commission under paragraph (1) of this subsection. Such report shall be transmitted no later than January 1, 1980.

EFFECTIVE DATE[13]

Sec. 16. This Act shall become effective one hundred and eighty days after enactment, except (a) that the Secretary of Labor may extend the delay in effective date of any provision of this Act up to an additional ninety days thereafter if he finds that

[11] Effective September 30, 1978.

[12] Effective April 6, 1978.

[13] The effective date of the provisions added by the Fair Labor Standards Amendments of 1974, which are shown in bold face type, was May 1, 1974. See section 29(a) of the Fair Labor Standards Amendments of 1974. The effective dates of the provisions added by the Age Discrimination in Employment Act Amendments of 1978, which are shown in italic type, are indicated in footnotes to each provision.

such time is necessary in permitting adjustments to the provisions hereof, and (b) that on or after the date of enactment the Secretary of Labor is authorized to issue such rules and regulations as may be necessary to carry out its provisions.

APPROPRIATIONS

Sec. 17. There are hereby authorized to be appropriated such sums as may be necessary to carry out this Act.[14]

Approved December 15, 1967.

[14]Section 7 of the Age Discrimination in Employment Act Amendments of 1978 amended this section by eliminating the $5 million authorization ceiling on appropriations.

Additional Provisions of the Age Discrimination in Employment Act Amendments of 1978

(92 Stat. 189)

[PUBLIC LAW 95-256]

[95TH CONGRESS, 2D SESSION]

AN ACT

To amend the Age Discrimination in Employment Act of 1967 to extend the age group of employees who are protected by the provisions of such Act, and for other purposes.

Be it enacted by the Senate and House of Representatives of the United States of America in Congress assembled, That this Act may be cited as the "Age Discrimination in Employment Act Amendments of 1978".

[Sections 2 through 4, 5(a), 6 and 7 of the Age Discrimination in Employment Act Amendments of 1978 amend the Age Discrimination in Employment Act of 1967, and are incorporated in their proper place in the Act. Where the effective dates of these amendments are not part of the Act proper, they are noted in footnotes. Section 5(b), (c) and (d) of the 1978 Amendments amend title 5 of the United States Code, and are set forth below.]

FEDERAL GOVERNMENT EMPLOYMENT

Sec. 5.[15]**

(b)(1) Section 3322 of title 5, United States Code, relating to temporary appointments after age 70, is repealed.

(2) The analysis for chapter 33 of title 5, United States Code, is amended by striking out the item relating to section 3322.

---

[15] The amendments in Section 5(b), (c) and (d) take effect on September 30, 1978.

(c) Section 8335 of title 5, United States Code, relating to mandatory separation, is amended—

(1) by striking out subsections (a), (b), (c), (d), and (e) thereof;

(2) by redesignating subsections (f) and (g) as subsections (a) and (b), respectively; and

(3) by adding after subsection (b), as so redesignated, the following new subsections:

"(c) An employee of the Alaska Railroad in Alaska and an employee who is a citizen of the United States employed on the Isthmus of Panama by the Panama Canal Company or the Canal Zone Government, who becomes 62 years of age and completes 15 years of service in Alaska or on the Isthmus of Panama shall be automatically separated from the service. The separation is effective on the last day of the month in which the employee becomes age 62 or completes 15 years of service in Alaska or on the Isthmus of Panama if then over that age. The employing office shall notify the employee in writing of the date of separation at least 60 days in advance thereof. Action to separate the employee is not effective, without the consent of the employee, until the last day of the month in which the 60-day notice expires.

"(d) The President, by Executive order, may exempt an employee from automatic separation under this section when he determines the public interest so requires".

(d) Section 8339(d) of title 5, United States Code, relating to computation of annuity, is amended by striking out "section 8335(g)" and inserting in lieu thereof "section 8335(b)".

7
FLEXIBILITY IN RETIREMENT: U.S. AND INTERNATIONAL EXPERIENCE

Malcolm H. Morrison, Ph.D.

Throughout the industrialized world the growth of the aged population continues to be accompanied by the trend of early retirement. However, the rapidly escalating costs of public and private pension systems, the continuing pattern of high rates of inflation, and increasing social awareness have resulted in numerous proposals for increasing the development and implementation of flexible retirement options for older workers. These alternatives permit greater individual choice as to the time and degree of retirement and sometimes provide extended employment options for older workers. It is likely that flexible retirement will increase in the future in response to changing social and economic circumstances. This chapter discusses the emergence of alternative work patterns, outlines policies and programs which emphasize flexible retirement options, examines responses by governments, employers and older persons, and suggests further research to identify flexible worklife alternatives for older persons.

FLEXIBLE DISTRIBUTION OF WORK, EDUCATION AND LEISURE*

Over the past 75 years, industrialization accompanied by significant economic growth has resulted in a substantial reduction in the proportion of time spent at work. For the most part, this reduction

---

* I am indebted to Dr. Fred Best and Dr. Barry Stern for suggesting the basic outline of this discussion.

has resulted from a major decline in weekly hours worked. In fact, the average U.S. workweek has declined from approximately 60 hours to 39 hours over the past century. (Hedges and Moore, 1971) Over the last 40 years, however, the workweek has remained quite stable and most of the reduction in working time has been in the form of vacations and holidays. (Owen, 1976) In addition, the growth of nonwork time has expanded to encompass increased periods of *schooling* (usually early in life) and *retirement* during the later years of life. The result of these patterns has been the development of the linear life pattern—going to school in youth, working during middle years, and retiring in old age. To some extent this pattern of life scheduling can be viewed as a result of the natural requirements of the life cycle and a response to conditions of industrialization. However, it appears that the emergence of the linear life pattern is primarily the result of expansion of nonwork time and competition for work between age groups. (Best and Stern, 1976) To a considerable degree, the compression of work activity primarily into midlife is the result of factors of advanced industrialization which have resulted in job shortages and the creation of policies to preserve job opportunities for persons in the middle of the life cycle.

Suggestions have been made that the continuation and extension of the linear life pattern will intensify certain social problems particularly related to jobs for youth and older workers (Best and Stern, 1976). Of course, as earlier chapters have demonstrated, the continuous encouragement of early retirement is already resulting in rapidly escalating support costs for the remaining workforce.

The current linear life pattern may in fact be dysfunctional for several working age groups, young, middle-aged and old—who must share the available job opportunities. Of course, the basic shortage of jobs in the United States continues to result in serious employment problems for youth and older workers who are most seriously affected by the linear life approach. Furthermore, evidence is available which indicates serious inequities in the distribution of work *within* age groups. First, statistics demonstrate that a large proportion of new jobs created between 1960 and 1970 were in the low skill, low pay category and went to youths under age 25 and mature women. A similar trend occurs for minority group workers who were less well represented in midlevel jobs and had disproportionate representation in lower level jobs. In general, growth in youth employment continues to be in low-level jobs with little career potential. (Freedman, 1976) In addition, jobs are not equitably distributed within the largest group of workers aged 25–65. Persons holding the lowest status positions have both less leisure time and the least educational benefits. (Quinn and Sheppard, 1974) Of course, the availability of employment for older workers is severely constrained by early retirement policies and the lure of presumably sufficient pension benefits. In addition, serious negative attitudinal barriers influence employer hiring and job retention policies neither of which are structured to benefit older workers.

Several serious problems now exist coincidentally with the strong linear life pattern. Among these are: (1) severe competition for jobs by members of the post-war cohorts, trained minority group job seekers, and women labor force reentrants; (2) continuing job shortages; and (3) increasing desire of all age groups for job equality despite present inequities. If the current linear pattern of distribution of work, education and leisure continues, the above mentioned problems are likely to increase in intensity with the likely exacerbation of problems of youth and older workers. The various inequities in work distribution related to the linear life pattern are already resulting in a growing support burden (particularly for retired and disabled workers) on the remaining workforce. The retention or enhancement of the present regularized linear, education-work-retirement pattern with extensions of periods of nonwork will result in even higher support costs for workers *and* increase tensions between groups of workers. A pattern involving more flexible distribution of education, work and leisure which would re-distribute the extended periods of nonwork time now spent in youth and older age to the middle years of life (for pursuing education, leisure or part-time employment) is a reasonable response to the dysfunctional aspects of the current linear life pattern. (Best and Stern, 1976)

There are indications that such a nonlinear pattern would meet with support from various types of workers, especially students, women, and older workers who could most benefit by implementation of alternative work patterns. Studies by Best and Stern (1977) also indicate that prime-age workers also prefer additional flexibility in work scheduling with the most popular approach being a modified cyclic life pattern with extended periods of free time in midlife *and* tapered or phased retirement.

While in principle many workers appear ready to alter the current rigid worklife patterns, there is no general agreement as to the best approaches to take in creating more flexible worklife options. Recommendations include approaches to redistribution of work (shorter workweeks, job sharing, part-time employment, public service jobs, short-time compensation programs, flexible retirement programs, etc.); leisure (extending vacation time, more liberal leave of absence provisions, flexible retirement programs); and education (voucher plans, paid or unpaid educational leave, work sabbaticals, utilization of unemployment insurance to support education and training). (Best and Stern, 1976) Obviously these proposals are not mutually exclusive, a change in one area will effect a change in the others.

Many of the above policies do not enjoy any real measure of public support particularly from organized labor interests who fear that such piecemeal redistributive steps might be harmful to full-time regular employees and might be utilized by business firms to reduce employment and/or fringe benefits. In addition, while the idea of providing more flexibility in work life through a more equitable distribution of work, leisure and education between young, middle-aged, and older workers, is appealing, the development of a national policy to restructure and redistribute employment opportunity is quite unlikely. Fortunately, however, there is far less opposition to the creation of modified worklife patterns for older employees many of whom wish to retain some connection to employment.

RETIREMENT PATTERNS

The gradual institutionalization of retirement has resulted in making retirement policy an issue of major national concern. Attention is now focused on the problems of maintaining the financial stability of the Social Security system, regulating the provision of private pension benefits (Employee Retirement Income Security Act) and assuring the "right" to employment for older workers (Age Discrimination in Employment Act). Recent legislation—Age Discrimination in Employment Act amendments of 1978—prohibiting mandatory retirement before age 70 for most private sector employees, has served to intensify concern with labor force participation by present and future cohorts of older workers. The changing composition of the U.S. work force and the influence of this new legislation are being widely discussed with relation to adjustments in corporate personnel and pension policies. Despite the continued prevalence of the early retirement trend, there are a number of factors which are likely to result in later retirement for a growing proportion of the older work force in the years ahead. Among the most important of these are the gradual aging of the population and workforce, longer life expectancy, and the concomitant increasing financial support burden for a growing older population.

In most countries with "mature" pension systems, the continuous aging of the population accompanied by increasingly earlier retirement by many workers is already resulting in serious economic pressure on shrinking work forces to finance growing retirement benefit payments. Over the past 20 years most industrialized countries have introduced a variety of so-called "flexible" retirement provisions in public pension systems. Almost all of these policies allow for early retirement before the normal retirement age in order to provide benefits to workers who have had hazardous employment, suffer health problems, or prolonged unemployment. Such early retirement policies have been based on the presumed need to provide job opportunities for younger labor force entrants. They, of course, demonstrate one aspect of the linear life pattern approach— extending the period of retirement. Continuation of the trend of lowered retirement age will increase the financing problems of pension systems. Some have predicted that this will result in a slowing of the early retirement trend as more experimentation with later retirement takes place. (Tracy, 1978, Rehn, 1977) Thus far few countries have responded to this problem by developing flexible public retirement pension policies which encourage continued employment of older workers, nor have many business and governmental organizations developed pension and personnel policies which reflect this objective.

Due to the relatively recent recognition of the problems of aging workforces, the concept of "flexible retirement" has not as yet been clearly defined nor relevant policy options identified. In fact, the amount of research and experimentation conducted thus far has been quite limited. There remain many unanswered questions where empirical research data are lacking. We do not, for example, have comprehensive data on U.S. or foreign firms providing flexible retirement options, nor do we know how many employees have access to or would take advantage of such options if they were available. We have only limited information on the potential response of U.S. workers to the legislation raising the age for mandatory retirement to seventy. Furthermore, there has been little if any policy analysis in the area of creating more flexibility through modification of public and private pension policies. Obtaining answers to these questions will require substantial research effort. Some initial research on age discrimination, involuntary retirement, and part-time employment opportunities is under way (U.S. Department of Labor, 1980; U.S. Department of Health and Human Services, 1979, 1980) but the development of public retirement policy and corporate personnel and pension policy to expand flexible retirement options will require more focused research studies which examine both institutional policies and individual preferences.

Despite these informational limitations it is useful to review recent evidence concerning the preferred form of labor force participation by older workers, examine various flexible retirement policies and programs now functioning and suggest how managements can best prepare organizations in adapting to the upcoming aging of the workforce.

OLDER EMPLOYEE PREFERENCES

Evidence presented in earlier chapters has demonstrated that while increasing numbers of older employees are choosing early retirement, many older individuals may desire to continue to work on a part-time basis. While the early retirement trend is clearly predominant, there is some question as to whether the expressed part-time employment preferences of older employees are being actualized through employment. Evidence suggests that although more older persons wish to work part-time, many cannot locate such employment. They either retire completely, lose their jobs and experience great difficulty in finding subsequent employment, or (in a small number of cases) continue to work full time. While some have speculated that raising the age for mandatory retirement, increasing Social Security benefits if retirement is delayed, and worsening economic conditions will lead to increased part-time employment of older workers, the emergence of such a trend is far from certain. Early studies of the consequences of a higher mandatory retirement age indicate that the early retirement trend is continuing unabated. (Copperman, 1979, Spencer Associates, 1979)

The barriers to employment faced by older workers whether "substantive" or "attitudinal" are not likely to disappear in the near future. Older workers are frequently less well educated and more likely to experience skill obsolescence than younger persons. Irrespective of health status, employers continue to apply negative stereotypes to older workers, limiting their chances for retention and/or initial employment. Employers also believe that costs for fringe benefits are higher for older employees—especially new hires. Determining whether fringe benefit costs are greater for older employees is difficult since various insurance benefits are often determined based on corporate experience—"experience rated" (not based on ages of employees) and since pension benefit formulas are not necessarily more costly for older employees. Furthermore, the Age Discrimination in Employment Act does not require accrual of pension benefits beyond the normal retirement age in the pension plan. Therefore, older employees may be retained without any additional pension costs to firms. While some initial studies are under way which will investigate fringe benefit costs for older employees, this area will require far more detailed research before reliable conclusions as to costs can be suggested.

Today there are approximately 24 million persons over age 65 in this country—10.5 percent of the total population. In 1979, one quarter of all federal outlays directly benefited the aged through Social Security, Medicare, federal employee retirement, and various welfare programs. By the year 2000, there will be 32 million persons over age 65—13 percent of the total population. Projections indicate that 32 percent of all Federal outlays will then be expended for benefits to this population. By 2025, projections indicate that benefits for the aged will reach 63 percent of total Federal spending if present trends continue. (Storey and Hendricks, 1979) The financial consequences of rapidly escalating costs for retirement benefits are already causing deep concern for government policy planners. Due to indexing for inflation, these costs continue to rise increasing the fixed costs for government outlays. A continuation of current retirement patterns will only aggravate these financial support problems and intensify the search for alternatives to limit the trend of rapidly increasing expenditures.

One possible approach to limiting or at a minimum "spreading-out" the cost of future retirement payments would involve a shift of the traditional full retirement pattern toward *transitional* or *phased retirement* where older workers might gradually reduce working hours over a period of years before becoming "fully retired." Such an approach might be coupled with the development of a partial pension system which could supplement wages earned from part-time employment with partial pension payments. Both of these approaches of course represent a substantial departure from current policies and are more complex than such adjustments as raising the minimum age for receipt of Social Security benefits or shifting the financing of retirement payments from payroll to general revenue taxes. Yet, adjusting the linear life plan to create retirement flexibility would be a far more significant reform which could clearly benefit millions of middle-aged and older employees and assist the economy in adjusting to fewer younger labor force entrants in the years ahead. Movement in the direction of flexible retirement programs requires that older workers be provided with opportunities and incentive to stay in the labor force. Any significant modification of the early retirement trend will involve: (a) The actual availability of older employees for employment at least on a part-time basis; (b) the provision of incentives for continued employment through public (and possibly private) pension systems; and (c) provision of flexible work arrangements by employers.

PART-TIME EMPLOYMENT

Most studies of retirement behavior have not investigated the extent to which part-time work might have been chosen if such an option had been available. While the major reasons for retirement have been identified and explained (Quinn, 1977, Burkhauser, 1978), the desire for part-time work may well be affected by labor force effects of the Social Security system. Specifically, the *retirement test* provision of the law was liberalized (1977) so that a worker entitled to Social Security benefits at age 65 may earn up to $4000 with no benefit reduction. Above this amount, benefits are reduced $1 for every $2 earned. This exempt earning amount is scheduled to rise by $500 per year to reach $6000 in 1982, after which it will rise automatically with increases in the general level of earnings. In addition, in 1978, provisions raising the *increment* for delayed retirement from 1 percent to 3 percent of the annual benefit were enacted. These provisions will undoubtedly result in a continuation or enhancement of prior worker response to liberalizations of the retirement test—an increase in the propensity to retire. However, the increase in the level of earnings exempt from the retirement test will probably lead to more older workers continuing their participation in the labor force on a part-time basis. (Pellichio, 1978)

In addition to Social Security effects, it is clear that mandatory retirement rules have also had an impact on the retirement decision. While some researchers have suggested that this impact is minor because a large majority of workers retire *before* the effective mandatory retirement age, this does not demonstrate that compulsory retirement ages have no effect on retirement behavior. In fact, the existence of mandatory retirement ages may have strong anticipatory effects on employee behavior as the mandatory age is approached. (Data from the Social Security Administration Survey of Newly Entitled Beneficiaries show that compulsory retirement was cited by half of all workers who claimed a Social Security benefit at age 65—U.S. Department of Health, Education and Welfare, 1976.) In addition, Department of Labor studies of private pension plan provisions demonstrate that nearly half of these plans contain mandatory retirement provisions usually applicable at age 65 (Kittner, 1977). Of course, the passage of the 1978 Amendments to the Age Discrimination in Employment Act now make it unlawful for a private pension plan to retain a mandatory retirement age of less than 70. Although this provision may not have any *immediate* effects on retirement behavior, its longer term impact may be significant in encouraging retention of employment by more older persons.

Since most older persons probably leave their full-time jobs because of mandatory retirement and economic reasons such as pension eligibility (as well as declining health), the crucial question is whether they are interested in continued employment on a full or part-time basis? Unfortunately, clear research evidence on this question is lacking. Of particular importance is the lack of data as to the proportion of older persons who leave the labor force and do not in fact desire work *of any type.*

Studies now in progress (U.S. Department of Labor, 1980) are beginning to investigate the preferences of older employees for continued employment on a part-time basis. Far more research is necessary in this area in order to identify the actual preferences of upcoming cohorts of older workers.

At present about 14.5 percent of all nonagricultural wage and salary employees (11 million workers) work part-time by choice in the United States. Only 5 percent of such workers are 65 years of age or over. Among all older persons working part-time (whether by choice or not) however, nearly 50 percent are voluntarily employed part-time—the highest percentage of any age group. Of persons over age 60 and not in the labor force but desiring employment, half perceive that employers will consider them too old, and an additional 25 percent think there are no jobs available. Thus, nearly 80 percent of persons who desire employment believe they cannot get a job and presumably reduce their job search activities. Of course these beliefs are in fact supported by mandatory retirement policies and negative stereotypes of older employees held by employers. (U.S. Department of Labor, 1978)

The clearest indication of older worker preferences comes from national opinion surveys conducted by Louis Harris and Associates in 1974 and 1978 (National Council on the Aging, 1975; Harris, 1979). The results indicate that: (a) Large majorities of current and retired employees and business leaders are opposed to any mandatory retirement age; (b) about half of all current employees say they would prefer to work either full or part-time as an alternative to retirement; (c) about half of current retirees say they would prefer to be working; and (d) most older workers still plan to retire between ages 60–65. These preferences imply that while workers apparently intend to retire *initially,* a significant number anticipate a subsequent return to work. While these preferences cannot be assumed to reflect actual behavior, they indicate a significant desire by current and retired workers for flexible employment opportunities.

In Europe there is a very pronounced trend of part-time work among older men. In 1975, 53 percent of men working part-time were over age 55, 47 percent were 60 years or over and 36 percent were over age 65. (Robinson, 1979)

In summary, the available data indicate that an increasing number of current and retired workers suggest that they are interested in continued employment, that many older persons who now work part-time do so voluntarily and that older persons have a higher probability of choosing part-time employment than any other age group. When these findings are viewed in light of recent changes in Social Security provisions, Age Discrimination legislation and continuing inflationary economic conditions, it is apparent that more and more older workers are likely to desire opportunities to continue employment. Many will prefer part-time work opportunities because of a desire to make a transition between full time employment and full retirement.

Despite the seemingly irreversible trend toward early retirement, several recent developments in the U.S. and abroad suggest that retirement policies may gradually be modified to encourage and accommodate more flexible retirement. In some countries (mainly in Europe) public pension systems are being modified to provide increments in final pension benefits and establish partial pension programs that allow a gradual transition to retirement. In a few instances (particularly in the United States) private pension coverage has been extended beyond the usual retirement age by business firms. Such inducements to remain employed are likely to become more prevalent as the cost of supporting an increasing retired population rises. Decisions to remain employed at least part-time are likely to increase due to the interaction of individual preferences and wider employment opportunities. Public pension policy may also be further modified to provide additional inducement to stay in the labor force through an increase in the age of eligibility for receipt of benefits or the establishment of a partial pension option for older workers who wish to work part-time.

FLEXIBLE RETIREMENT OPTIONS

In order to develop options for flexible work opportunities for older persons, experimentation with a variety of approaches is desirable. Programs can be introduced easily by employers and unions *without disrupting usual employment practices* and yet represent real options for older employees. Of course, such options should not be introduced without giving careful consideration to effects on employee benefit programs and personnel policies. It is important to recognize that since major public pension policy changes are unlikely in the near term, developments in flexible retirement options will be more influenced by innovations in personnel and private pension plan policies than by government regulatory requirements.

Some of the policies and programs that might be adopted were mentioned earlier. Since evidence indicates that there is a growing desire for individual flexibility of retirement at both earlier and later ages it has been suggested that: (1) Retirement should occur as a transitional or phased process with workers permitted to taper off employment both before and after the "regular" retirement age; (2) that the option of temporary retirement might be introduced in which a period of retirement is followed by a return to work; and (3) that continuation of full-time employment be possible for older workers. These policies introduce flexibility into the retirement process, a goal supported by both medical and psychological research which indicates that health may be adversely affected by a sharp discontinuance between work and retirement and that a transitional period can be of significant benefit. In summary, four major retirement options can be suggested as providing a meaningful approach to flexibility: early retirement; retirement at the "normal" age when full benefits are available from public and/or private pension systems; transitional or phased retirement involving a period of permanent part-time work before full retirement; and a continuation of employment (full or part-time) beyond the regular retirement age. (For other options involving major modifications of the public pension system adoption of periodic worklife sabbatical leaves see Morrison, 1978.)

Current experience indicates that there are two approaches for creating more retirement flexibility: corporate personnel and private pension policies and public pension policies.

PERSONNEL AND PENSION POLICIES

Throughout the world, business organizations have generally taken the lead in developing flexible retirement approaches. While the current level of development can only be considered experimental, these policies and programs serve as models for future expansion and modification. In the United States, for example, the results of recent surveys of employers demonstrate that employers are in the process of initiating changes in personnel and pension policies which may introduce more flexibility in the retirement process.

1. In a national mail survey of 1636 firms and a telephone survey of 256 larger (more than 500 employees) firms contacted in the spring of 1979, Copperman, Montgomery and Keast (1979) reported that between 50-60 percent of firms *permitted* pension benefit accruals after the normal retirement age for workers continuing employment. This may not be a general pattern in industry. Furthermore, despite the availability of such benefit accruals, very few employees remain employed beyond the normal retirement age in pension plans and thus few utilize this option. They further found that about 11 percent of all firms had or were implementing flexible work hours (flexitime) programs, 17 percent had permanent part-time employment programs, and 5 percent had phased retirement programs. Overall 15 percent of all employers surveyed had or were implementing some type of alternative work schedule policies. It is important to note that while most employers expected a *small number* of their employees to continue to work past the age of 65 in response to the new ADEA age 70 mandatory retirement age, 90 percent of the employers expected that such continued employment would be quite minimal. It is interesting to note, however, that when queried about potential effects of continued *inflation* on retirement behavior of employees, 23 percent of all firms expect that more employees will forego early retirement and 48 percent expect that more employees will wish to continue working past the normal retirement age.

2. Similar findings resulted in a survey conducted in August, 1979 by the Bureau of National Affairs. (Bureau of National Affairs, 1979) A total of 267 medium- to large-size organizations were surveyed about retirement policies and programs. This study indicated that 15 percent of the employers had established some type of phased retirement program for all employees or specific groups of employees. (These programs are considerably more likely in nonbusiness organizations—hospitals, universities, government agencies.) In addition, 52 percent of all firms use retirees as consultants and 62 percent may recall retired employees to work for short

time periods. Again, in this survey most firms (86 percent) report no or very little effect of the change in the mandatory retirement age. The study suggests that the reason for this is that thus far few employees have actually been affected by the change. However, about 20 percent of the firms have experienced an increase in the number of workers staying on beyond the normal retirement age. Finally, almost 30 percent had made changes in their retirement programs over the last two years, and an additional 32 percent expect to make changes in the near future. Modifications most frequently involve improved insurance benefits for retirees, medical insurance, life insurance, etc., and development of retirement preparation programs, which more and more firms cite as important to develop and implement.

The studies conducted thus far have not been representative of all U.S. employers, and have not investigated employee plans, attitudes and behavior in responding to the new mandatory retirement age, changes in Social Security law and continuing inflation. The major national study of age discrimination and involuntary retirement now being conducted by the U.S. Department of Labor (1980) will establish definitive baseline information on a unique linked nationally representative sample of 6000 employees and their employers. The results of this study will therefore provide the most definitive information on current and planned employer personnel and pension policies and employee plans and preferences regarding retirement. While it is unlikely that this study's major findings will significantly differ from the surveys reported above, the amount of detailed information developed will be far greater and the basis for assessing changes over time in employer policies and employee preferences and actual retirement behavior will be established.

The major methods now used by U.S. employers to provide flexible retirement options include: (1) Reduced work-week schedules (four-day or three-day week) prior to retirement; (2) extra vacation time in years prior to retirement; (3) reduced hours of work; (4) job transfer programs; (5) employee consultants; (6) temporary part-time work for retired employees, and (7) payroll transfer programs (rehiring an older employee through a private employment service). Flexible retirement programs developed in Europe include: special job allotments for older workers, job redesign and special unemployment allowances in West Germany; various work-hour reduction programs in France (including days off per week, extra vacation time, and paid leave); establishing older worker quotas with government subsidies for hiring and extended unemployment benefits in Japan; and other innovations such as mobility allowances, retraining programs and specialized employment services utilized particularly in Scandinavia and West Germany. Some of these types of programs are beginning to be experimented with in the United States—such as reduced work hours approaches—while others, including job allotments, retraining and mobility allowances, government subsidies, and specialized employment services have received little attention. To a considerable extent, the pervasiveness of the early retirement trend, coupled with severe youth unemployment difficulties has resulted in only limited U.S. government attention to the problems of older workers. However, the increasing aging of the population, accompanied by dramatic increases in retirement support costs will undoubtedly result in a gradual reallocation of employment and training resources toward middle-aged and older workers.

PUBLIC PENSION POLICIES

Many countries have attempted to encourage continued employment at older ages by providing a bonus in final pension benefit for deferral of retirement beyond the regular age when full benefits may be claimed (usually 65–67). Norway, for example, provides a 9 percent and Sweden a 7 percent annual bonus for as many as three years' deferral of retirement. Germany, Britain and France also offer such incentives. In the U.S., recent Social Security legislation, beginning in 1982, mandates a 3 percent increment in final benefit amount for each year retirement is deferred between ages 65–70.

Evidence indicates these presumed inducements to employment have had little effect on the older work force. This is probably the case because early retirement options and incentives, offered in both public and private pension systems, have an over-riding effect on inducing people to leave the labor force.

Another technique presumably intended to induce labor force participation is utilization of earnings limits and marginal tax rates for money earned while receiving retirement benefits. Evidence indicates these approaches, known popularly as "retirement tests," result only in a bunching of earnings just below the amount at which retirement benefits will be reduced because of excess income.

Liberalization of the tests seems to result in more people leaving the labor force to draw retirement benefits while maintaining limited earnings from employment (Sander, 1968, 1970). The opposite of the desired effect is therefore accomplished: Rather than encouraging employment, the retirement test provides an additional incentive to leave the labor force early to begin drawing pension benefits, while allowing for limited earnings (up to a maximum where a marginal tax rate is imposed) for persons able to secure appropriate employment.

More successful public pension policies for flexible retirement have been developed in Sweden and Norway. In both countries, the public pension program offers a *partial pension option* allowing a gradual transition to retirement and time to adjust to a lower level of income (Tracy, 1978). These programs may also serve the additional objective of opening full-time positions to younger workers, though neither country suggests it as a major goal.

The Swedish system, the most well-developed, provides an example of the types of flexible innovations that can be introduced. While Sweden has a regular retirement age of 65, it is possible to draw full or half pensions as early as age 60, with benefit reduction of six percent annually for each year prior to 65. It is also possible to postpone retirement between ages 65–70, with a 7 percent annual benefit increment; additional pension credits may be earned while drawing half pension between ages 60–65. Also, from ages 60–70, it is possible to interrupt retirement benefits as desired to change from full to half pension.

Thus, the regular pension program offers considerable flexibility. In addition, a new National Partial Pension Program, initiated in 1976, directly facilitates the transition from work to retirement. This program was established in response to findings of gerontologists, physicians, psychologists, and some trade unions showing that the opportunity to taper off work directly benefits retirement adjustment and health. All salaried employees and wage earners are covered by the new system—about 200,000 persons.

The partial pension may be obtained between ages 60–65, provided the individual transfers to part-time work averaging 17 hours per week. The pension income level is 65 percent of the income loss sustained by taking part-time work; available income from partial pension and part-time work generally represents 85–90 percent of earlier full-time income. The partial pension does not reduce the pension available under the regular pension system, and those wishing to continue work after age 65 may do so by replacing the partial pension with half pension under the regular system.

In May 1978, less than 2 years after its introduction, almost 40,000 pensioners (20 percent of those eligible) had enrolled in the program, and the number continues to increase (Crona, 1978). The degree of flexibility it permits and its incorporation within the national public pension system make the Swedish plan important. Similar policy innovations should be explored and considered in the U.S., where substantial increases in pension costs are already being experienced.

CONCLUSION

In the U.S. and abroad, the aging of populations has been accompanied by a major trend toward early retirement. Now, however, various flexible retirement approaches are being discussed and in some cases implemented. Generally, these allow for increased choice as to the time of retirement and provide for various forms of continued employment for older workers.

In the U.S., approaches by business, government and educational institutions include eliminating a mandatory retirement age and establishing specialized programs such as part-time employment, payroll transfer, reduced work hours and retirement assessment. In Europe, innovations such as mobility allowances, employer subsidies, retraining, older worker quota systems, specialized employment services and phased-retirement programs are in use. In both the U.S. and Europe, some forms of flexible retirement (usually early retirement) are mandated by public pension programs.

These recent initiatives represent the beginning of an overall adjustment to changing demographic trends and economic conditions. In the future, larger numbers of older persons will be in good health and interested in continuing in some form of employment. Though the supply of such workers is likely to increase gradually at first, as time passes more will desire to continue employment. More-over, as pension costs continue to escalate, public policies are likely to mandate a later retirement age to reduce economic burdens on younger workers and to finance retirement pension payments.

All these developments require that much more attention be de-voted to examining new work arrangements for older persons, in-cluding part-time work, job sharing, partial retirement, midlife sab-baticals, job adjustment, shifting and retraining—all potentially useful personnel practices for older workers. To implement any of the programs in a particular organizational setting, a review of work force characteristics and current personnel and pension policies is usually necessary. Requisite to successful implementation of flexible retirement policies is an accommodation to the employers' needs, the employees' preferences and the particular work environment charac-teristics of the organization.

REFERENCES

Best, Fred and Stern, Barry. Education, work and leisure: Must they come in that order? *Monthly Labor Review,* July 1977.

Best, Fred and Stern, Barry. Lifetime distribution of education, work and leisure: Research, speculations and policy implications of changing life patterns, Institute for Educational Leadership, The George Washington University, December 1976.

Bureau of National Affairs. ASPA-BHA Survey No. 39, retirement policies and programs, Bureau of National Affairs, Washington, D.C. 1980.

Burkhauser, Richard. The pension acceptance decision of older men, *Journal of Human Resources,* Vol. 14, No. 2, 1979.

Copperman, Lois F., Montgomery, Douglas D., and Keast, Fred D. The impact of the age discrimination in employment act amendments of 1978 on the private business community, Institute on Aging, Portland State University, 1979, Portland, Oregon.

Crona, C. Partial Retirement in Sweden—Development and Experiences, Ninth World Congress of Sociology, Uppsala, Sweden, August 1978.

Freedman, Marsha. *Labor Markets, Segments and Shelters,* New York: Allanheld, Osman & Co., 1976.

Harris, Louis and Associates. American attitudes toward pensions and retirement, Johnson & Higgins, New York, 1979.

Hedges, Janice and Moore, Geoffrey. Trends in labor and leisure, *Monthly Labor Review,* February 1971.

Kittner, Dorothy R. Forced retirement: How common is it? *Monthly Labor Review,* December 1977.

Morrison, Malcolm. Flexible distribution of work, leisure and education: Potentials for the aging, *Aging and Income,* (B. Herzog, Ed.) Human Sciences Press, New York, 1978.

National Council on the Aging/Louis Harris and Associates, *The Myth and Reality of Aging in America,* Washington, D.C., National Council on the Aging, 1974.

Owen, John D. Workweeks and leisure: An analysis of trends, 1948-1975, *Monthly Labor Review,* August 1976.

Pellechio, Anthony J. The Social Security earnings test, labor supply distortions and foregone payroll tax revenue, National Bureau of Economic Research Working Paper No. 272, Cambridge, Massachusetts, August 1978.

Quinn, Robert and Shepperd, Linda. *The 1972-73 Quality of Employment Survey,* Ann Arbor, Michigan: Institute for Social Research University of Michigan, 1974.

Quinn, Joseph F. Microeconomic determinants of early retirement: A cross-sectional view of white married men, *Journal of Human Resources,* 12, 1977.

Rehn, Gosta. Towards a society of free choice, in Comparing Public Policies (J. J. Wiatr and R. Rose, Eds.), Ossolineum, Wroclaw, 1977.

Robinson, Olive. Part time employment in the European community, *International Labor Review,* May-June 1979.

Sander, K. The retirement test: Its effect on older workers' earnings *Social Security Bulletin,* June, 1968.

———. "The Effects of the 1966 Retirement Test Changes on Workers Aged 65-72," *Research and Statistics Note No. 1,* Social Security Administration, 1970.

Spencer Associates, Inc. ADEA impact on retirement trends seen as minimal to date, EPBR Research Reports, 123.1-1, 9-79. Charles D. Spencer Associates, Inc., Chicago, Illinois, 1979.

Storey, James R. and Hendricks, Gary. Retirement income issues in an aging society, The Urban Institute, Washington, D.C., 1979.

Tracy, Martin. Flexible retirement features abroad, *Social Security Bulletin,* May 1978.

U.S. Department of Health, Education and Welfare, Administration-on-Aging, Direct and indirect effects of increasing or eliminating the mandatory retirement age, Cross-national study of part-time employment for the elderly, 1979; Flexible retirement programs for older workers, 1980.

U.S. Department of Health, and Human Services, Social Security Administration. Almost 65: Baseline data from the retirement history survey, Washington, D.C.: U.S. Government Printing Office, 1976.

U.S. Department of Health, Education and Welfare, Social Security Administration. Reaching retirement age: Findings from the SNEB 1968-1970, Washington, D.C.: U.S. Government Printing Office, 1976.

U.S. Department of Labor, Bureau of Labor Statistics. *Employment and Earnings,* January 1978, **25**(1), Washington, D.C.: U.S. Government Printing Office, 1978.

U.S. Department of Labor, Employment and Training Administration. *Employment and Training Report of the President,* 1979.

U.S. Department of Labor. Studies of involuntary retirement and the effects of raising the mandatory retirement age limit, 1980.

CONCLUSION: THE FUTURE
OF RETIREMENT

Over the past 40 years retirement institutions and policies have developed in an ad-hoc, uncoordinated manner resulting in current patterns of retirement behavior. The most fundamental characteristic of these patterns is increasing early retirement throughout the labor force. Due to the general aging of the work force, this retirement pattern is resulting in rapidly increasing pension costs which will rise even higher because of adjustments required to meet the costs of inflation. Low fertility and improved mortality will reduce the ratio of working age persons (aged 22–64) to retirement age persons (65 and over), from 5.0 in 1975 to 3.0 in 2025. Thus, if present trends continue, there will be fewer workers available to pay for the increasing retirement benefits required by the larger older retired population.

Because of these trends, it is very likely that the current institution of retirement and the policies and programs which support it will undergo significant change in the years ahead. It certainly is unlikely that policy makers will accept the projected large increase in the proportion of the government budget allocated to retirement payments, without consideration of alternatives to reduce the growth of this type of allocation. In addition to the serious growing financial support burden for the retired, other significant factors which will influence a change in retirement policy include: (1) The increasing number of working women and their inequitable treatment by the Social Security system; (2) continued high inflation without effective price controls which may result in greater dependence on the inflation-indexed Social Security system; (3) lack of coordination of various retirement systems resulting in multiple pension coverage of some limited groups of workers and little or no coverage of other groups; (4) overlaps between Social Security and welfare programs; (5) rapid rise in costs of disability and health insurance for retirees; (6) inadequate funding of private pension systems; (7) effects of major increases in Social Security taxes on wages, on integration of private plans with Social Security; and (8) tax and investment consequences of the growth of pension fund capital. Consideration of these factors demonstrates that the future of retirement is of great significance not only for current and future older persons but also for the larger number of younger working persons who must provide support for the older population.

It is clear that a continuation of current retirement policies will result in very serious economic and social consequences for our society. The combination of demographic changes, high rates of inflation, efforts to control rising costs of retirement benefits, the early retirement trend, and the interrelated effects of current pension system functioning, however, will clearly result in significant changes in retirement policies and programs in the years ahead. At present no less than six major studies/policy analyses are being conducted by the Federal government to examine retirement policies and programs. (Advisory Council on Social Security, National Commission on Social Security, Universal Coverage Study, Study to Eliminate Dependency and Sex Discrimination Under Social Security, President's Commission on Pension Policy, Study of Age Discrimination in Employment) Additional studies are also being conducted by private sector research organizations, individual companies, and university research centers. Many, if not most, of these studies focus on six key questions identified by Storey and Hendricks (1979):

- When should nondisabled workers retire?
- What proportion of a worker's former earnings should be replaced in retirement?
- How should retirement benefits be adjusted for inflation or economic growth?
- How should the financing of retirement benefits be shared?
- How should the various retirement systems be coordinated?
- How should retirement and social welfare needs be rationalized?

To these questions must be added the important concern with the extent to which older persons can choose to allocate their time between employment and leisure. That is, how should retirement policy be designed in order to provide opportunities for part-time employment with partial retirement to allow for a transition between fulltime work and full retirement? This question raises the most important underlying issue regarding the future of retirement policy: what should be our long run goals for retirement in the United States? To answer this question, a comprehensive approach to retirement and pension policy issues is essential. Developing a consensus regarding appropriate answers to key policy questions requires above all, an accurate base of information upon which policy alternatives can be evaluated. Such an information base cannot be developed only through independent studies of individual issues such as public pension financing alternatives, retirement ages, pension integration, coverage, wage replacement, age discrimination, labor force participation, etc. While such studies are essential, judgments as to the effects of policy options will not be accurate unless comprehensive models of the functioning of current retirement policies are utilized. Unfortunately, such models and data collection efforts which must underlie them are not available primarily because of the complexities involved but also due to the fragmentation of policy-making in this area. If baseline measurements of the effects of current policies and programs can be developed on an integrated basis, representing an analysis of the interrelationships of retirement systems, then comprehensive assessments of various policy and program options could be made. Since there are a variety of goals involved, including income adequacy, funding, inflation indexing, retirement age, employment incentives, system coordination, etc., a comprehensive model could permit analysis of a variety of proposals to achieve such goals in terms of their interrelated effects. Also, policy proposals could be evaluated in terms of assessing their likely effects on various objectives both in the near term future and over longer time periods. The present studies now underway may well provide an opportunity to develop a more comprehensive informational base for evaluating policy choices.

An underlying assumption of this book has been the belief that a national re-evaluation of retirement policy is necessary and essential in order for our society to adapt to changing social circumstances and economic conditions. The data cited throughout the preceding chapters provide ample evidence of major changes now under way in terms of demographic, economic and social variables. While it is clear that we do not presently have one uniform national retirement policy, it is also evident that most of our current uncoordinated policies result in the major trend of early retirement. This trend is beginning to be perceived as dysfunctional mainly because of increasing pension costs. Of course, it may also be dysfunctional because it limits the human potential of millions of persons who could contribute to productivity if provided with the opportunity.

To a considerable extent, current retirement behavior reflects the incentives provided by current policies. These policies may be based on the perceived need to remove older workers from the labor force in order to "make room" for younger and middle-aged employees. It is clear that we may be approaching the limit of marginal utility for such policies. Every person who retires requires support from the remaining work force. As the tax burden for this support increases, workers suffer reductions in quality of life. Current economic conditions of inflation and declining productivity further reduce quality of life and lower expectations for future growth and accompanying economic and social benefits.

A major question that confronts our society is whether we will consciously act to develop and implement a retirement policy which emphasizes more balance in utilizing the capacities of the available workforce, or continue our present approach of reacting to limited aspects of the problem with stop-gap measures designed to temporarily remedy the most immediate problems. Thus far, the reactive approach has led only to proposals for shifting the financial burden of retirement support from reliance on one method of taxation to another. Such measures of course will not resolve the growing financial crisis and are based primarily on *acceptance* of current retirement policies and the behavior that they mandate. A more comprehensive analysis of our emerging retirement crisis demonstrates that dealing only with the income support aspects of the problem will not alter the basic dilemma—the appropriate utilization of the productive capacity of human capital. In order to create a new retirement future, the issue of encouraging the employment of older workers must be satisfactorily resolved. National policies must be devised to

1. Modify public pension systems to provide for partial retirement options;
2. Encourage the utilization of pension system incentives for developing transitional retirement programs for employees;
3. Encourage employers to adopt personnel policies permitting greater flexibility for older workers;
4. Create more balance in the sharing of the responsibility for income support for the retired;
5. Encourage the development of programs which involve flexible worklife approaches which are not based on the traditional linear life plan of education, work and retirement.

The extent to which such policies can be developed and adopted is determined to a great degree by the information provided to public policy makers, particularly members of Congress and professional specialists in government agencies which administer retirement related programs. Our present policies have to a great degree been shaped by legislators who have usually been provided with limited information on narrow issues related only to specific legislative jurisdictions. Thus it is not surprising that policies are uncoordinated and have led to unintended social and economic consequences. Although an overall multifaceted retirement policy strategy and program is far from being available at present, a conceptual understanding of the linkages between pension, employment and retirement policy is clearly a necessity if a new retirement policy is to be developed on an incremental basis. The provision of this conceptual background to public and private policy makers is of crucial importance if our future retirement policy is to be designed to balance the objectives of financial support and employment opportunity.

INDEX